The Postgraduate Research Handbook

Succeed with your MA, MPhil, EdD and PhD

Gina Wisker

palgrave

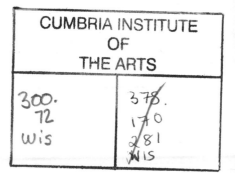

First published 2001 by
PALGRAVE
Houndmills, Basingstoke, Hampshire RG21 6XS and
175 Fifth Avenue, New York, N.Y. 10010
Companies and representatives throughout the world

PALGRAVE is the new global academic imprint of
St. Martin's press LLC Scholarly and Reference Division and
Palgrave Publishers Ltd (formerly Macmillan Press Ltd).

ISBN 0–333–74777–1 paperback

This book is printed on paper suitable for recycling and
made from fully managed and sustained forest sources.

A catalogue record for this book is available
from the British Library.

10   9   8   7
10 09 08 07 06 05 04

Printed in Great Britain by
Creative, Print and Design (Ebbw Vale), Wales

Contents

Stage 4 Support, Progress, Analysis, Writing up, the Viva, Presentations and Afterwards

Acknowledgements

I have enjoyed working on this book and am grateful for all the insights provided by the many research students who have worked with me, using and commenting on the materials as they developed into the book. Particular thanks go to the several cohorts of research students from Israel undertaking PhDs with us at Anglia, to my colleagues Dr Gillian Robinson and Dr Vernon Trafford for their advice with materials, to Lindsay Barnes and Nicola Skinner for their dedicated hard work on layouts, and to my family, Alistair, my husband and Liam and Kitt, my two sons for their support and tolerance. Finally, thanks to Margaret Bartley and other colleagues at Palgrave who have supported and commented along the way.

Cambridge, 2001

List of Figures

1 Introduction

If you are thinking of starting to research for an MA, MPhil or PhD, then this book should help you at each stage of your work. Initially, it will help you to decide what and how you want to research, where you would like to undertake your research qualification and study, and how to work with a supervisor. Then it will tackle how to keep the momentum going over time and how to analyse your findings and draw conclusions from these. Finally, it will help you to see how to produce a good quality dissertation or thesis which, we hope, will pass.

Starting to undertake a research degree is a very exciting and also a rather daunting undertaking, because you know that it is a next step up in your learning. You will probably have heard of friends or colleagues who started a large piece of research once, took years and years over it and never finished. But you will also know people who have really enjoyed and benefited from undertaking a research degree. My own experience as a part-time, female research student working at a distance from my supervisor and home university as well as combining a full-time job (and commuting) with study, certainly had its ups and downs. It did, however, change my life and it changed my sense of my own achievements. I have never regretted the work and have always been pleased I gained the degrees (first an MA, then a PhD). It is through this experience that I wanted to write this book, as well as out of the exciting and fruitful work I have been involved in with research students and supervisors over the past few years, particularly a large cohort of professional part-time research students from Israel, and with supervisors new to supervising in my own university (Anglia Polytechnic University). The intention is to enable you to see clearly what you want to research, how to go about it and how to work successfully towards achieving your aims.

The book draws on good practice developed at a wide variety of universities in Australia, the USA and the UK. I am grateful to colleagues from Australia, the UK, Israel and lately South Africa, who have engaged

1

in immensely useful conversations with me, pointing me towards local good practice and sharing their own strategies. Most recently this led to a companion book for supervisors entitled *Good Practice in Postgraduate Supervision* (Wisker and Sutcliffe 1999), and some of the ideas in that could also be useful to you in your work with your supervisor.

Of course, you will receive a great deal of support and guidance from your university and your supervisor(s). Having this book as a guide-book should, however, help you to take control of and responsibility for your own learning and to know what kinds of questions to ask as much as what the answers to some of those question are, as you proceed on your research journey.

One of the biggest growth areas in higher education is postgraduate work. More students than ever before are deciding to continue with their studies, or to return to postgraduate study to research for a qual-ification, after some time in paid or voluntary work or bringing up chil-dren. There is now a diverse group of students seeking postgraduate study and it is no longer only the lifetime career academic who seeks research study qualifications. There is also much international move-ment as many research students wish to gain the enriching experience of studying in another country, most commonly the UK, the USA and Australia. The greatest growth in groups of research students is that of women, and women returners in particular, who often combine study with jobs and domestic responsibilities. Many other students under-take research when they have retired from full-time employment. They too, like so many others engaged in research, are seizing the opportu-nity to 'do something for themselves at last'. The diversity of research students has helped to bring about development and change in research supervision practices and in universities' practices of support for and recognition of the needs of research students. This book takes note of the differences in demands of students from different cultural contexts and takes into account different social, age and gender back-grounds. It also takes note of the different kinds of postgraduate research study in which students are engaged.

Students embarking on research for qualifications are considered in this book in three related groups: those working towards their Master's, particularly the MA, and those working for an MPhil or a PhD, with the latter qualifications substantially different from the former for reasons of length, depth, and originality. Some students study on taught courses at all three levels while others undertake research-based studies. At PhD and MPhil level there is also, more recently, the development of a professional doctorate, sometimes called an EdD (education doctorate), where appropriate, or a doctorate in professional practice. These developments recognise the integration of and synergy between professional practice, employment and work-related study and research, and they are often different in shape from established research. Doctorates by publication have also recently been recognised and these, too, are different in shape. However, all involve research, and anyone undertaking any one of these qualifications will find this book useful. We will be looking at these variants and concentrating on what is in common between them, that is, *the process and the practice of research*, which is the main focus of this book.

The book really starts where I know I did, and where so many of my own research students began, with some basic advice, some questions to answer and things to think about. The opening sections of each chapter outline the issues to be discussed. There are reflective questions to consider and some strategies, plans and exercises to try out which aim to get you to concentrate on planning and managing your research. The more complex developments are in the middle of each chapter and a conclusion sums up main points covered. The book as a whole follows the line of development of a research project, whether a relatively short-term project for an MA (probably around a year's work), or a longer project for MPhil and PhD (between three and six or more years' work, depending on whether you carry out full- or part-time research). You will need to pick and choose your way around the book as different questions arise for you in your work. Treat it, in other words, as a useful sourcebook, like any other in your research. It is one to which you can refer when you need to, but which also provides an underpinning to your study.

Each chapter asks you to become involved in reflective (or active) tasks to help you to focus further on your work. These should aid the reflection on the progress and process of *your research* – activities which in themselves are a key to good research.

▶ What the book does not do

This book cannot guarantee you success. The hard work still rests with you. As you develop your own working relationships with supervisors, your research area and university, and as you also develop autonomy, you will appreciate that there could not be a manual which successfully guaranteed that at this level. It is a complex, original and creative activity.

This book is specifically addressed at social science and humanities students; it does not aim to guide science students, although those undertaking health-related research should find it useful (and scientists might find some parts useful too).

▶ What the book does and how it is structured

The book gives basic advice as well as signposts to more specialist research methods and I hope that you will find that it is accessible and clear in its presentation, and includes the basic points you will need to look at in your research. There are four parts:

1 Starting research
2 Getting going – supervisors, methods and time
3 More detailed research methods – maintaining momentum
4 Support, progress, analysis, writing up, the viva, presentations and afterwards.

There are 'task' boxes to enable you to consider how research methods could work for you and to help you with your thinking towards your research projects. The book endeavours to direct you towards reading which leads you to further *specialist research methods training*. It does not try to replicate here the books that train the use of, for example, statistics, but instead asks fundamental questions that enable you to make some choices about appropriate methods and underpinning methodologies.

In outline it:

•   takes you through generic decisions about titles, areas of study, the methods and methodology of research, timing, contracts, and so on
•   deals with issues and practices common across different subject areas and levels in the social sciences and humanities
•   branches out, where relevant, to consider the different levels of Master's, MPhil and PhD It defines the kind of difference related to original work or work which contributes to the PhD, and the issues around contribution to practice and experience which much

Master's work now involves. It also looks at how to ensure this all takes place
* consistently reflects on the different needs of international students.

You will see the book is structured in relation to the four phases of a research student's work, that is:

Part 1   Starting research
This concentrates on:

* starting your own research
* choosing universities
* choosing topics
* defining the area and asking research questions

Part 2   Getting going – supervisors, methods and time

* understanding and taking control of your own learning
* getting into good study habits and managing time
* literature reviews, notes and referencing
* selecting research methodologies, theories, methods and practices
* starting to work with your supervisor – agendas and contracts

Part 3   More detailed research methods –
maintaining momentum

* maintenance and development of ideas and research practices, restructuring and refocusing issues and practices
* continuing to maintain good working relations and supervisions with your supervisor(s)
* restructuring to taking into account findings and new questions, new reading and ideas, and so on
* maintaining momentum
* ensuring pilot studies inform further developments, analysing your data and producing and building on your findings
* recuperating after difficulties with data and respondents
* making a leap in conceptual awareness
* dealing with underlying values, knowledge and structure-based difficulties

Part 4   Support, progress, analysis, writing up, the viva, presentations and afterwards

- analysing data
- writing transfer documents, progress reports
- supportive research cultures
- building in time for seen and unforeseen problems
- what makes a good quality research piece, especially a PhD
- editing
- re-editing to keep to length
- ensure organisation develops thesis
- ensure thesis raises and deals with problems
- diagram design and presentations
- protocols
- submission formats
- vivas
- rewriting and resubmission if it goes wrong
- conference presentation
- publication
- the difference between MPhil- and PhD-level work

Outside the research, the writing up and the viva, the book then looks briefly at presentations, conferences and publications – getting your work out into the broader research area – and life after research, that is, what you might do next.

Good luck! I hope you find the book helps you achieve your aims in your research.

Further reading

Wisker, G., & Sutcliffe, N. (eds) (1999). *Good Practice in Postgraduate Supervision*. SEDA Occasional Paper 106. Birmingham: SEDA.

Stage 1
Starting Research

2 Starting Your Postgraduate Research

This chapter looks at:

- Why undertake a research degree?
- Reasons for undertaking a research degree now
- Auditing your research skills

▶ Why do an MA, MPhil or PhD?

- Is this the right time for you to start and if so, why?
- What are your reasons (both personal and occupationally related) for going into research?

Postgraduate study is an opportunity for personal skills development and for professional recognition and status. It is challenging and demanding. Being involved in developing and working on a project, or increasingly, in taught courses with a dissertation element that you have chosen (at least partly), is very exciting. You are at last able to concentrate on one of the most interesting things in your life and to watch it grow and develop. There is no doubt that this kind and level of study involves you in a great deal of hard work and time, but it aids your personal growth and helps self-awareness and self-actualisation. If it is a clearly and fully conceived project it will make intellectual demands of you as regards dealing with complex concepts, ethics and issues to do with the handling and interpretation of different kinds of data. It will also demand a high level of communication and expression skills from you because others (everyone from the window cleaner and your mother to the great authority on the subject) will want to know what you are doing, both in informal and formal exchanges. You will need to keep clear goals and clear expression constantly in mind, without letting the desire for clarity lead to undue simplicity.

One question you could ask yourself is whether postgraduate study is the best way to further your interest in the area or subject in which you wish to research. Perhaps your interests would be better served in a form that required less stringent data management or bibliographical work and did not have to conform to the extensive commitment, deliberation and institutional regulations with which a postgraduate qualification will be involved. Perhaps the project you have in mind might be better served by being explored through a book or a report.

However, postgraduate study might be exactly what you seek now. It is demanding, rewarding and creative and can help you to develop an alternative sense of identity as you become involved in your work.

It is also a big challenge to your intellect and determination and you might well fear failure. It is important, then, that you are sure you want to start this work, know what it entails and can commit to it with enthusiasm and determination and are motivated to continue with it. You will need a good support network of others who believe in and will help motivate you, and who are willing to help you use the necessary problem-solving strategies to work out ways of dealing with and over-coming various problems as you meet them. And you will meet them! That is the nature of research and also part of its stimulating challenge. The only reasons to give up are if the research information is clearly flawed and the hypotheses upon which it was founded are clearly incorrect, or if all the other priorities in your life take over. However, in the former case you could recast the research, and in the latter, formally enquire about deferral. Neither are really reasons to give up. Having said this, you will be surprised how many students do actually fail to finish their research. If you have committed yourself far enough to read a book on studying and working for a research degree, you are probably already lessening your chances of being part of that group. You are spending time considering the challenges of the tasks ahead and the planning and hard work which contribute to your success. You are also starting to learn more about how *you* learn and study as a research student. This contributes positively to your success because it will allow you to be personally aware of your learning and to take control of this process yourself.

Undertaking postgraduate research is exciting and personally and professionally rewarding. Success leads to greater self-esteem and whether or not it eventually aids promotion or the acquisition of a new job, it increases professional credibility and status. You might well be rather nervous about undertaking such a big step, taking on what could, certainly for PhD and MPhil work, be a long-term commitment (MPhils often last three years full time and six years part time, and so do PhDs, while MAs last one to two and a half years). It is certainly true that this undertaking will expect you to take a step up in terms of the level at which you have been working. There will have been previous such steps, between GCSE and A level, for example, and A level or equivalent and first-degree study. You would do well to remind yourself how you recognised the step up, the differences in levels demanded of you and to consider how you managed the step. You can also remind yourself that you have been successful in making these steps and have already written substantial pieces of work. This will help firmly establish your confidence as well as give you some insight into your own sense of how you work well.

If you are undertaking an MPhil or PhD, these questions about research background and skills are absolutely central. Your main activity is research. For MA students, research is a part of each element or essay and is the crucial element to the final dissertation.

Task

In order to benefit from your own previous research experiences and draw out your research abilities, ask yourself:

- What previous experience of research do you have? For example, research carried out for a dissertation, for publication, for internal papers, for Master's or other postgraduate qualifications, in your role – discovering practices and supporting developments.
- Was it scientific research, social science research or humanities research?
- Was it research to feed into or underpin your daily work, new processes and practices, for a professional activity such as a report?
- Was it research carried out for interest alone?
- Was it market research, research into choices people make, attitudes or behaviours?
- Was it research into the background of something or someone, for work, for pleasure, for your family or for interest?
- Was it teaching and educational research – to underpin teaching practices?
- Was it more general research – to find out about buying a house, about your family tree or local history, to discover different costing and different opportunities in house development or holiday buying?

All of these kinds of research, broadly speaking, use humanities and social science research strategies that involve identifying issues, problems, questions and sub-questions and setting out to investigate them, asking questions of different data and people in different ways, and coming to some, probably temporary, partial conclusions. They might have led to a change in practice, to information on which to base a development at work, to insight gained into why certain things always happen or certain people did or do certain things in certain ways, and they could have resulted in information presented in many different ways, including reports and information sheets, or even in essays – but this last is less likely unless they were related to an academic context.

Task – characteristics of research

- What would you say were the main characteristics of your previous research – for example, a problem, questions, a need, right timing, finding out information, ordering the information and organising it into an argument to persuade yourself or others?
- How do your previous experiences of research relate to or differ from the research you would like to undertake?
- Think about research you have undertaken previously. What would you say were the successful research elements and practices in any of these activities?
- Could you define them and transfer them to your plans for research now?

▶ Planning, key issues and suggestions

This section looks at:

- planning your research – the first stages
- contributing to research culture – originality
- developing a hypothesis and questions
- defining research outcomes
- defining each stage of the research process
- suggested research skills

Planning your research – the first stages

Planning your research and replanning it as you proceed are essential elements in a good research project and a good research degree. As you begin to define your research area and the kinds of methodologies and methods you intend to use, who to work with, where to work and who can be supportive of you, you need to be clear about why you want to undertake the research and what you hope to find out. Think of your interest, which fuels this research, as a guiding piece of motivation. You will need to think strategically and conceptually and to manage both long-term activities and short-term work. Some of these elements are covered in the latter part of the book.

Contributing to research culture – originality

You need initially to concentrate on the accurate definition and description of the research by selecting an appropriate title and asking yourself why this research is important. What can it contribute to knowledge and/or change? The Swinnerton Dyer report (1982) comments about postgraduate research:

> the choice of research topic should be heavily influenced by the staff and, where appropriate, also from outside the academic institution; this is to ensure that the topic is a suitable subject for research training, that it is likely to prove a rewarding investigation, that it is of practical benefit where this is possible, that competent supervision is available and that the work can be completed within the time available. (Dyer 1982)

Defining your research area, choosing your title and asking your main research questions are essential points of entrance into the research process.

What the Swinnerton Dyer report suggests, also, is that MA, MPhil and PhD research is not an end in itself. It is actually a training ground for researchers. The hope is that you will establish sound practices during your course and transfer these to further research afterwards.

Developing a hypothesis and questions

Task

Consider:
    Where do your work and your ideas fit in so far? What are you clear about from this list of first stages of research?

- Define your area.
- What do you want to research into?
- Decide on a title that gives you enough scope to ask research questions but does not attempt research of too great a scope.
- Develop a hypothesis or research question.
- Set up a plan of activities and sort out where the resources and information might lie.
- Plan the time – and the critical path.
- See funding and support.
- Seek supervision.
- Seek a support group or person, if appropriate.
- Get started on the literature search, the reading, the initial plans, the first supervision, and the writing up of the first and subsequent drafts of the proposal for university agreement.

Now look at the very first stages.

Consider:

- What will your research area and title be?
- What questions and concerns do you have about developing good research practices in your situation?
- How can you work to overcome any problems?
- What needs do you perceive?
- Share your ideas and initial plans with a colleague (if you can).

The areas of developing your research are covered fully in the chapters which follow, but it is useful to consider now what you want to research into, where you want to carry out your work and what kind of research degree you want to undertake. These thoughts, as well as some idea about the problems and benefits of research, should inform your use of the chapters to follow, and then inform your work.

What follows are some suggestions about key issues in successful research practices, largely emanating from Australia. These should provide a guide for good practice and good experience throughout your study.

Defining research outcomes

- The research student should ensure that they are engaged on a promising topic that might fairly be expected to produce sound results and within the agreed time frame.
- Students should work with their supervisors to develop standards of achievement that will result in a good quality thesis. (*University of Queensland Calendar*)

Ask yourself if your research is promising or rich enough and likely to produce sound results. Will it be completed within the time allowed?

It is important that the supervisor works with the student to look closely at the first stages of development of the research project proposal. It is also important that both student and supervisor agree that this is a promising, manageable project that *should* achieve a good quality thesis. Once you have thought through and settled on your responses to the lists (above) you might want to share them with your supervisor(s).

Defining and managing each stage of the supervising process – systems, problems, good practice

Once the supervisor has been chosen or assigned, and contacts made, there follow several informal interviews or discussions, some of which might be by phone or letter. The early development of an outline of your postgraduate research hypothesis, ideas, concerns and research questions follow. It is important also to start to read widely within the appropriate literature and to start to develop a literature research base. You will need to use your own sense of what realistic and good quality research you have worked with in the past and to consult with your supervisor and colleagues to produce what looks like a viable project based on the quality of the research questions, the methodology, your ability to organise ideas and your discoveries to date. You will need to show imagination and realism, and the ability to change and develop ideas in relation to what you are discovering.

The next stage of the activity is to move towards establishing the procedure for the research, the design of the actual research work you will undertake which, particularly in a social sciences- or health-related research project, should contain:

- a description of the theoretical or conceptual framework
- a list of potential reading and other sources of evidence evidence/authority

- the methodologies to be used
- the research design and research questions.
- an outline of the analytical techniques

There should also be:

- a timetable for the completion of stages of the work
- a draft set of contents which helps you to define the major areas of work, and research questions informing the whole.

Some of the stages and some of the responsibilities include:

- network planning or critical path analysis
- setting objectives
- ordering research activities
- estimating the time each stage of the research should take
- deciding on and ordering/getting hold of the necessary facilities and resources
- drawing up a realistic schedule which will (of course) be changed with developments, setbacks and changes in circumstances.

See Chapter 7 on balancing demands and Chapter 8 on time management.

Once this schedule has been decided and planned, it then needs to be actioned. You will need to seek support from your supervisor and other research student colleagues in developing your research. You need to ensure you:

- are realistic about your critical path and schedule and can plan an appropriate course of study
- meet your supervisor at regular intervals to discuss and guide the progress of your work
- seek opportunities to take part in the university's research culture – give papers, consult with peers, attend conferences, and so on
- consider, plan and seek advice from other students and the university's published guidelines on the scope and presentation of the thesis, on format, length, layout, dates and various regulations.
- Consider and plan publications likely to arise from the work (much of this emerges as you carry out the work)
- agree with your supervisor that they will see and comment (helpfully, constructively and critically) on drafts of the major sections of the thesis as these are prepared

- encourage supervisors to comment helpfully, constructively and critically on the draft of the completed thesis before it is submitted.

Being aware of these stages and taking notice of the advice can help supervisor and student develop a harmonious working relationship, with clear patterns of working and clear expectations of each other's responsibilities. However, there are some specific areas in which research students can have problems in their research, or with their supervisor, and these too need considering in relation to working successfully with your supervisor for success in research.

There are many potential difficulties in relation to supervisors and resources. You might like to think about how to overcome some of these (should they emerge!) before embarking on your research. Look also at later chapters (such as Chapter 6) which discuss the managing of your supervisor to consider how to overcome common problems in this area.

Some broad areas which could cause concern are:

- inappropriate/undoable/excessively complex research questions and/or research plans
- management and planning, if these are unrealistic
- difficulties with acquiring data, or analysing and managing it
- relationships with supervisors
- life outside research preventing a full and successful focus on your work.

There are also some difficulties that could arise because of the kinds of learning styles and approaches which students take – see Chapter 9 for some thoughts and suggestions about this.

Common problems
Research has shown that students have problems with:

- research questions and areas which do not yield enough information or have been inappropriately posed – asking for accumulations of information rather than questioning and suggesting – so that the work becomes dull and descriptive
- access to research subjects, contacts and contexts – often this seems guaranteed at the outset of the work, but situations change. Sometimes the people, information, scenarios, and so on, disap-

pear, or you are no longer in a situation to access them (or sur-
prisingly, they are refused to you early on or part of the way through
your work)

- personality factors: neglect by the supervisor, a clash of personalities, barriers to communication arising from age, class, gender,
race, differences in approach to work
- professional factors: a misinformed supervisor or one without sufficient knowledge in the area supervised
- a supervisor with few genuine research interests, or ones which
differ fundamentally from those of the student
- organisational factors: the supervisor having too many students to
supervise; the supervisor being too busy with administration; the
supervisor's inability to manage their research group or their
numbers of researchers efficiently
- departmental facilities and arrangements isolating the student
- lack of a genuine research culture – lack of others to work with and
talk to, to share excitement, discoveries, setbacks, problems, developments, strategies and solutions
- inadequate support services and provision of equipment
- difficulties with other life demands and crises that do not allow you
enough time to develop the research.

You will need to consider how you might avoid or overcome these
potential problems and pitfalls.

Some student dissatisfaction with the development of their work
and with relations with supervisors can be avoided if there is clear and
open communication on all aspects of the project and if, overall,
there is structure without a straitjacket, that is, with a framework for
supervision and studies which facilitates rather than hinders students'
development and creativity. Such a structure will enable students to
develop their autonomy, to become sure of the rules and resources,
and of the intellectual and systematic support they need to do so.
It will also help students to be treated equally fairly when being
supervised, even in cases where they have personality clashes with
supervisors.

To avoid problems, both research students and supervisors have
to make it very clear to each other at the outset where the different
responsibilities lie and to agree what roles and responsibilities they will
each take on. It is in the spirit of this need that the idea of developing
contracts emerges (see Chapter 6). It is in the spirit of an ongoing need

for support and discussion – which is not always possible from the supervisor – that the idea of peer support systems and co-counselling has developed (see Chapter 10). There could be some difficulties for distance research students whether in the UK or abroad, and distance systems should be set up to cope with such problems. A different kind of pacing of agreed activities has to be set up and maintained for supervising relations at a distance. Some of these needs can be satisfied by the development of contracts, and some others by peer support networks and structures.

Research students need to develop autonomy. They need to plan and action their research projects and to use the support of the supervisor and research colleagues to guide them, help clarify difficult issues, test off hypotheses and the importance of data, and support and redirect them in crises if necessary.

Autonomy, negotiation and the development of shared responsibilities should result from the establishment of sound research practices and a good, clear relationship with your supervisor(s). This puts the supervisor in a position as facilitator, and you in a position where you are well informed, sure of what to expect in the nature of supervision, well aware of rules and formats, dates, what you can ask your supervisor, and so on. This usually results in successful supervisory relationships. Equally important are peer groups that help students to share ideas and develop a sense both of communicative peer support and of ownership of their work. A useful addition to formal, timetabled supervision sessions, peer- and group-based sessions and systems can make life easier and much more productive all round. A lower dropout rate and better quality of work are predictable, tangible results.

Task

Consider:

- Are there any problems you foresee?
- What can you do to avoid or cope with them?
- What do you need to do immediately to set up good working relationships?

Research skills – are you ready for this?

Task

You might well already have many research skills. You need to assess and measure these and so you will find it useful to audit your skills. Most universities offer research methods and skills training. Find out if yours does. You might specify needs, such as training with social science research analysis packages (SPSS). Alternatively, your needs might be more general, for example, acquiring and managing knowledge. Here are some of the research skills you will need. Audit them now. Mark the extent of your current skills and your skills needs. [1 = need to develop, 2 = some skills, 3 = quite confident, 4 = confident, 5 = a strength of mine.]

Project planning	1	2	3	4	5
Time management	1	2	3	4	5
Knowledge retrieval	1	2	3	4	5
Knowledge management	1	2	3	4	5
Analytical skills	1	2	3	4	5
Calculation skills	1	2	3	4	5
Interpretation skills	1	2	3	4	5
Evaluative thinking	1	2	3	4	5
Problem solving in different contexts	1	2	3	4	5
Creative thinking	1	2	3	4	5
Reading for different purposes	1	2	3	4	5
Reviewing the literature critically	1	2	3	4	5
Writing for different audiences	1	2	3	4	5
Writing theses and articles	1	2	3	4	5
Structuring and presenting papers	1	2	3	4	5
Managing discussion	1	2	3	4	5

You might well have underestimated or even overestimated your skills in some areas and you might also think that skills developed so far just will not be relevant at this level of research. Be realistic. Think of instances in your study life and everyday life when you have used such skills and could transfer them to a research context. For example, if you have run a family budget you might be better skilled at calculating than you imagine. If you have carried out literature reviews for an undergraduate essay, or written a journalistic piece, these too are skills which can be developed and transferred. If you find genuine gaps in skills, then seize opportunities to work with others who have these skills. Seize development and training opportunities – develop, build and reflect on your skills as you carry out your research work. Some of the chapters in this book aim to help you develop some of these skills, so you should find the tasks helpful.

Conclusion – a few points to remember

- Postgraduate study is a challenging opportunity for personal skills development
- Pick the right research qualification route for *you*
- Spot and work to avoid or overcome potential pitfalls
- Audit and update your research skills and recognise what you already have experience with in relation to research.

Further reading
Swinnerton-Dyer, H. P. F. (1982). *Report of the Working Party on Postgraduate Education*. London: HMSO.

3 Choosing the Right Research Degree

Selecting the right research degree and institution is vital.

> *This chapter looks at:*
>
> * *Types and varieties of research degree – and choice*
> * *Choosing your university and supervisor*

▶ Types of degree

This book largely concentrates on research projects, reports, dissertations and theses which are all part of MA, MPhil and PhD work. Practice-based doctorates of all sorts also often involve coursework elements but include a research-based dissertation. The chapter (15) on practice-based research and action research will also comment on balancing your coursework and your research, should you be undertaking this kind of a coursework and/or practice-based postgraduate qualification. The reason for focusing most heavily here on the research element of whatever postgraduate degree you are undertaking is that this most often constitutes a large-scale, new kind of undertaking for students, while coursework, although possibly of a different kind at postgraduate level, is more recognisable and possibly more manageable, resembling undergraduate essay work. The size of the thesis (often 80 000 words) is such a significant leap in terms of mass, extent, depth, and potential for conceptual complexity and detail, that it constitutes a real development of a kind of study for students and very different kinds of study practices, over time, than do extended essays, even at Master's level (most often these are 5000 words – more like an undergraduate dissertation than a thesis).

Before you embark on your research, you need to decide which is the right kind of research degree course for you. It might be that you decide to undertake a degree that offers more opportunity for taught work than concentrating on a dissertation or thesis alone. This is possible now even at PhD level (the EdD). If you choose a taught degree, you will still need to think about the dissertation or thesis element, and this book can help you with that. Consider which kind of research degree suits you by looking at the definitions and discussions below.

MA

Master's degrees are more usually a taught option. They frequently provide the opportunity to spend some time on research methods that help future research. If you decide to undertake an MA, consider whether a part-time or full-time course would suit you and your other commitments. Do ensure that there is a research-based dissertation or similar, because these are seen as guarantors of the level and quality of the work produced. Should you decide to undertake further research, you will be expected to have completed a dissertation to show that you are capable of an extended piece of research work (around 15 000–20 000 words).

MPhil

An MPhil is often seen as a stopping-off point before a PhD The MPhil is actually an opportunity for a very highly focused piece of research, often a single case study. A single issue, problem or concern often provides the focus for an MPhil, which involves research, but without the depth and the wide contribution and research culture of the PhD They tend to last from two or three years to five or six years (depending on whether it is full or part time), (length 50 000–60 000 words or more).

PhD

A PhD is a contribution to research development culture. It is a significant step forward in the work done in a specific area which is disciplinary or interdisciplinary based. PhDs tend to be larger, broader, and more original than MPhils, to cover more ground whether in breadth or depth, and to contribute something new, well founded and grounded. They also tend to last from three years (full time) to six or more (part time) so are substantial time commitments (length 50 000–80 000 words).

▶ Varieties of research degree

There are now, in many universities (probably mainly the 'modern' universities), real opportunities for doctorate study in particular, which are flexible, responsive and creative, and often also practice-based in many instances.

PhD by publication
Over a dozen universities in the UK now recognise the PhD by publication. Normally this involves pulling together a variety of small and large publications with a common theme and supplying an appropriate analytical and critical commentary of about 10 000 words to accompany the submission. The coherence of the submission is crucial. There need to be common themes and arguments running through the publications rather than an attempt to gain recognition for all you have previously published (at whatever level). Most often this form of PhD will be accompanied by a mini-thesis or commentary that sets out to prove the coherence of the whole and links all the work together.

Creative PhDs/MPhils/MAs
Many students now choose to produce something original and creative in response to a question, and to write an analytical discussion of how they see the creative work reflecting and moving forward the concerns, perspectives and needs. In the fine arts, women's studies, performing arts and other creative areas this is an essential way of recognising the kinds of thought and work which arise in the subject area. A firm theoretical and critical grounding is essential in these theses, often accompanied by creative works which otherwise would not be very easily analysable or explicable (sculptures, videos, collections of creative writing, stitchcraft, and so on).

Practice-based PhDs and the EdD
Several universities across the world, principally in Australia and some parts of the UK, have recognised the usefulness of the practice-based PhD In some instances this is an educational doctorate. It also appears in several other subjects, chiefly social work, business, management and health practice. Practice-based PhDs involve both a research element and a practice element. Often the research is into elements of practice and forwards understanding of that practice, leading to change. Essentially, this kind of PhD grew out of the aim for change rather than research for itself, and so in terms of shape the PhD will

have a large element of recommendations and action leading from its findings or will chart and explore reasons for certain practice developments and their effects. Practice-based doctorates are doctorates which 'represent inquiries by professional practitioners (for example, teachers, nurses, civil servants, police, doctors) into an aspect of their own practice' (Winter and Sabiechowska 1999).

This kind of research degree requires different kind of planning and supervising. It involves coursework as well as research, and it requires different kinds of supervisors and different-minded examiners who understand the practice base and the effective aims of the PhD The EdD is an educationally related version of this practice-based PhD.

The doctorate in education (EdD)

Education practitioners in particular often choose to take an education doctorate, which is offered by several universities including APU (Anglia Polytechnic University) and the OU (Open University).

It is aimed at professional development, involves much taught face-to-face work, operates using cohorts of student groups, and is assessed by several staged pieces of work, building up to a longer thesis. As such, then, it offers an opportunity to take professional issues, developments or problems and base elements of the research around these. For further details of the OU EdD see Chapters 22 and 23.

Task

Consider:

- Which sort of research degree suits you now? Why?
- Might you want to undertake a further research degree afterwards? Why?

▶ Choosing your university and supervisor

When you choose your university for your research degree, you need to take several factors into account:

- suitability for your kind of research
- accessibility

- facilities
- reputation for completion
- reputation of supervisors in your field
- reputation for support – training and quality of supervisors
- reputation for quality of research culture – publications, named people prominent in their fields, conferences, and so on
- your own feelings and intuition – can you spend what could be a considerable amount of your time here?

Often students select the supervisor for their specialism before choosing the university. Other students prefer to remain with the university at which they completed undergraduate study, or to deliberately move to somewhere new.

If you are a research student from overseas, it is also important to ask:

- What are the facilities for overseas students?
- Is there accommodation?
- Is there an international office or its equivalent?
- What is the university's reputation for support for international students?

Look up the university on the internet or through the central applications system (in the UK this is UCAS), seek out people who know people who have been there, or visit it if you can. Of course, if it is your local university or one in which you have already studied, you will already know the answers to many of the above questions, but you might not actually know how well the university does support its research students in terms of:

- accommodation
- a research structure – training, seminars, work-in-progress meetings, a location for students, for example, with comfortable chairs, a drinks machine and a noticeboard
- computer facilities, library support, and so on.

You might also not know about the reputation of the university elsewhere in terms of the subject area in which you seek to research, and you will probably not know the individual reputation of the supervisors you seek out. Some information, both formal and informal, can be gained by calling or visiting the departmental office of the department in which you will be based, by visiting the graduate office and by talking with current research students. All of these, as well as published materials, can yield answers to these questions. Then you can make your own mind up. Often mature students study for their research degrees at their local university and have no other alternative because they need to fit in with domestic and work demands. Others can move to universities other than the nearest that welcome them. Nearest does not mean best, nor does it mean worst. Your local university might well be the best for the work you wish to carry out. You need to carry out some research to find out what suits you, what will support you and who can supervise you.

Universities are keen to take on research students for several reasons. Their presence contributes to the development and recognition of a research culture which ensures a high level of intellectual activity, exchange, development and practice within the university culture as a whole, and embraces staff and undergraduates as well as research students. Staff are often very keen to take on research students for this reason and also because the most interesting, high-level, intellectual, in-depth learning conversations they have are, for the most part, with their research students. Good research students contribute to the research assessment exercise (RAE) in the UK, and to similar cultures in Australia, the USA and Europe, and so enhance the university's research rating, internationally as well as nationally, which attracts funding and students. Some research students actually come with research funds and international research students often pay high fees for the privilege of being supervised in their research.

However, some universities do not provide the necessary support which enables research students to successfully engage in their research. Some departments and supervisors have poor reputations for providing the kind of support which helps research students (see Denis Lawton in Graves and Varma 1997: 5).

Some supervisors take on more research students than they can actually cope with, in terms of giving the appropriate amount of time and attention to each one. Ideally, a supervisor should have no more than ten students at any one time. You might find that the supervisor you choose has too many students to take you on (see Chapter 4).

You will probably be asked for interview and you can ask questions about support and facilities at that stage. You will also be expected to discuss your research proposal fully with your prospective supervisor. It will therefore be very useful to have a sense of the questions you wish to ask underpinning your research, and the methods you will use in your research. The clearer you are about the questions and methods you feel are central to your work, the more likely you are to be able to ask appropriate questions, and to be accepted.

Task

Consider:

- What do you know about the university of your choice? And what is its reputation concerning research students?
- What do you know already about the department and the research culture?
- What do you know about your future potential supervisor?
- How can you go about finding answers to these questions?

Conclusion

This chapter should have helped you to choose:

- The right kind of research degree for your purposes and time available
- The right university.

Further reading

Graves, N., & Varma, V. (eds) (1997). *Working for a Doctorate: A Guide for the Humanities and Social Sciences*. London: Routledge.

Winter, R., & Sabiechowska, P. (1999) *Professional Experience and the Investigative Imagination*. London: Routledge.

4 Choosing Your Supervisor

Managing your supervisor(s) well and developing and maintaining a supportive, positive, constructively critical relationship over time is essential to help you produce a good quality thesis.

This chapter looks at:

- *Finding the right supervisor(s)*
- *Initial contacts and contracts – first sessions*
- *The nature of the supervisory relationship*
- *What you can expect from your supervisor(s)*
- *Learning contracts*
- *Stages of the supervisory process*
- *Supervisions at a distance*

▶ Introduction

The relationship between you and your supervisor or supervisors is a very important one and it is essential that you can get on with them personally, without necessarily being the best of friends, and can respect them in terms of scholarship, academic credibility and their practices. Many students select a specific person to be their supervisor because they know their work. You need to set up contacts in advance and develop a working link with such a prospective supervisor. Some students even cross the world (or move around the country) to be able to work with the supervisor they want. Often, however, you have little choice over who can supervise you because of the limited range of specialisms available or the specific nature of the research project.

In other instances, you could find the department and university normally match students with supervisors based on university knowledge of specialisms. If you have selected one or a number of possible universities (perhaps because of location or if other family members and friends study there or live nearby) you could find out about potential supervisors and their specialisms by looking up departmental web pages which usually indicate research and publication interests. For international students in particular, this can help provide a 'flavour' of the department and narrow down on or save on costly visits. If you can take an active part in the selection of who supervises you, you need to take some of the following issues into consideration. Do remember that sometimes the most eminent person is the busiest and can afford the least time for supervision, while the least experienced might give you more time. Sometimes we pick our supervisors for their specialist knowledge, at other times for their experience in the dominant methodologies we are going to use. If you are expected to have several supervisors, that is, a director of studies, a second supervisor and even an external adviser/supervisor, it is as well to think in terms of balancing the characteristics of a good supervisor in this choice: i.e. accessibility, communication skills, researh skills, reputation.

Task

In relation to your project, consider a supervisor:

- who is eminent in the field and so would be well aware of the latest reading, contacts and ideas
- who is using the kinds of methodologies you want to use and can help you with these
- who has the time and commitment to supervise you
- who is reliable, trustworthy and clear in their relations with you
- who is dependable
- with whom you get on professionally
- who is available
- with whom you can actually keep in contact, even if they are not close to you geographically.

▶ Choosing your supervisor, and internal regulations

In the outlining and development of your initial proposal and the scheme of your project you will need to follow the internal regulations.

In many of the new universities it is common for there to be a director of studies, first supervisor, and a second internal supervisor plus an external supervisor. The first supervisor – director of studies – might be in a position to suggest the other two, or you might have some suggestions. It is a good idea to pick someone who is interested in the same ideas and area but perhaps who can also contribute different skills, for example, methodology skills and different contacts. The external supervisor is also useful for their relative objectivity and other contacts and angles on the research.

You will need to draw up a credible and viable research outline and discussion of whatever length is required by the internal processes. You will need a clear initial idea of the methodology you intend to use to gather the necessary data and to ascertain the kinds of research questions and kinds of outcomes expected, and the kinds of probable skills needed such as data-gathering and processing skills. You need to spend some time on considering your underpinning beliefs and ideology and the theory and concepts you wish to use and can foresee.

Task

Consider:

- Who do you think you can ask to be your supervisor, or who have you been allocated?
- What do you know about their specialisms, the number of students they are supervising and their personality?
- Have you already met, and started to plan your research?
- When can you meet them?
- What do you feel you need to know immediately?

Once you have approached a supervisor and/or they have approached/ been allocated to you (whatever the process is in your case and that of your university), you need to get a clear definition of how much and how far you supervisor can and will work with you on your project and to contract with them over responsibilities.

Often the second supervisor is chosen for:

- expertise in methodology
- expertise in methods
- overall knowledge of university processes.

▶ Working with your supervisors: initial contracts and contacts

Title and scope of the project

Discuss the overall project with your supervisor and ask for their support in defining and clarifying the research title, the research questions and getting started in terms of reading and contracts. Remember how important it is to get your title right.

Good practice working with supervisors – regularity and kind of supervisions, at what stages

You need to draw up a formal or informal learning contract with your supervisor. A learning contract is like a legal contract (but less punitive and mostly informally binding) that you agree between you which sets out what you each expect of each other in terms of work, communication and responsibility. As you discuss your roles and draw this up as an informal contract, it helps you to make explicit your expectations, the frequency and kind of supervision, and what to avoid.

Try and agree on a clear plan of when you will see your supervisor and what stages of work are expected and when. It is important to set up regular supervisions in the early stages of your work, and these will probably become less frequent once you are fully engrossed. After the first stages, you will need to see your supervisor regularly, both (at not too close intervals) to keep a check on what you are involved in, and to ask them questions, to hear about further sources and contacts. They will also need to be closely involved when you are developing complex concepts, to check whether your interpretation of the reading and data is seemingly appropriate and successful so far. It is important that you remember that, although you are under the direction of a supervisor, your research is *your* activity. The autonomous student who nonetheless ensures that they abide by the rules, keeping in regular communication, checking their results and writing up appropriately, is the student who is genuinely undertaking their own research. You need to keep a firm balance between managing necessary autonomy and individual, independent research, without losing touch with your supervisor and the demands of the university regulations.

▶ Managing your supervisor

This section covers:

- Getting on with supervisors
- What can go wrong
- What you can reasonably expect
- Managing difficult and changing relationships

Students have problems with:
   Personality factors:

- neglect by supervisor
- clash of personalities
- barriers to communication arising from age, class, race, gender, and so on
- differences in approach to work.

Professional factors:

- a misinformed supervisor or one without sufficient knowledge in the area supervised
- a supervisor with few genuine research interests, or ones which differ fundamentally from those of the student.

Organisational factors:

- a supervisor having too many students to supervise
- a supervisor too busy with administration
- a supervisor's inability to manage their research group or their numbers of researchers efficiently
- departmental facilities and arrangements isolating the student
- inadequate support services and provision of equipment.

Research suggests that student dissatisfaction with the development of their work, and with relations with supervisors, can be avoided if there is clear and open communication on all aspects of the project. Also, overall, there needs to be structure without a straitjacket, that is, a framework for supervision and studies which facilitates rather than hinders students' development and creativity. A sound structure helps students to be aware of rules, demands and constraints, time limits and protocols. Within this structure they feel supported intellectually by supervisors and can develop their own individual, independent research as far as is possible. Structures also ensure fair play and provide systems for dealing with problems such as personality clashes, and misunderstandings about roles and work responsibilities.

To avoid these kinds of problems, both researcher and supervisors need to make it very clear to each other at the outset where the different responsibilities lie and to agree what roles and responsibilities they will each take on. It is in the spirit of this need that the idea of developing *contracts* emerges. It is in the spirit of an ongoing need for support and discussion, which the supervisor cannot always supply, that the idea of *peer support systems* and *co-counselling* has developed. It is in the spirit of the difficulties of distance research students, whether in the UK or abroad, that distance systems to cope with such problems and a different kind of pacing of agreed activities have to be set up and maintained. Some of these needs can be satisfied by the development of contracts, and some others by peer support networks and structures.

Research students need to develop autonomy. They need to plan and action their research projects and to use the support of the supervisor and research colleagues to guide them, help clarify difficult issues, test hypotheses and the importance of data, support and redirect in crises if necessary.

Autonomy, negotiation and the development of shared responsibilities should result from the establishment of sound research practices and good, clear relationships with supervisors which put the supervisor in a position as facilitator, and the student in a position where they are well informed, sure of what to expect in the nature of supervision, well aware of rules and formats, dates, what they can ask of their supervisor and where their peer groups can help them to share ideas and develop with a sense of both communicative peer support and of ownership of their work. As useful additions to formal, timetabled supervision sessions, peer- and group-based sessions and systems can make life easier and much more productive all round, and a lower drop-out rate and better quality of work are predictable, tangible outcomes.

Task

Consider:

- Are there any problems which you foresee?
- What can you do to avoid or cope with them?
- What do you need to do immediately to set up good working relationships?

▶ Things to ask/not to ask your supervisor(s)

What you can reasonably expect

It is good to have a clear relationship with your supervisor, with clear parameters. Here are some of the situations in which you can or can't reasonably expect help.

- Ask them to help clarify stages of the research.
- Ask them to put you in touch with information, people who can give you information and books that they know of.

But:

- Don't expect them to do the research for you.
- Don't let them do the research for you.
- Don't be steamrollered into something totally irrelevant to your project but topical for them.

Before supervisions, decide:

- what questions you need to look at
- what problems you have
- what you feel you can ask from them
- what outcomes you have in mind, for example, what you would like to achieve from this particular supervision at this point in your research. It might be assurance that your direction is right, that your data is interesting and valid, or a chance to test out a hypothesis, consult on a problem, or it might be to check out parts of what you have written with the supervisor to see if they feel that it makes sense, is fluent, and is written for the right audience.

Drawing up an agenda for each meeting, however informal, can help you both to focus on the important current and longer-term issues. If possible, consult with your supervisor beforehand to see what is on both your agendas, and so start the process of concentrating on the work to be discussed in advance.

▶ Planning to get the most from your supervisor

- Try to agree on well spaced-out supervisions, properly timetabled, not ad hoc chats (these are helpful too, but should not be confused with proper supervisions).

- Get clear instructions.
- Get hold of the rules and regulations yourself too, and check with other researchers.
- Make sure you understand about length requirements, protocols, timings and facilities.
- Try and get on with your supervisor without becoming too friendly, so that you can both be honestly (constructively) critical.
- But remember that they have lots of other people to work with – other students, other pressing calls on their time – so ensure your time with them is quality time.
- This is high-level work – you are largely autonomous, but the supervisor shares ultimate responsibility for the quality of work – so you need to negotiate decisions and quality throughout.
- It is important to ensure clear communication and understanding of what is expected, in terms of levels of thought, practice and product. All of these need to be checked out at the start, through-out the project, and at the end before it is written up.
- Don't take anything for granted.
- Find anything such as regulations or dates out for yourself as well, so you are not too dependent. You need to know these things as they affect your timing, and your work overall.
- Check with other researchers about stages, problems and quality.

▶ What research students can expect of supervisors – a brief summary

While this is not an exhaustive list, it can give you an idea of rights and responsibilities. Knowledge of these expectations and interactions can help form the basis of a mutually successful supervisory relationship. You can expect your supervisor(s):

- *To supervise* – guide as to structure, scope, decisions about meth-odology, and so on. You can expect to be told if your work goes off course, seems misguided, is likely to be too adventurous and enor-mous in scope, and so on. Supervisors cannot give this kind of guidance without seeing and discussing the work in progress. They should be asked for this kind of guidance.
- *To read your work thoroughly, and in advance.* It is important then to agree a time for the supervision, select the work on which you would like advice and comment, send this to the supervisor, and if

possible indicate in what areas you would like this advice and comment. It is important to send selected items, but mention the areas that need curtailing and shaping.

- *To be available when needed.* They need to mutually plan regular supervisions, but students need to know that their supervisors are approachable in between these more formal sessions if necessary, to ask key questions, through a 'surgery' or other system.
- *To be friendly, open and supportive.* Academic issues need discussion, but it is important to establish a consultative, supportive relationship as well.
- *To be constructively critical.* Students can expect praise to be given where relevant, and criticism toned to the constructive rather than the harsh, to enable change. If you do not receive helpful information and feedback you might become discouraged. Gradually you will need less of it as autonomy and judgement develop.
- *To have a good knowledge of the research area.* If the supervisor is not an expert, provided the student has access to others who are, and the division of responsibilities between first and second supervisor is clearly made, a supervisor whose specialism is related but not absolutely centred on the student's exact topic can still supervise and support.
- *To structure the supervision, and ongoing relationship*, so that it is relatively easy to exchange ideas.
- *To know how to ask open questions, how to draw out ideas and problems and how to elicit information, even if the student finds communication difficult.* Some of this can be facilitated by working for some of the time with more than one student present, to aid discussion. If a student works with a supervisor who does not ask useful questions they should learn to ask them themselves and elicit information and comment in that way. You might also need to interact with other students supervised by the same supervisor, or on a similar topic, and discuss these kinds of questions and share information and ideas. This is particularly useful if the supervisor is not very practised in asking useful questions and prompting you.
- *To have sufficient interest in their research to put more information such as reading, resources and contacts their way.*
- *To encourage you to attend appropriate conferences and introduce you to others in their field.* Supervisors should encourage students to publish parts of their work and support them in the writing and

editing processes. However, it is important to measure the amount of work put up for publication, and you should seek advice on this. Too much work published from the thesis before submission might endanger the originality of the thesis itself, and too many publications on only tangential topics will probably take your mind off your main focus. A balance needs to be kept between publishing and saving the work for the thesis, and supervisors should advise on this.

• *To be sufficiently involved in their success to help you focus on directing your work later for a publication, promotion or job.* However, supervisors are rarely able to actually provide the job themselves, so depending on them too much on this area can be an error. They can always be asked to be referees, and to give advice on jobs sought, later (see Moses 1989).

Some of these expectations are really a description of how the supervision can enable the student to enter the research culture and gain from its opportunities, with supervisor(s') support. Some others are about the precise direction, teasing out of complex conceptualising and research questioning, and editing of parts of the written thesis which are probably the major part of the supervisor's role. In some instances, such as science students working in research labs, or social science students on project groups, working daily alongside their supervisor and others, it is difficult to insist on a complex and conceptually taxing supervision when you meet all the time. However, it is important to focus just on your own work. Arrange specific times for supervisions with the kind of agenda discussed above, at different stages in your research.

Working closely with your supervisor, it is more probable that they will suggest conferences and publication opportunities, sometimes the kind of joint publication which helps a student gain a reputation from the coupling of their name with that of the established supervisor. Be careful in such instances that you are not having your work merely 'stolen'.

▶ Stages of supervisions – what you might expect at different stages

At different stages of the supervision process supervisors should support students' work and advise in different ways, while maintaining a close but not too intrusive eye on the general way in which their work is developing. If it feels helpful, it might be an idea to check with your supervisor whether they are happy to take the following responsibilities and elements of their role on board, and what is expected of you in your work. This too will form the basis of a formal or informal learning contract, and give each of you an idea of what to expect from the other.

The beginning of the supervisory process
Supervisors should be expected to:

- help define and clarify a title
- suggest and evaluate proposed methodologies
- ensure students carry out any necessary preliminary other skill development and study, for example, research methods, statistics training
- help shape initial plans
- help refine and define the field, methodology, scope and nature of the research
- encourage realistic approaches and hopes
- put contacts and reading your way
- encourage early outlines, and the refining of these outlines
- encourage the development of good time-management habits
- set up a pattern of supervisions early on, which can be modified with need
- put you in touch with other research students
- help design useful learning situations for you, and take advantage of openings which could help you develop.

Ongoing – in the middle stages of your work
The supervisor should be expected to:

- stay in touch but not over-intrude unless necessary
- care about the development of the research and work on it
- encourage conversations which enable you to conceptualise and deal with difficult underpinning ideas and constructions of knowledge
- establish a role model of modes of research, of ethical decision making, of commitment and perseverance, of being realistic, and so on
- teach the craft of research – that is, ensuring students are aware

of the importance of setting up well-defined ethical experiments, manage data appropriately and fairly, produce sound reports and a well-argued, well-documented, well-evidenced thesis
- read your work thoroughly
- consider your questions, and the questions you should be asking
- help tease out difficult issues and problems
- give constructive criticism
- wean you away into autonomy gently and gradually
- encourage your academic role development
- encourage you to keep very good notes and references
- support you realistically through any crises in the work.

Towards the final stages of your work
The supervisor should be expected to:

- encourage you to start to write up as soon as you can, and alter it if necessary (but don't leave it too late)
- encourage you to edit
- encourage you to disseminate at conferences and through publications as soon as you and your data are ready, and help you with this without taking over
- encourage you to produce a well-presented final thesis
- encourage you to prepare thoroughly and fully for the viva, to believe in yourself and to consider possible questions
- encourage you to move on further, as appropriate, in the field when you have achieved your postgraduate qualification.

The relationship with your supervisor(s) is a long-term one and is essentially designed to help you to become a sound and successful researcher. You need to ensure that you do not depend too much on the supervisor(s), and do not take too much for granted. It is essential to be open and frank about mutual expectations and needs. Consider what Ingrid Moses has to say about the start of the project in particular, from the supervisor's point of view:

> Becoming a supervisor is a two-way process. Openness in the initial discussions may prevent years of frustration for you and the student if your personality and learning–teaching styles are mismatched and no common style or ground is found. Openness about your own and the student's competence may prevent the student from withdrawing or failing. (Moses 1989: 10)

Task

Consider:

- What do you really want to achieve in your research?
- How can your supervisors help you to achieve this?
- Who else can help you?

▶ Planning work and supervisions

Task

Consider:

- What kind of agenda will you need to sort out with your supervisor at the early meetings?
- What is essential in a learning contract between you?
- What do you want to ensure happens?
- What do you want to ensure does not happen?

Considering some of these issues and practices should help you with the planning and managing of your research, and your supervisor. You have a right to adequate and good quality supervision. You will also find it useful to get into good working habits with your supervisor(s) and maintain good relations with them so that you can exchange ideas, seek and use suggestions, and avoid any personality clashes. You will also find it useful to ensure that you get in touch with other peers, seek and maintain peer support for research in progress work (see Chapter 10) and troubleshoot. But it is up to you to manage your project and your time and to have a clear idea of what your goals are. You should also be realistic with what you plan, how you work, when things are going wrong and how to readjust, when things are going well, how to ensure that you produce a conceptually complex enough, well-researched, well-expressed and argued, well-presented postgraduate research project which genuinely contributes to research in the field. This can and should be a very satisfying process and experience.

Task

Consider:

- Who can you approach to be your supervisor(s)?
- Who might advise you on supervisor(s) to approach?
- Have you already been allocated a supervisor?
- Does the supervisor you have agreed to work with/think you will be working with have the right mix of methodologies, time, willingness, and so on? If not, who could be brought in to balance this lack?

You will need to have these issues clear in your own mind before you start to work with your supervisor(s) so you know what to aim for, what to avoid or overcome, and what kind of help you will find useful. Of course, some of your needs will change during the project and you will need to continue and develop a supportive/constructively critical dialogue with your supervisor(s) to enable you in your work.

Decide on how you want to and need to develop your skills, what to ensure happens and what to avoid. Concentrate on what you can you do in terms of:

- time management
- project management
- self-management
- management of your supervisor.

Before going to the first supervision you need to decide what kinds of activities you will be involved in with your supervisor(s) in the first supervision, what your agenda is, what your short- and longer-term aims are and how you would like the supervisory relationship to work. It is important to set the tone right at the first meeting, and to establish a formal or informal contract between you about mutual working practices, and expectations from the supervisory process.

You might well plan to set up a learning contract with your supervisor(s) on your first meeting. These greatly enable smooth working practices between you and clarify what kinds of 'ground rules' of expectations and behaviours you will be working towards over time (it is a long-term relationship, remember).

Conclusion

We have looked at:

- Choosing your supervisor
- Working with internal regulations
- What you can and cannot expect from your supervisor
- Potential difficulties with supervisors and how to avoid them

Further reading

Moses, I. (1989). *Supervising Postgraduates*. Sydney: HERDSA.

5 Writing a Research Proposal

This chapter looks at:

- *What does a good research proposal look like?*
- *Stages and elements of a research proposal*
- *Submission*

Your research proposal is the main base upon which a supervisor and a research degree committee can begin to judge the value or potential of your research work. Many universities now demand a great deal of work prior to the submission of a research proposal, which in the past might well have been little more than an indicative title.

Drawing up a research proposal is the first main task you will be involved in with your supervisor. Depending on your university regulations, the norm is to register for your research degree if it is an MPhil or a PhD, then develop the proposal, then have registration confirmed when the proposal is accepted – which could be a process lasting anything from three months to a year in some instances. For students studying for an MA or other Master's and writing a dissertation, you will already be on the course, and drawing up a proposal with your supervisor is an ongoing, rather swift process with a usually early deadline to begin the work and a set deadline to hand it all in. Do check on university regulations very early in advance as you enter your research degree.

Before you submit your research proposal formally, you will need to carry out a substantial amount of early research work, some literature review and searching, and to identify the theoretical and methodological underpinnings to your work.

What are the theoretical bases and contexts for your work? With much PhD research in particular and some MPhil and Master's work, the interdisciplinary nature of the research means that there will be several theoretical contexts and areas with which your work will be related and out of which it will grow. You need to determine and focus on the methods, beliefs and ways of constructing and discussing knowledge and ideas which you will need to be familiar with. You need to be able to show you can work with these to achieve your research outcomes.

You will need to seek support from your supervisor in the development of a proposal of sufficient quality and to convince a research degrees committee that you have the potential to carry out research at the level you seek. Master's research proposals often go before field or subject committees, while MPhils and PhDs go before full research degree committees (or whatever carries out that function in your university), where they will be read carefully by internal and external readers and by the committee. The latter can ask some very helpful things about questions, aims, methods, theoretical underpinning and that fundamental question – so what? That is, what will this piece of research lead to or contribute to?

The research proposal is a carefully crafted piece of work. It is also a very useful foundation from which to develop your ideas and arguments. You will be able to use it to help you plan your work and study programme and to draft your chapters. Some of the problems you might encounter in your early literature review could lead to central underpinning questions running throughout the research. The issues you deal with in order to write the proposal will also run throughout it. It is a stage and a substantial piece of work from which you will draw in the future. You will also have to recognise that it is a compromise. Of course, by producing a detailed plan like this, you might well feel you are in a 'straitjacket' and this should be avoided. You will discover other information and arguments, you will find some of what you seek is not there, you will change your mind and your emphases and you will find also that the time planning skips, changes, and so on. But the proposal is a draft outline and it will be worked with in the future in a dynamic way. For the proposal acceptance process, it is absolutely essential and it is a most useful base for future work.

▶ What do you want to research? How you can draw up a good proposal

When you embark on your proposal, you are expected to identify your main research questions and sub-questions, to clarify for yourself:

▶ What are you looking for?
▶ What do you seek to prove/investigate?
▶ What will you consider the relationship between?
▶ What will you contribute to?
▶ What will you change?
▶ What difference will your research make? Why does it 'matter'?

The proposal

In your proposal you will need to address the following areas (or similar):

Indicative title
What will you call the dissertation/thesis? It is better to pose questions and to make a suggestion about links in argument rather than to give a single word or area of study.

Aim and focus of the study
These should suggest the underlying research area and your main question and sub-questions. Eventually it hopes to form the abstract of your thesis. Think about it carefully. What are you really exploring, arguing, trying to find out and hoping to find out, then suggest? What links with what in your mind?

Context for the research
What issues, problems, history, background and others' questions provide a context, an academic culture, ongoing set of questions, thoughts and discoveries for your own work? How is it contributing to academic work in this area and to the body of research and knowledge in this area?

Theoretical perspectives and interpretations
Where have you taken your theories from – from what kind of framework? What are the underpinning theoretical perspectives informing your ideas? For example, you might use feminist or Marxist theoretical perspectives and work on organisational analysis, phenomenography, and so on. Be careful to indicate not only which theories and theoretical perspectives inform your work but how they are combined and how they relate to and direct or drive your unique (or quite unique) piece of research.

Research methodology and methods

What is the research methodology, or research methodologies under-pinning your research? What methods or vehicles and strategies are you going to use and why? How do they link with and help inform and develop each other?

You will need to know exactly why you have chosen, for example, questionnaires or interviews because of the way they can help you get to and find out about your research object. Your questions and your conceptual framework need explaining. You should be able to clearly indicate how your chosen methods should enable you to investigate your chosen questions and subject area. The sample, your timings and methods of analysis need defining.

Research design

How will you go about collecting information and carrying out litera-ture searches? Provide an outline of the different activities you will undertake at what points in your research and do a critical path analy-sis of this, that is, first activities (usually a literature search), then the research activities.

Ethical considerations

Many dissertations and theses have ethical considerations, and these will be particularly complex when you are using human subjects. Obvi-ously if you are involved in medical research this would be so, but it is also true of protecting the identities of those who give you informa-tion from questionnaires, focus groups and interviews. You will need to take care when asking certain sorts of personal questions or using documents that refer to people, alive or dead. You also need to indi-cate due care and concern for procedures when dealing with those who are dead, and with certain subjects. Some research, for example that of nurses in hospital, might be covered by an already established code, such as the Helsinki Agreement, so you need to say so. There will prob-ably be other issues to take into account which specifically relate to your work. Other ethical issues arise when working with animals, with confidential material (however old) or with children. Look up your uni-versity's code of ethics for guidance. (See Chapters 16 and 24, which have sections on ethics).

Outline plan of study

This part of the proposal asks you to indicate what you think would be the timeline for your research activities, and/or main features of each of your chapters. It would be useful to revisit this at different points in your ongoing research and consider how they are developing and if any early findings are changing these. It cannot be rigidly adhered to, but it is a useful scheme.

Justification for level of award

An MA, MPhil or PhD usually involves this question. You will need to describe and discuss what you feel your research will contribute to the field of knowledge, the development of arguments and the research culture. What kinds of practices or thoughts and arguments can it move forward? How can it make a difference? Why does it matter and why is it obviously at this level? Is it serious, broad, deep-questioning and original enough?

Primary references

10 or 12 of these will be included in your submission. Do make sure they represent key texts, the range of your theoretical areas, and some up-to-date examples.

You need to be in agreement with your supervisor about your proposal as it forms the basis of your future work. You also need to be agreed about the proposal before it goes before any research degrees committees as it will be thoroughly read, probably by both an internal and an external referee who will have points to make about the viability, the expression and the methodology. It is tempting if the research proposal is accepted just to ignore the questions asked at a research degrees committee, but in fact some of the questions about contexts, methods, and so on, are going to be very helpful, probably in the formation of arguments and in the discovery of information and ideas, so they are useful to take on board. While early supervisions should help develop the proposal, a supervision after the committee have commented will help refine it further so you can get started formally on your research. At the same time as committees consider proposals, students usually get going reading more and focusing clearly.

Task

- Produce a draft proposal/plan.
- Look carefully through this draft plan and discuss it with a reliable colleague or friend.

- See if you can justify and explain each part of it to them/to yourself.
- What questions and gaps do you have?
- What is still to be fleshed out?
- Draw up a plan of action to work on the elements that are not fully developed.

Draw up your own draft proposal under the following headings. Remember these are as yet notes which you can flesh out.

Draft proposal

- indicative title
- aim and focus of the study
- questions
- sub-questions
- context for the research
- theoretical perspectives and interpretations
- research methodology
- research methods
- research design (stages of your work – over time)
- ethical considerations
- outline plan of study

Timeline for activities in the research

1 from . . . . . to . . . . .
2 from . . . . . to . . . . .
3 from . . . . . to . . . . .
4 from . . . . . to . . . . .
5 from . . . . . to . . . . .

- Draft chapters and areas
- justification for level of award
- primary texts

Does this make perfect, coherent sense to you? And to your colleagues? Talk it through with a friend, colleague or family member, and of course, with your supervisor!

Conclusion

We have considered how you go about putting together a research proposal. At all levels such proposals are needed, sometimes in a formal (PhD, MPhil) and sometimes a shorter or less formal shape (MA). Writing them helps you to be clear about how your research questions and conceptual framework (of ideas, arguments, theories and methods) run throughout your proposed research. For MPhil/PhD most universities demand a lengthy proposal (about four pages), and this could take up to six months to refine and perfect. You will be researching alongside this writing, but probably will have your proposal agreed (and probably changed a little or a lot) by a research degrees committee before you are formally and finally registered. Sometimes registration can be backdated. Sometimes you might have to resubmit the proposal. This is perfectly normal. You need to get it right, as it informs all you do – so don't be too upset if it is sent back for rewriting – it will encourage you to be clearer, more coherent, and more likely to produce a successful piece of research which matters.

Stage 2

Getting Going – Supervisors, Methods and Time

6 Managing Your Supervisor(s)

This chapter looks at:

- *Meetings*
- *Learning contracts*
- *Supervisory arrangements at a distance*
- *Ongoing arrangements*

▶ Planning work and supervisions

Task

Consider:

- What kind of agenda will you need to sort out with your supervisor at the early meetings?
- What is essential in a learning contract between you?
- What do you want to ensure happens?
- What do you want to ensure does not happen?

Considering some of these issues and practices should help you with the planning and managing of your research, and your supervisor. You have a right to adequate and good quality supervision. You will find it useful to get into good working habits with your supervisor(s) and maintain good relations with them so that you can exchange ideas, seek and use suggestions, and avoid any personality clashes. You will also find it useful to get in touch with other peers and seek and maintain peer support for research in progress work (see Chapter 10 on peer-support systems) and to troubleshoot. But it is up to you to manage your project and your time and to have a clear idea of what your goals are. You should also be realistic with what you plan, how you work and how to readjust when things are going wrong, when things are going well, how to ensure that you produce a conceptually complex enough, well-researched, well-expressed and argued, well-presented postgraduate research project which genuinely contributes to research in the field. This can and should be a very satisfying process and experience.

Before going to the first supervision you need to decide what kinds of activities you will be involved in with your supervisor(s) in the first supervision, what your agenda is, what your short- and longer-term aims are and how you would like the supervisory relationship to work. It is important to set the tone right at the first meeting, and to establish a formal or informal contract between you about mutual working practices, and expectations from the supervisory process.

You might well plan to set up a learning contract with your supervisor(s) on your first meeting. These greatly enable smooth working practices between you and clarify what kinds of 'ground rules' of expectations and behaviours you will be working to over time (it is a long-term relationship, remember).

The first supervision will take place before you have submitted your proposal and had it accepted by the research degrees committee, or whichever university group at your university makes decisions about the viability of research degree proposals. You need to draw up your own agenda for this meeting concentrating on:

- getting to know each other
- sounding out the supervisor with regard to their availability and suitability, their enthusiasm and their initial responses to your project
- drawing up an initial draft proposal in outline
- drafting a title
  (see Chapter 5 for details on how to go about these last two activities)
- you will find it useful to talk through the aims and outcomes you have in mind, the kind of methodologies you intend to use, and any of the needs or problems you foresee (see Chapter 9).

In your first supervisory conversation you can judge your supervisor's initial responses to your ideas and ways of thinking, and to what extent they can offer further reading, contacts, and suggestions about methodologies and their viability. For instance, it might be at this very early stage that the supervisor advises you to go beyond using a questionnaire only for data collection, or asks you some thought-provoking questions about controversies in the subject in which you are working, or tests your responses about how to deal with ethical issues, and so on.

It is important that a very early supervision with your first supervisor/director of studies also includes your second supervisor so that there can be some development of agreement as to the different, complementary roles they play in relation to your work, and how you and they are going to work together. If these working relationships are not made clear early on, you could find that you receive contradictory advice and are caught in the middle of their debates. This needs to be handled with sensitivity.

At the first meeting with your supervisor you can also decide together what form your future supervisions could take, their frequency, and, in this first instance, the next stages towards preparing the proposal. A learning contract can help to clarify and formalise some of these practices of working together.

▶ Learning contracts

Research students are undertaking a long piece of work with many stages, at any one of which they might need guidance and help. Sometimes you work closely with your supervisor, or see them frequently, but sometimes supervisors and research students hardly cross paths and you might both be unsure of how often you should be meeting. It is important, for the sake of clarity and equality, that there should be learning contracts, clearly defining how much time, and what kind of support the supervisor(s) can offer, and what the expected behaviours of each of you are. Learning contracts can be drawn up which make expectations explicit, such as frequency of supervisions and the production of stages of work. These can help everyone involved in the supervisory equation to manage their work, and to point out problems fairly objectively. A learning contract is like a legal contract (but less punitive and mostly informally binding) agreed between you, which sets out what you each expect of each other in terms of work, communication and responsibility. As you discuss your roles and draw up this informal contract, it helps you to make explicit your expectations of the frequency and kind of supervision, and outline what to avoid. Another shape to a learning contract is less about expected roles and behaviours or 'grand roles' for the supervisory relationship and more about ensuring you have clear goals and outcomes and a clear idea of how to achieve these. You will need to decide what sort of contract enables you and your supervisor to establish ground rules and working procedures. You might decide to just use the contract for yourself and mention it informally to your supervisor.

Why use learning contracts?

Research has shown that when adults learn on their own initiative, for reasons of personal development (see Brookfield 1986, Rogers 1989 and Tight 1983), they can do so within a loose structure. However, when the purpose is to improve competence in a job or engage in a profession, or develop a longer-term project (such as a research qualification), then the needs and expectations of other groups must be taken into account and the structure needs to be more explicit.

Learning contracts (see Anderson et al. 1996) also provide a vehicle for the mutual planning of learning experiences by the research student and supervisor. By participating in this process, the research student can feel that they own the plan and therefore can be more committed to the learning.

Guidelines for developing a learning contract

Once you have agreed a learning contract, you need to fill it out in some detail for yourself.

A learning contract can be thought of as having six stages:

1 Learning needs

The learning needs are the gap between where you are now and where you need, or want, to be. The gap to be bridged for you as a researcher involves both training to equip yourself with research skills (such as IT skills and presentation and viva skills, as well as statistical analysis and library research skills, and so on) and the various stages of the research which it is hoped will yield the findings useful for your research degree submission.

2 Learning outcomes

The next step is to specify exactly what you need to learn in order to fill the learning gap. This involves describing what will be *learned*, not the strategies adopted. This is an account of the specific skills and levels

you need to develop to be successful in undertaking your research –
quite apart from whether you discover what you seek in the work.

3 Learning resources and strategy
Work out what materials will be needed and who might be involved to
help you meet each of these outcomes. Note what approaches will be
used. You need to identify stages of the research, who can help you,
what is needed, what needs to be in place, who needs to be involved,
and so on.

4 Evidence of accomplishment
You will need to decide what can be counted as evidence of achievement of the stages of the research and the outcomes. You could point
to various findings and analyses for the research and also to publication, conference presentations, and so on. The transfer document or
research report (depending on which you need to complete) will also
be evidence of achievement of certain stages in your work.

5 Review
Review the contract with friends or colleagues to check how clear,
appropriate and convincing they find it, and whether they think anything has been omitted.

6 Carry out the contract and evaluate your success at each stage
One such learning contract for research degree supervisions could look
like the one below (but there are many alternatives, and you will need
to decide on what suits your situation and that of your supervisors).
You might find it useful to start to fill out the blank learning contract
from your point of view before your first meeting with your supervisor.
To be sensitive to the relationship, it would be a good idea to ask if
a learning contract might help clarify the way you will work with
supervisors and then show them an example, rather than arriving with
one half completed! It should be negotiated between you, but is *not*
a necessity.

*Learning contracts (bare outline of kind of contents of a typical
contract):*

- Defining goals, aims and outcomes
- Agreeing goals, aims and outcomes with the supervisor
- Recognising and planning appropriate learning tasks, activities

which will help achieve these goals, aims and outcomes, for example, involvement in research seminars and training courses

- Drawing up/finding/agreeing a specific time plan for activities which contribute to stages of the research and to training, presentation, and so on
- Drawing up/finding/agreeing a set of achievement measures which will enable you to measure off your achievements – in training and in stages of the research
- Evaluating – reflecting on further needs for learning – both training for the research and stages of the research work.

Agreement between learner and supervisor.

A working example of a learning contract

Research student:
First Supervisor/Director of Studies:
Second Supervisor:
External Supervisor:
Title/research topic:

Date of registration:
Approximate proposed date of completion:
Agreed frequency of supervisions:

Research student

I agree to:

- agree meeting dates and attend meetings well prepared
- maintain a steady working pattern
- send chapter drafts/work as agreed two weeks in advance of each supervision for comment and discussion
- suggest issues, questions and concerns for discussion arising from work in progress or contained in the chapter drafts for an agenda for the supervision
- seek, consider and take advice on aspects of conceptual issues, reading, methodology, progress, writing up, publication and presentations, as appropriate, from the supervisor
- inform the supervisor(s) immediately of any major problems in the research, changes in workload which affect the research, and personal issues which affect it, for example, house moves, job changes and so on

- provide draft progress reports every six months to aid scheduling, replanning and monitoring of progress.

Supervisor

I agree to:

- agree meeting dates and prepare to consider key issues, overall work and future developments
- read and comment on chapter drafts/work as agreed in advance of each supervision for comment and discussion
- suggest issues, questions and concerns for discussion arising from work in progress or contained in the chapter drafts for an agenda for the supervision
- offer advice on aspects of conceptual issues, reading, methodology, progress, writing up, publication and presentations and so on, as appropriate
- suggest appropriate reading, contacts, and methodologies
- inform research student immediately of any major problems in the research, changes in workload which affect the research, and personal issues which affect it, for example, sabbatical absences, job changes, and so on
- ask for and comment on draft progress reports every six months to aid scheduling, replanning and monitoring of progress
- advise on writing up, conferences, opportunities for publication and presentation, and so on.

Signed .... Date ....

Addresses and contact points:

Research student   First Supervisor   Second Supervisor   External

This is a very prescriptive learning contract. You might want to develop a more open-ended one which largely concentrates on defining the ends/outcomes you wish to achieve and then negotiates (with your supervisor) and defines the routes you will take to get there, and also specifies how you will know when you have achieved your outcome. Obviously, achievement of the research degree will be the major outcome, but there will be others along the way and these are important to try and identify.

Learning contracts are a learner-centred way of encouraging learners to identify and be involved in their own programme planning, recognising their learning outcomes and objectives, and becoming fully involved in their own learning, recognising and working on developing their learning approaches and styles, making the most of their learning opportunities and monitoring their own learning needs and achievements. As such, then, it is a key, new learning strategy related to experiential and work-based learning, and personal monitoring and management of learning. Certainly, if you are involved in a work-based or professional doctorate, you will want to develop a learning contract. It is also useful for all those undertaking research work since it causes you to plan in negotiation with your supervisor and to make perfectly clear what the time, tasks, roles, outcomes, assessment and products look like at each stage.

If learners are to develop the skills of planning and carrying out a self-directed learning project, then they need not only the empowerment to do so, but a framework in which to learn. This framework is a learning contract.

A learning contract can be:

- informal
- formal
- an implicit self-contract.

See p. 61 for a draft learning contract to complete.

▶ Involving your supervisor(s)

There is also often a concern about how much supervisors are actually involved in the work students carry out. They are important in helping to shape and structure the work, and in providing support, information and guidance, but they must not actually do the work for the students. When the drafts of the thesis finally come in, it is important that the supervisor encourages some of the editing but does not actually carry it out themselves. Discussing fundamental theories and the meaning of what has been discovered is helpful, but final expression and editing is not. It starts to take the ownership of the work away from the student. The supervisor is the repository of knowledge about rules and regulations concerning expression, layout, and so on, but it is important that you have the written information about these details

Task

Your draft learning contract (please complete)

Draft learning contract

Name: ....

Supervisor: ....

- Defining goals, aims and outcomes.
  Agreeing goals, aims and outcomes: (a) training and (b) stages of the research:
  (a)
  1
  2
  3
  4
  5
  (b)
  1
  2
  3
  4
  5
  6
  7
- Recognising and planning appropriate learning tasks.
  Tasks and activities:
  1
  2
  3
  4
  5
- Time plan for activities.
  Dates: activity:
  Dates: activity:
  Dates: activity:
  Dates: activity:
- I will know I have achieved these outcomes when:
  1
  2
  3
  4
  5
- Evaluating learning and reflecting on further needs for learning: (complete this when contract completed – a self-reflection exercise)
  Agreement between ....
  And ....

Date: ....

and access to central information as well, as supervisors can forget and give erroneous or sketchy information at times. With information and formalised rules and systems of support established, understood and available, you are then empowered and responsible to make choices, develop and express ideas and finally, to check that expression yourself in the final draft of the thesis.

▶ Getting on well with your supervisor(s), establishing and maintaining good working relationships while avoiding personality clashes and coping with absences

Some of the concerns that research students have voiced are to do with personality clashes, for example, with the recalcitrant or interfering supervisor who can't let them get on with anything and checks their every move. Maintaining a steady rate of work can be difficult in these instances. You need to ensure that you have clear working relations with your supervisor, do not intrude on their personal lives, and manage to keep the balance between friendship and a professional working relationship so that neither of you relax too much and forget to concentrate on the timing and management of each aspect of the research. If you do not get along with your supervisor it is important to remain cordial at least, because social impasses will affect your work adversely. Interpersonal relations need handling with sensitivity. You also need to make sure that preoccupied supervisors still concentrate on your work, that very eminent ones who travel to conferences and go away a lot still give you the time you need, as agreed, and that those whose working situations change (sabbaticals, retirement, new job responsibilities, and so on) renegotiate their working relationship contract with you to enable you to continue with their support. If they retire/leave their job and cannot continue to supervise you (the two do not necessarily follow), then the supervisor needs to ensure that someone else with equal commitment takes the supervision process on.

Questions
▶ What would you do if you found you did not personally get along with your supervisor(s)? Does this matter?
▶ If your supervisor left for a sabbatical year/six months abroad, what would you do?

▶ If you realised that good practices of meeting for supervisions had lapsed, what would you do?

▶ If you developed disagreements about the emphasis of the thesis, interpretation of information, underpinning concepts, and so on, what would you do?

To avoid these kinds of problems, supervisors have to make it very clear to students at the outset where the different responsibilities lie and agree with them what roles and responsibilities they will each take on. It is in the spirit of this need that the idea of developing contracts emerges. However, there can always be changes in either working relationships or in access.

It is important to:

• Ensure that your right to adequate supervisions is not jeopardised because of staff absence. In these instances you might need to discuss with the supervisor(s) who will replace them in their supervision of you, whether in their absence they can continue to support you through visits and regular e-mail and phone contact, or whether they have a trustworthy, like-minded colleague who could take the supervision over.

• Ensure that you get on with your supervisor(s) but make it clear politely and assertively when you disagree with good reason; when you need clarification and they do not seem to have been fully clear with you; when you need information and guidance and this is not forthcoming or you have not fully understood, and when there are certain developments in which you believe which they seem to overlook or undervalue. If you actually 'fall out' or have quite strong disagreements you will need to sort this out. Write a letter, then make an appointment to resolve the difficulties. Again, ensure you are assertive but polite, do not lose your temper, but get a fair deal. If there are extreme working relationship problems with your supervisor you need to ensure you confidentially discuss these with the supervisor, then with the subject leader or research head, as appropriate, so that your work is not jeopardised by a clash of personalities or clash of emphasis in the work.

It has been acknowledged that a supervisor cannot always supply the support and discussion required, which has led to the development of peer-support systems and co-counselling (see Chapter 10).

▶ Supervisory arrangements at a distance

There are many successful practices and also difficulties for distance research students, whether in the UK or overseas, and distance contact and supervisions systems need setting up to cope with any problems. A different kind of pacing of agreed activities has to be set up and maintained. Some of these particular needs can be satisfied by the development of contracts, and good distance supervision and contact systems, and others by peer support networks and structures. If you are working at a great distance from all your supervisors you need to ensure that you maintain regular contact and update them on your work, ask the necessary questions and discuss conceptual issues, data findings, the directions of the research, and so on. Some of this will happen in face-to-face supervisions, arranged well in advance, and just as straightforwardly as it would for supervisors and students who work closely together. You can phone or e-mail and/or write to set up supervisions in line with the learning contract you have drawn up. Often, distances ensure that when you do meet it is real quality time, because it has been quite an investment on your part to find the time to travel the distance. The supervisor is making an investment here, too – they will prepare for supervisions by reading your work, finding useful current writings, and setting aside their time for you.

Videoconferencing

In some instances students can be supervised through videoconferencing. This is more face-to-face than an e-mail contact but much more complex to set up. There are some supervisory teams who meet regularly by videoconference, with the supervisor fielding questions, causing and facilitating debate between the research group and updating them all on developments. This can support a research culture and lead to a well-managed work rhythm. Some of these videoconference links are European and international.

Good practice with videoconference supervision

For supervision by videoconference, you and your supervisor need to do the following:

- Plan commitments to meeting at specified times.
- Book videoconference rooms, preferably with refreshments.
- Send work – drafts, plans, questions, reading between you in advance for a focus.

- Set on an agenda – time is precious.
- Ensure a friendly technician can be called on for help if the line goes down.
- Keep good eye contact. Start with social comments, then ask specific questions.
- Give the supervisor time to pause to think before answering.
- Try not to talk over each other – because of time lapses and the lack of interaction possible in videoconferencing, this is more likely to happen than in face-to-face supervisions.
- Agree what you have decided and repeat it back (you cannot show it to them unless you have a visualiser connected to the videoconference system).
- Ensure a clean, friendly end to the videoconference and 'sign-off' as you switch off (as it becomes either messy, or rather abrupt).
- You could fax or e-mail agreed points immediately after the videoconference.

E-mail supervision

In order to keep a regular discussion going it is useful to use e-mail. There are many distance discussions that take place by e-mail or fax, backed up with some visits for full-blown supervisions. If the supervisor is in another country then the e-mail contact is essential and the face-to-face supervisory contacts will be condensed into the periods when you can both be in the same country. Make e-mail contacts lucid, short and precise, with some friendly tone to establish a personal touch. Try not to get involved in excessively chatty discussions but to concentrate on asking questions and seeking information and reporting on findings for comment.

E-mail is quite an insistent medium. If you make contact too frequently the supervisor will feel harassed. If you make contact too infrequently the supervisor will feel guilty (and so will you), wondering what you are up to. Regular brief contact with some very full discussions on work in progress at regular intervals will maintain a sense of a working relationship over time and space.

Good practice with e-mail supervision

- Keep regular contact for both social comments and progress checks.
- Try to test out the kind of tone that enables you and your supervisor to be both (a) friendly and (b) focused in your exchanges.

- Send short messages with explicit questions.
- Reply to questions in texts sent to you by interleaving in capitals (or bold, or in colour).
- Send chapters in draft, by attachment. Ask for comments back by interleaving in text (in bold, capitals, or in colour).
- Print off exchanges as a record to refer to where necessary.
- Send draft materials to both supervisors and send copies of questions and comments to both, indicating where a response is needed.

Group/project team supervisions

Videoconference group supervisions are not the only group supervisions which are logical and useful. In some subject areas, for example practical science or medicine, there are likely to be several students working on a related project. In these cases it would be useful to hold regular group project supervisions at which students can share ideas, problems and questions, and the supervisor can say just once some of the things they would otherwise need to say to each individual, about learning outcomes, length of the thesis, time, protocols, question framing, strategies, reading, and so on. In other subject areas there might be only one student working in a specific area, but there will probably be a few working in cognate areas or areas which are otherwise related, whether in terms of methodology being used, or in terms of subject or discipline. It would be just as useful in these instances to bring these students together regularly or occasionally for group supervisions. This is not to substitute for individual supervisions but to augment them and provide a sense of sharing and support and peer responsibility. You and the other students will often get as much (though sometimes different things) out of sharing your own questions and ideas and work in progress with each other as in discussing it with the supervisors, and the group session enables you at the same time to keep updated on progress, and gives you the opportunity to ask questions and seek to develop ideas. What can also be encouraged is meeting together in self-help peer-group sessions (see Chapter 10 on self-help groups and self-managed sessions).

▶ **Key points**

1   Find the right supervisor(s). It is important to find supervisors who have the time, the right knowledge and the commitment to work with you productively.
2   Abilities and expertise can be shared out among a supervisory

team. You need a director of studies/first supervisor, and possibly also a second supervisor and an external one.

3 Initial contacts and contracts are important. Establish workable learning contracts so you decide and agree on the regularity and shape of supervisions, and your commitments to an agenda, work production, and so on.

4 Ensure you discuss the title and scope of the project at your first session.

5 The nature of the supervisory relationship is important. Set up regular sessions, make relationships clear, ask for help with planning the scope of the project, reading, contacts, and so on.

6 What you can expect from your supervisor(s) needs clarifying. You can expect support, clarity, direction, support over sharing information, management of ideas and concepts, ideas about presentations and publications, and guidance over the examination process.

7 Stages of the supervisory process need clarifying. The supervisor(s) are involved at the title, planning, literature search, methodology, draft data collection and pilots, drafting, presentations and publications, writing up and editing, viva and after stages.

8 Do establish and maintain good working relationships to ensure full support through all of these stages. Handle any difficulties in relationships with sensitivity and assertiveness.

9 Supervisions at a distance are a possibility. Set up e-mail contacts, video links, regular contacts and visits, quality time.

10 Also ensure peer group support is in place.

Conclusion

We have looked at:

- Managing your supervisor(s) well and developing and maintaining a supportive, positive, constructively critical relationship over time is essential to help you produce a good quality thesis
- Ground rules and learning contracts are vehicles to help this but less formal agreements can serve the same ends
- Students studying at a distance and/or part-time, possibly in an international context, need to establish good contact systems, for-example, e-mail, and set up a support network at home/amongst their peers

Further reading

Anderson, G., Boud, D., & Sampson, J. (eds.) (1996). *Learning Contracts: A Practical Guide*. London: Kogan Page.

Brookfield, S. D. (1986). *Understanding and Facilitating Adult Learning: Comprehensive Analysis of Principles and Effective Practices*. Milton Keynes: Open University Press.

Rogers, J. (1989). *Adults Learning*. Buckingham: Open University Press.

Tight, M. (1983). *Education for Adults Volume 2: Opportunities for Adult Education*. London: Routledge.

7 Managing the Balancing Act

'If you want a job done well, give it to a busy person.'

This chapter looks at:

- *Balancing the demands, pleasures and problems of research, home, social/leisure and work*
- *Transferring skills from one sphere to the other – or not*
- *An audit of demands, skills, pleasures and problems*
- *Relating research to home and work demands*

The old adage about giving jobs to busy people certainly rings true when we think about the variety of tasks and roles we have to balance, especially when embarking upon part-time research. You could be reminded of a circus performer balancing and twirling plates, keeping each one twirling just fast enough so that it does not fall and smash into pieces.

Being able to manage a variety of roles and tasks at any one time is a feat of flexibility and diversity. We do have to be careful, however, that it does not become a millstone around our necks, and that we do not hamper our own quality of life or the quality of our work by trying to do too much at the same time. Balance is essential. Some of the issues we need to think about, then, are stress and time management, identifying the kinds of roles and needs which are in the balancing act for each of us, learning to support each other and developing coping and planning strategies for ourselves and others. We also need to learn to say 'no' sometimes when there are too many demands placed upon us at home or at work which will make our research impossible. Similarly, there will be times when the research has to take second place to home and work demands. In order to minimise the stress and the disappointments this can bring, you need to plan ahead and spot the clear moments of conflict of interest and effort so that you can negotiate and balance your activities.

If you are intent upon becoming an academic of some sort after your research, or of continuing to research in your work, to write and publish, you will find the skills you develop for balancing your different roles and demands absolutely essential in the future, too.

▶ Balancing what?

Most part-time researchers in higher education balance at least two other roles quite apart from that of researcher. They have a job, full- or part-time, and a set of domestic responsibilities, family, parents, partners, and sometimes a host of pets and close friends besides. For international students working on their research in another host country, there can be stresses of homesickness, distance demands which are difficult to meet, and the occasional, perhaps unforeseen need to return home. We all need to juggle a variety of demands. Many of us also balance various roles within our jobs, coping with the complexities, for example, of balancing teaching with administration, and both of these with research. Increasingly more demands are being made on us to take on and develop the various roles related to our jobs. If we are academics already there is increasing pressure to research, and if we want to further our careers, we all have to take on more administrative responsibilities whether we teach and research as well or not. Other balancing acts include juggling the demands made by the various people to whom we report, and those whom we supervise, as well as those with whom we work closely, other administrative and support staff, personal assistants, secretarial and clerical and technical staff, and other staff with whom we work. The tensions and demands of these often tend to build up at the same time, so that we are faced with a variety of heavy demands at particular points during the year.

If you are not actually involved in working in an academic environment, then this can be both a blessing and an increased difficulty. On the one hand, others might have little or no idea of the kinds of demands and stresses (as well as the joys and celebrations) associated with your research work. They might envy you it, be distanced from you because you have developed an alternative 'other' life, or simply fail to see why you bother. All of these responses undermine our sense of the value of our research, and they can be augmented by some deliberately hostile or destructive responses, in the worst cases.

At work:

- It is important to negotiate with those with whom you work and to explain the demands of the research in which you are involved without boring them or requesting special privileges.
- It is also important, if the research is work-related, that you both negotiate some support and time in which to carry out and ensure that your colleagues can see that the work is not just for personal satisfaction but also for the good of the company/ organisation/workplace.

At home and socially:

- Try and gain the support of family members and friends for the research you are involved in – explain the demands to them, negotiate the pressures and support needed
- Try not to let your involvement in research undermine your relationships
- Try not to let your involvement in research take all your time or you will find you lose your friends, alienate your family, and become rather boring company! You might well get bored with yourself too – so it is a good idea to try and balance the pleasures and demands rather than putting off all your social activities and your domestic responsibilities (if you could). When involved in research it is often very pleasant to be able to escape and become another person, enjoy yourself, talk, socialise, relax, become involved in sport and leisure – this all uses different parts of your brain and your energy. And if you do not have any other pursuits and involvements you might think of developing some to relieve the tensions and stresses and provide different stimuli and rewards.

▶ Varieties of roles and activities – an audit

In order to begin to review the variety of role demands and various elements in the balancing act of balancing research, work and home/other, it is useful to review where our particular responsibilities and activities, strengths, rewards and demands lie in our lives. One way of doing

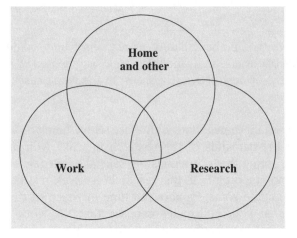

FIGURE 7.1 BALANCING SPHERES OF ACTIVITY

Audit task

- What skills, problems, demands and strengths, or rewards, and so on, appear in each of the circles?
- What overlaps are there?
- Are there any strengths and enjoyments which appear in one area which could usefully be developed and used in the other – for example, a skill in home activities, time and task management (sorting out a family – food, domestic management, rota of jobs, and so on) – which could be built on to help you handle those specific developments and demands in your research?
- Then consider whether there are any specific outlets and areas of relaxation, personal development and enjoyment, which appear in 'home' or 'other' or your work which can balance some of the tensions and demands of the research, because they let you develop such skills or because they provide an opportunity to do something completely different.
- The clue is to decide what kind of part all these areas play in your life and note in what ways unstressful, sporting or social activities, or alternative demanding roles, help to offset the stresses and demands of the research, those of research the demands of your job, and so on.
- If you find that there is an overload of similar demands or of damaging conflicting demands in the various different strands and areas of your life, you will probably need to think about changing things, about coping with the clashes.
- Sometimes merely recognising potential clashes and benefits is enough to help you start balancing and appreciating each for their own merits.
- A successful research project can, for example, provide you with a long-term sense of identity and fulfilment set against an undemanding or unrewarding job.

this is initially to look at the skills, activities, roles, demands and pleasures identified under the three interesting categories (see Figure 7.1) of home/other, work, and research.

Once you have started to fill in your own version of this figure, you need to ask yourself some questions to work out ways of balancing your demands, and recognising the kinds of pressures and also the skills and enjoyments which appear in each sphere, which could either be usefully cross-fertilised, or kept very separate (you will need to decide this for yourself).

▶ What kind of balancing act suits you?

Balancing rather than collapsing under the stress

We are all different people and the kinds of balancing acts we can cope with will vary as much as do our personalities. The main point is to recognise what you thrive on, and what to avoid. I know that I thrive on variety but with some overlap. If I am involved in many different activities, if some of them have a common theme of skills or interest, I can carry out a certain balancing act because the overlap and the interfaces will help me to keep various activities all running at once. There are dangers in everything being connected and everything relying on the same sorts of skills and contacts, producing the same sorts of demands and responsibilities, however, in case the collapse of one area infects all the others. When I was studying for my own PhD it had very little to do with my work life or my home life for much of the time and provided an alternative way of thinking and behaving, an alternative identity for me. The research I carry out now is of both sorts, sometimes coping with everything, sometimes very definitely an intellectual escape.

You will also need to review the role different kinds of leisure activities play in your life when you are involved in research. Not everyone you meet will want to hear all about your latest discovery or how you file your index cards. You will probably want to keep some leisure interests separate and develop others related to the research. Many people make friends in the university library, the coffee room, the lab. However, the fact that you might make these friends could be a concern for friends and family who will wonder whether your involvement in a research culture socially will take you away from them intellectually and emotionally. You will need to put yourself in their shoes and consider how to handle this possible friction.

Balancing research and teaching – for academics involved in research projects

If you are expected to carry out both research and teaching, you will probably also have those other domestic and outside responsibilities going alongside to consider, but let us look at the research and teaching issues first. There are contradictory findings about the success of various balancing acts. Margherita Rendel's research (Rendel 1986) suggests that women with domestic responsibilities actually produce proportionally more research and published papers than do single men. An interesting example of a successful balancing act which gives some of us heart! This is contradicted by Over (1982) in his study of psychologists, but there are subject differences which could account for the overall differences in these two sets of findings. Shirley Fisher (Fisher 1994) comments that domestic responsibilities may play a big part in the discrepancies found between publication and research rates of men and women: 'The difference in publication rates may reflect the dual role of women in that rearing children even with back-up services may create overload' (p. 58). However, currently there are increasing loads being placed on both men and women. More and more in higher education, we are being asked to publish and to research, and always on top of heavy teaching and administrative loads. Fisher (1994) looked at the difficulties university staff are having in managing the different demands on their time and divided groups of academic staff up in relation to the their expectations, their role demands, and the stress these caused. Staff were grouped according to their sense of identity as researcher/administrator/teacher, teacher/administrator/researcher or administrator/researcher/teacher, each role balance reflecting how the staff member saw their priorities and the demands of the job. Asking academics what caused stress for them in this complex balancing act, Fisher found that research was frequently prioritised as the activity academics most wished to be involved in, but the one which caused most stress because it could only be performed in very congenial circumstances. As demands increased to produce research output under the research assessment exercises, payoffs increased, but so did stress, at least for some.

Your success in balancing the various elements of your work, research, domestic and other commitments will depend to a great extent on your time management, and on the support of others around you. It will also depend on your determination to carry on with the research. Sometimes research work has to take a back seat because of work or domestic demands – do not worry about this. Keep it in your head, review it from time to time, and promise yourself that you will get back to it. Plan this in, and get back to it. It is an important part of your identity and you cannot let it go without a personal sense of loss. So work on retaining it beyond the crisis or crises – *but do not be put off*: certainly most part-time and many full-time researchers have a succession of demands and problems which prevent them from putting all their efforts all of the time into the research work.

Conclusion

We have looked at the following key points:

- Why you need to balance work, home and research demands
- How to plan and balance

Further reading
Fisher, S. (1994). *Stress in Academic Life*. Buckingham: Open University Press.

Over, R. (1982). Does research productivity decline with age? *Higher Education* 11: 511–20.

Rendel, M. (1986). How many women academics 1912–1977? In R. Deem (ed.), *Schooling for Women's Work*. London: Routledge.

8 Managing Your Time and Tasks

This chapter covers different kinds of time planning and time, task and stress management on a one-year (MA) or three-year-plus research degree (MPhil or PhD full- or part-time), considering how to fit in not only research but domestic and work pressures where appropriate. (See Chapter 7 for further consideration of managing the balancing act of research, work and domestic and other responsibilities.)

This chapter looks at:

- *Realistically planning stages of research*
- *Fitting in with institutional demands on time*
- *Availability of resources*
- *Planning field work and data collection*
- *Managing time and stress with domestic commitments*
- *Other work commitments*
- *Long-, medium- and short-term strategy planning*
- *Working with others and fitting them into the planning*
- *Coping with setbacks*
- *Critical path analysis of research processes*

Undertaking research for a postgraduate qualification is a very time-consuming activity. However, it will probably have to be carried on alongside many other commitments, such as full- or part-time work, and to home and family or other domestic responsibilities. It is essential that you use the time available to you well, and that you gain support from others in doing so. You need to ensure that you plan the stages of the research carefully so that the longer-term activities such as experiments, ordering materials, travel abroad or around the country, and presenting the final written draft in perfect condition are all costed in terms of time. There is no point in wasting time awaiting materials or results when you could, with good planning, be getting on with other elements of the research. There is also no point in rushing because of bad planning, because a rushed piece of postgraduate research usually lacks a conceptual underpinning which has been carefully worked out throughout, with clear organisation and sound referencing and expression. It will also lack that final presentational polish which helps to convince its readers and assessors that this is a piece of work of quality which can contribute usefully and well to knowledge and understanding in the field.

▶ Good planning: long, medium- and short-term time management

It is essential that you plan well and manage your time carefully:

- Look back over the information on stages of the research project and the kinds of demands involved.
- Develop a plan and programme considering your overall project and the ultimate aims.
- Outline your long-term planning aims and outcomes.
- Outline your long-term activities and end results.
- See the whole project in outline.

Not all you predict will actually happen, but you need an idea of the whole project in terms of the time and stages of activities involved in order to use time effectively, to revise plans if necessary, to develop, and to spot problems. To do this it is helpful to look towards the end results of the project and track backwards, putting in place different elements of research activity, support, acquisition of materials and resources and writing.

Now look more specifically at long-, medium- and short-term planning, carrying out a critical path analysis which helps you to spot points at which there will be too many things to do, potential problems and waiting time so that, once spotted, these times can be used effectively.

Overall planning and the cycle of research

It is helpful to think about the research in terms of a cycle which moves on, progressing at each stage and informing each stage with the

Task

Consider:

- When you need to write up by.
- What you will need to process before you write up.
- Who and what you will need to set in motion to help you to write up eventually.
- What machinery/texts/paper, and so on, are necessary to help you to produce the finished project.

experiences of previous stages of the cycle. This can be set against the rather linear time-planning activity already completed and so can help you to plan your time effectively.

The research cycle is rather like Kolb's experiential learning cycle which underpins action research (see Figure 8.1).

Eventually this leads to conclusions and writing up. In full the development process looks more like the following:

Stage one

- Initial ideas and hypotheses
- Title and research questions to structure the research activities
- Plan
- Carry out various preliminary activities, for example, literature searches.

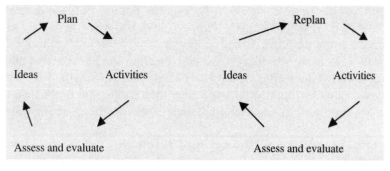

FIGURE 8.1 KOLB'S EXPERIENTIAL LEARNING CYCLE (KOLB 1984)

Stage two

- Alter plan – firm up stages
- Carry out activities – for example, reading, interviews, drawing up and using questionnaires, or other experiments, in stages
- After each stage reflect, evaluate, see how it shapes the whole research
- Write up any findings in draft form
- Reflect.

Stage three

- Replan and move on
- Draft
- Carry out research activities
- Reflect, evaluate
- Get ideas and findings and arguments in perspective, modify if necessary
- Produce results.

Stage four

- Write up and edit
- Final write-up
- Submission of thesis
- Examination and viva.

Both your supervisor and any supportive research group of which you are a part can help you at each of these stages, in different ways. Other colleagues unrelated to the research can also be helpful some-times in putting contacts or reading your way, or suggesting other approaches or interpretations. Friends and relatives can provide a different kind of support and help. When you see the different stages you can also spot what kinds of support you need to seek. Sometimes it is support in clarifying methodology, interpreting data, learning new skills, talking through difficult concepts, overcoming intellectual hurdles, helping to solve problems, helping to spot issues which have not been taken into consideration, thinking of other ways of finding out answers, and providing professional, psychological and emotional support in times of pressure or when things are not going very well.

▶ Time and task management and planning – action

- Draw up plans – start this process now.
- Although you probably cannot produce a refined plan at the beginning of your project, start the process off and then spend time finishing off the plans for long- and medium-term planning as soon as you can. Take advice from colleagues or partners to whom you might show the plan.

Task

Consider:

Long-term planning – what needs to be done over the next few years? Where are the high points, suspected moments of difficulty and overload, and where do other activities in which you are involved produce time-consuming work or demands which will affect how much work you can put into your research?

Medium-term planning – draw this up on a chart, track it in stages of actions in a diary/on a calendar. Perhaps look at a single year.

This way you can spot:

- forward planning needs
- some of the problems
- some of the really hectic periods
- some of the quieter periods
- what activities need to be carried out over the next few months
- what other activities will make demands on your time coincidentally.

This kind of planning helps you to visualise the work needed, to take control over the time and neither feel overwhelmed by so much to do in so much time, nor pressurised. Planning gives you the control. With this medium- and long-term planning in place you can usefully manage time to fill the quiet periods with more routine activities or activities which need completion at some point and can be carried out in a quieter moment. You can also plan ahead and carry out some small preparatory tasks, such as continued reading, ordering resources, ringing up people you need to make appointments with, and sorting and cataloguing data, in order to manage the more hectic moments so that you do not feel overwhelmed.

Look backwards from your **long-term plan** to see when:

- stages of activities can be slotted in
- and contacts established
- and things/activities bid for, organised or agreed
- and visits made
- and materials ordered
- and people consulted
- and problems of different stages addressed.

In this context plan **medium-term activities**, for example:

- fixing up supervisions
- gathering data
- managing money
- setting up experiments
- organising visits
- producing and processing questionnaires
- organising interviews
- piloting stages
- drafting parts of the thesis
- presenting to colleagues in progress seminars and sessions – presenting parts of the work to others at conferences
- writing up some elements of the work into publishable papers.

Critical path analysis can help both your long- and short-term planning.

Consider when other pressures might upset your research plans and plan ahead to leave some space, to avoid crises, to tackle problems in advance.

Use systems of 'bring forward' dates in diaries reminding you of when to order something, start a process, start to clear time and space for a difficult piece of work coming up. Then start to write up certain elements and book space with your supervisor in advance for them to see your work.

▶ Critical path analysis

This is an example of a critical path analysis, in this instance planning towards the delivery of a presentation. Look at how the different stages of work are fitted in around foreseen and unforeseen demands and problems. (This example does not actually include domestic and full-time work demands and problems which you might well have to include). When you have considered this example it would be useful to draw up your own critical path analysis, possibly in the form of a small chart (see Figure 8.2).

Now draw up and plan your own critical path analysis. You might like to take the full planned time for your PhD/MPhil/MA or just until the end of the year (or some other appropriate slice of time).

Consider what demands, activities, pressures and problems could affect your time in relation to:

- the research work itself
- other work – paid or unpaid
- domestic and social responsibilities
- the work loads and demands of those who work with you/for you/to you/who you work for in relation to the research – for however small an amount of time (for example, technicians, reprographics, media)
- anything or anyone else connected with the research – subjects, animals, plants, calls on machinery and equipment.

Seeing the critical path visually will probably initially be something of a shock – there never seems to be enough time and there are many pressures involved. It will help you to plan realistically and to avoid

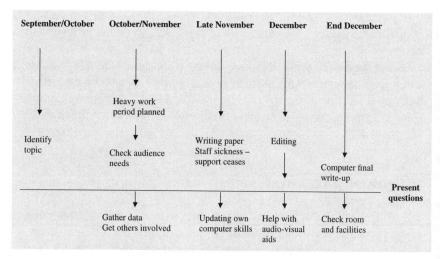

FIGURE 8.2 PREPARING A PRESENTATION – A MODEL CRITICAL PATH ANALYSIS

real pressure points (and so relieve stress and help ensure better quality deep learning and work).

▶ Consulting others

Now that you have begun the process of long- and medium-term planning, discuss it with a colleague or partner.

Task

Ask yourself and ask each other:

- Is it realistic?
- Is it full enough?
- What moments of pressure have been overlooked?
- What essential ongoing activities have been left out?
- Who else needs to be brought in, at what stages?
- What resource needs are not yet planned for?
- What crises are not yet spotted?
- Is too little time left for some activities which might need repeating or checking, or which could go wrong and throw the planning out?
- Have you given some thought to when you might be able to see your supervisor and for what kinds of meeting?
- What else?
- Co-counselling – give each other advice on refining the longer- and medium-term plans.

▶ Managing time with domestic and other work commitments

You will already have been planning some of these into your critical path analysis work. In order to help you consider their importance it is useful to consider:

- Who are the main people in your domestic and social life to whom you have commitments of time?
- How much can you negotiate with them for specific and ongoing periods of time in which to work?
- Can you organise rotas for chores and visits, make deals with others to be involved in domestic and social activities, particularly at

moments of 'quality time', and keep other times clear for your work?

Most research students find that their work encroaches on their domestic and social life, so you will need to take this into considera-tion and weigh up the respective benefits of domestic and social activ-ities and those of your research. You will need to relax as well as fulfil commitments and will possibly tend to resent the research if it domi-nates all aspects of your life to the detriment of others which stimu-late and relax or entertain and respond in different ways. Everyone's circumstances are different but you might find it useful to consider demands on your time in relation to sets of overlapping circles, pin-pointing where demands impinge on each other and where there are clear spaces and trade-offs.

▶ Short-term planning and 'to do' lists

With the longer- and medium-term plans visualised and in place (although they will certainly change) you can plan short-term activities for tomorrow, this week, the weekend, and so on, with further elements of your research work.

You will need to produce 'to do' lists which you can fill daily/weekly with a variety of small, large, deep or relatively trivial and yet essential tasks:

- Listed and defined parts of the daily or weekly main research tasks, such as taking round questionnaires, continuing a literature search, writing up explanations of statistics, conducting focus group inter-views, and so on.
- Parts of essential ongoing regular activities, such as checking sources and monitoring experiments.
- Small, tedious but essential activities which could otherwise hold up your work, such as buying paper for the printer, keeping your card-index of sources and references tidy and up to date.
- Small parts of larger tasks, sometimes because large tasks cannot be completed unless smaller tasks are completed first, for example, learning how to operate software, phoning people back.
- Tackling parts of a problem which has been broken down into manageable sections.
- Continuing to think through difficult ideas and read and discuss them with colleagues.

Task

Consider (and then, if possible, discuss with a colleague):

- Do you already use 'to do' lists?
- How could they help you in your organisation and planning of the research work?

Draw up a 'to do' list for tomorrow in relation to fitting your research development work so far in with your other work. Consider things you need to find out, questions to ask, thinking and reading to do. When you have drawn up this draft list, assess its usefulness.

Conclusion

We have looked at the following key points:

- You will need to manage your time and tasks carefully in relation to the clear stages of your research
- Managing commitments to domestic and other work areas alongside your research commitments will lessen stress and clarify your different areas of the demands. Don't give up all your domestic and social interests, but do learn to time and schedule them in, in relation to your research, so that they don't cause more stress and you do fulfil commitments
- When planning don't forget that other people's time, commitments and skills will be involved, so do plan these in too
- Draw up and continue to map your work against and update your critical path analysis. Working with this in sight can often help you to see how you have progressed and what different parts of the work need to be set in motion when. It also helps you to re-plan and cope realistically after crises and difficulties

Further reading

Kolb, D. A. (1984). *Experiential Learning: Experience as the Source of Learning and Development.* Englewood Cliffs, NJ: Prentice-Hall.

9 Learning as a Research Student – Recognising Learning Approaches and Styles, Avoiding Pitfalls

> *This chapter looks at:*
>
> * *How do you approach your learning?*
> * *How do you conceptualise your research?*
> * *What possible pitfalls could arise from a mismatch between learning approaches and the demands of your research?*
> * *Using the research as learning questionnaire as a learning vehicle*

When you start your work as a research student, you are making a great leap upwards into a more complex and demanding level of learning, just as you did when starting a degree, or the work which preceded it. It is, therefore, very useful to find out more about the learning demands of the research-as-learning, and about your own preferred or usual learning styles, strategies and approaches in relation to those demands.

We do not know very much about how students learn and even less about how research students learn, but some of the theories and vehicles for finding out about student learning can help you to define your own learning style, your learning conceptions and approaches, and help you to work out how to learn from a variety of opportunities. These opportunities include experiences, information, events, situations and other people. This information can indicate to you how you learn already and how you might refocus to learn from people, documents and experiences from which you do not normally learn, and when you should adopt learning styles and approaches with which you are not familiar. It will help you to adapt your learning style and to recognise some of the potential strengths and weaknesses or pitfalls in your learning style and approach with regard to certain kinds of research activities.

The following areas of questioning will help you to think about:

- why you carry out your learning and research, that is, what motivates you (such as parental examples, a sense of duty, a sense of fulfilment)
- how you conceptualise your learning (such as seeing learning as accruing more knowledge about the world or enabling you to fit new understanding into a conceptual framework and link it to your experience)
- what kinds of learning and research approaches you take (such as accumulating information and data, relating ideas and information holistically)
- what sort of outcomes you seek (such as gaining status yourself, seeing the world differently, bringing about creative change).

See the Reflections on Learning Inventory (Meyer & Boulton-Lewis 1997, discussed in relation to postgraduate learning), Meyer & Kiley 1998 and Wisker 1999.

It is interesting to clarify these kinds of issues and practices for several reasons. Because learning as a postgraduate rather than an undergraduate or a professional makes new and different demands upon you, you might need to develop your learning strategies to cope with this. If you are an international student, culturally influenced learning expectations and behaviours might well differ in your research university from those back home. Increased awareness of current learning approaches and the demands on learning approach development made by postgraduate studies can lead to your developing the appropriate variety of learning approaches and behaviours demanded at this level. Research into student learning (Marton & Säljö 1976, Ramsden 1979, Entwistle & Ramsden 1983) has suggested that students broadly take on or more of three approaches to their learning. Very generally, these strategies comprise:

▶ Learning styles: deep, surface and strategic learning

Established research into student learning identifies two main learning styles – deep and surface learning (Marton & Säljö 1976, Ramsden

1979). It is suggested that 'traditional teaching' largely encourages surface learning, particularly in science subjects, but that deep learning produces better results and longer-lasting learning for the students.

1   The **surface or atomistic learner** tends to see knowledge as the acquisition of a number of facts, tasks and objectives are seen as discrete, as are the stages towards completion of a task, time is very important, and any personal relation to the work is considered inappropriate and even misguided. This kind of student relies a great deal on learning and memorising because they are not uniting ideas and facts, and they are not fitting new information into already developed learning or concept 'maps'.

2   The **deep or holistic learner** searches for the meaning which lies beyond or within the specific task, relates any discrete information given to a general, already established learning or concept map, relates new ideas and learning to prior experience and prior learning, moving this on as new information and ideas are added. They personalise learning tasks and integrate them. They see the whole problem, the general ideas and the main concept and fit the learning activity into these over frames of understanding and of personal experiential reference.

3   A third category of learning has also been identified – **strategic learning**. This is focusing on the end product, the marks, with the main aim being to pass. It means the student merely chases grades and only learns what looks necessary, thus there is no linking and little retention.

▶ Disciplines

Different discipline areas, and different parts of discipline areas, might be taught in a way that encourages either surface or deep learning. Ramsden (1979) shows that students can switch strategies, to suit tasks, whilst Thomas and Bain (1982) argue that students develop a certain learning style and do not change it. Biggs and Rihn (1984) show that while students might show tendencies for either sort of learning, it is both possible and desirable to encourage the development of deep learning approaches because these are overall the most successful learning approaches. Depth of processing implies meaningfulness in learning.

The empirical evidence would support these implications.

A deep learning strategy, based on wide reading, reading new knowledge to what is already known, and so on, results in better learning. 'Better' is described as complexity of outcomes (Biggs 1978, Marton & Säljö 1976): satisfaction with performance, (Biggs 1978, Ch. 6): self-rated performance in comparison with peers or examination results (Schmeck 1988, Svensson 1987, Thomas & Bain 1982, Watkins & Hattie 1981): 'not only does consistency exist over such varied ways of defining good quality learning, the measures of depth of processing are also quite diverse' (Biggs & Rihn 1984).

It is recognised that science students more usually adopt a surface approach and that the sciences tend to call for this, but research carried out by Svensson (1987) suggests that those who learn to adopt a deep approach gain better exam results in the end (or become better learners).

A useful learning activity to encourage is the development of an awareness of how you are learning.

These arguments show that learners who contextualise their learning relate it to themselves and their own world. They concentrate on how they are learning as well as what they are learning. They are higher achievers than those who are less aware of or consider irrelevant such consciousness and contextualisation. These concentrate instead on the acquisition of fairly disparate facts and the achievement of discrete tasks and objectives.

Students' approaches may differ at different times and in different learning situations. This may produce a diversity of learning cues for supervisors. Difficulties could arise if, particularly at postgraduate level, you adopt a consistently surface approach: accumulating information rather than cohering it into an interpretation which changes the way you see the subject or the world. These notions of broad approaches to learning have developed into fuller and more complex studies of students' learning and their variants. Your learning relates closely to the way in which you see the world and to the reasons for your undertaking research and the kinds of outcomes you seek from it. It is useful to consider why you are researching, how you conceptualise your research, how you go about it and what outcomes you seek. For example, if you find you are largely taking surface approaches, you could be left with the accumulation of large quantities of disparate data and little developed idea about how to fit it all together, or make meaning from it.

Task

- What kind of learning approach(es) do you normally take (deep, surface or strategic, or a combination)?
- What approaches do you seem to be taking as you start this new activity of research?
- Do you feel you might find it useful to develop some strategies now and if so, how and why?

▶ What kind of learner are you?

There are other theories which suggest tendencies towards learning styles, and spotting these in yourself can help you understand why you find it difficult to learn from some situations and in some contexts and easier in others. When you have such knowledge about your own learning you can choose to plan to your strengths and/or to work on your weaknesses and develop further the learning styles which are not the most obviously successful for you. You could ponder which of the following four main styles seem to suggest your kind of learning (see Honey & Mumford 1986).

Please consider Honey and Mumford's definitions of learning styles. If you want to complete their questionnaire and analyse your results for a more 'accurate' picture, this is readily available in their book *Using your Manual of Learning Styles* (1986).

▶ Learning styles

Each style has its own strengths and weaknesses. There are no 'good' or 'bad' styles. Your major styles will tell you what strengths you have as a learner, which things make it easier for you to learn and what you need to be wary of. For example, studying car mechanics will tend to favour pragmatists and English literature will tend to favour reflectors.

The greatest variety of learning opportunities are available to those who can, to some extent, operate in all styles, but who are clear, when facing a problem, which style is most effective for them.

Activists
Activists learn best from constant exposure to new experiences. They like to involve themselves in immediate experiences and are enthusi-

astic about anything new. They tend to act first and consider the consequences later. They enjoy new challenges but are soon bored with implementation and consolidation. They learn least well from activities that require them to take a passive role.

Reflectors

Reflectors learn best from activities that allow them space to ponder over experience and assimilate new information before making a considered judgement in their own time. They tend to be cautious and thoughtful, wishing to consider all the possible angles and implications before making a decision. They often spend a good deal of time listening and observing. They learn least well from activities that require rapid action with little time for planning.

Theorists

Theorists learn best from activities that allow them to integrate observations into logically sound theories. They like to think problems through in a step-by-step way, assimilating new information and experience into a tidy, rational scheme. They are good at analysis, and are comfortable using theories and models to explain things to themselves and others. They are less comfortable with subjective opinion or creative thinking. They learn least from situations they are unable to research in depth.

Pragmatists

Pragmatists learn best from activities that have a clear practical value and that allow ideas and approaches to be tested in practical settings. They tend to be down-to-earth people who like to get on with things. They also tend to be impatient with open-ended discussions. They learn least from situations where learning is not related to an immediate purpose.

Task

Consider:

- Which descriptions(s) of learning styles best fit you and your learning?
- Are there any situations or modes of research behaviour which you find you are naturally happier with? How do they relate to learning

Continued

style? (For example, if you are a theorist and low pragmatist you might tend to read excessively before starting any fieldwork or beginning to draw conclusions from findings.)
- Are there any learning styles you find you do not seem to be happy with or learn easily from?
- If you spot such an approach or research learning behaviour and, for example, find it difficult to learn from focusing deeply or reading and understanding complex theories, what might you do to strengthen your learning behaviour approach to carry out this kind of learning more successfully?

Although you have one or more supervisors, much of your research as learning will actually be carried out on your own, or on your own in a team. In order to be successful at MA, MPhil or PhD level, your research will need to have a great deal of self-direction, motivation and sticking power. You might find it useful to consider the theories of self-directed learning. How do these apply to your research as learning as a researcher? Research students are by definition adult learners. You might well be combining a professional context and/or professional experience with your research. You will certainly need to develop reflective practice and you are involved in lifelong learning – your research work will probably carry on in your own life and is usually a result of a certain thirst for learning.

▶ Self-directed learning

One of the aims of good learning experiences and activities is to encourage learners to become self-directed and lifelong learners; their self-direction indicating that they understand, own and control their own learning. Self-directed learning is defined as 'the adult's assumption of control over setting educational goals and generating personally meaningful evaluative criteria' (Brookfield 1986).

Self-directed learning is not a set of techniques but a process of learning which, by its very nature, fosters the critical questioning and reflection which should be the purpose of adult education.

These several related theories and practices of lifelong learning (experiential learning – Kolb 1984; reflective practice – Schön 1983; self-directed and lifelong learning) feed into basic assumptions and guidelines underlying success in learning, and in the setting up of learning experiences and the monitoring, evaluating and evidencing of learning.

- Learners are able to make use of their own experience as a starting point for new learning and as a reference point throughout the learning process.
- Learners are aware of their individual differences in learning styles and how to build on these or improve on their learning strategies and overcome their weaknesses.
- Learners exercise some control and responsibility for the direction of their own learning. These kinds of choices help them to become more self-directed and self-aware of their own learning needs and achievements.
- Learners are given opportunities and guidance for reflecting on their experience, whether from life, work, or the more formal learning situation, making it explicit and turning it into learning.
- Their learning is task- or problem-centred; in other words, learners are dealing with problems and issues that have immediate relevance and application.
- Their learning is active – they are able to learn by doing, with an opportunity to apply theory in practice.
- Learners are able to share ideas, feelings and learning experiences (past and present) with other people and to learn from their experiences and ideas.
- Learners are in a climate and learning context that is reassuring and conducive to learning. The learning programme needs to make outcomes, processes, expectations and criteria explicit so that anxieties about assessment procedures, fear of critical or punitive attitudes from tutor or group members, and lack of confidence in the purpose of the learning programme are avoided. These negative elements are not conducive to a good learning climate.
- Learners are involved in negotiating the learning, at all stages; learners should be encouraged to accept a share of the responsibility for the planning, operating and evaluation of a learning programme, and preferably have some choice over learning and assessment methods. With these suggestions in place, learners are more likely to be self-directing in their approach to learning tasks, to own and take responsibility for their learning, and to work effectively with others in developing and sharing learning. They are also

more likely to relate their learning to their experience both in everyday life and in their work and practice, and become true lifelong, reflective, self-directed and active learners.

Task

Consider the above descriptions of self-directed learning.

- What are the benefits to you of being a self-directed learner?
- How might you develop your skills as a self-directed learner?
- What could you ask from your supervisor to better enable you to become and continue as a self-directed learner?

You could:

- ensure you base your research work with your supervisor around the explicit use of a learning contract
- keep a log, diary or reflective journal of your research plans, problems, activities and findings
- recognise your own current and previous experience, where relevant, as a valuable contribution to your research processes, for example, if you manage a home or an office, you could transfer those organisational skills to record keeping and management of the research. If you are a keen observer of others you could develop this as a research strategy.

What other specific ideas do you have about your own self-directed learning as a researcher?

▶ Experiential learning

Kolb (1984) in particular (following Dewey 1963) developed a model for experiential learning which can be used to help learners recognise and build on:

(a) their experiences in everyday life, drawing learning from these and

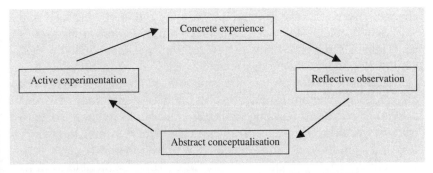

FIGURE 9.1 CONTINUOUS LEARNING (AFTER KOLB 1984)

(b) their learning experiences, both individual and in groups, in more formal learning contexts. The latter range from academic classrooms through to workplace training contexts.

Kolb defined experiential learning as 'the process whereby knowledge is created through the transformation of experience'. He also developed (1984) a useful diagram which explores how learners start from experience, move through stages of reflective observation and abstract conceptualisation, and then on to active experimentation. After this they begin a new cycle, and on again, building in each cycle on both their experience/experimentation, and their reflection and abstract conceptualisation (see Figure 9.1).

Continuous learning offers the opportunity for fresh, deeper meaning to develop. Other theorists add to the idea of experimentation that of 'play', or a creative release and exploration of ideas and practices (Gordon 1961, Melamed 1987). This could involve the use of imagination and emotions, metaphors, games and simulations, and other creative modelling processes, as well as releasing creative energies in brainstorming or problem-solving activities. During the activities themselves, adults often have flashes of understanding and insight, 'a-ha!' moments when ideas and experiences fall into place. When reflected on, these activities can lead to self-reflection and personal transformation (Mezirow 1985).

Reflective practice

Donald Schön, in *The Reflective Practitioner* (1983), establishes a theory of how professionals and practitioners learn from experience by arguing that professionals respond to and reflect on the varied experience which arises in their work. They then seek development and change. These reflective practitioners are more than merely technical solvers of problems. They use 'artistry' creatively to draw from a set of past examples and precedents to transfer from one situation to the next continually, and create and learn anew in each situation, bringing their past learning to bear on the new situation. While professional work and practice generate experience and knowledge naturally, it is important to make this learning explicit in a learning situation, so as to encourage learners to reflect on and articulate their learning from practice and from their work (see Evans & Varma 1990 and Winter 1995). For your own reflective practice, this will involve being able to draw out from your professional work and practice the learning experiences which relate to the research work you are undertaking.

Consider

- How might you develop your reflective practice? Is this relevant to your work as a researcher?
- How might experiential learning be used in your research? How might you build on your own experiences in your research?

You could actually base the start and progress of your research around Kolb's experiential learning cycle. See how and where you might enter the cycle and how your research progress can be changed by working out how you move through it. For example, one PhD student wants to research how the use of a particular piece of art therapy affects patients. She starts with her own concrete experience. This experience, from several years' practice, has given her hunches and insights. She moves to *reflective observation*, studying the therapy pattern and its effects on patients, analysing its elements. Then she produces some *abstract conceptualisation* of the way the patients work, the kinds of behaviours before, during and after it, and what this means for the patients' response and development. She reads theoretical works and feeds these insights into her own thinking and work. She uses the abstract conceptualisation to stand back and develop a *model* of patient treatment. Then she tries it out, in active experimentation. This is a piece of concrete experience. She notices what happens and studies it in *reflective observation*. The development is a cycle. You can use it in the actual research process by capturing it systematically and using theoretical underpinning and appropriate research methods.

▶ Research-as-learning: a specific learning styles questionnaire/activity for researchers

Look below at some of the definitions of conceptions of research and learning approaches in which postgraduates and researchers are involved. Can you complete the questionnaire and think about what this tells you about your own research strategies? Looking at your research topic and your proposed methods, could there be any moments of contradiction or potential clash?

Clashes are likely to take place, for example:

1 When an accumulation approach is largely adopted but a trans-formative aim is sought (how to move from accumulation of data to interpretation, analysis and decision making, leading to recommen-dations for action if there is little obvious connection between the stages).

2 When adopting a holistic or negative postmodern approach (Hodge 1995). In this, it seems that everything, such as findings and theories, is linked to everything else, but there are no clear set of mean-ings or obvious routes of interpretation. You could easily flounder amongst masses of fascinating data which link everything to everything else but provide little hint of how to make a decision or bring coher-ence and order. You may be unable to suggest and argue one interpre-tation through the information and theories over another (a kind of problematic relativism in the face of excess).

These are two very clear potential difficulties which can be spotted when scrutinising the research project on which you are engaged: your behaviour and your approaches to it. There could well be many others. It will be useful for you to consider potential clashes, limits and block-ages, and think about how you might develop your research proposals. Or possibly you could limit the area of your study or the variety of your research vehicle, or change the kind of research vehicle you are using from, for example, a largely quantitative to a mixture of quantitative and qualitative methods.

- How are you going to process, analyse and interpret the data that your research vehicles will produce for you?
- How might you direct the vast mass of information you are gath-ering and link ideas together?
- How are you going to make decisions about what to say about your

findings, how to interpret them, and make recommendations and suggestions for change and development as a result of these findings?

The following set of thoughts and two-part research-as-learning questionnaire should help you with this.

▶ The research-as-learning questionnaire: assumptions and questions – constructions of research in relation to self, understanding, beliefs, knowledge and the world

These are introductory ideas lying behind the questionnaire which suggest some researchers' beliefs underlying their approaches to research as learning.

Beliefs underlying research approaches and strategies
These could include:

* beliefs about knowledge and experience
* beliefs about personal subjectivity
* beliefs about categorical classification and pinning down of proof and real answers
* beliefs about involvement
* beliefs about the importance of creativity and originality rather than recording
* beliefs about the importance of research contributing to the improvement of human life.

What approaches and activities might different sorts of researchers take?

* positivistic researchers might record and expect solutions
* more holistic researchers might look at living responses, variables and the whole context
* professional, practice-based, creative/morally engaged researchers might seek some answers to effect change
* more predictive/descriptive researchers are positivistic, believing everything is discoverable, and they might take a more pragmatic approach to the right questions to produce the 'right' answers.

Questions about postgraduate research styles

Task

Complete the following questionnaire and then consider your pattern of responses.

Context: The aim of this short set of questions is to find out about you and your research so that you might understand your approaches. It will help you to gain insights into your beliefs, practices and approaches.

Title of research proposal (so far):

What are your main research questions? What are you seeking to find out?

Part 1
What is research?
Answering this question gives hints as to:

- beliefs
- values
- personal learning constructs
- world-views
- team-based interpretations of experience, approaches and findings – the way groups/cultural groups make meaning.

Part 2
In carrying out your research, which of these descriptions describes your activities? Please score them from:

1 – 'this does not describe my approaches and activities', to
5 – 'this describes my activities clearly'.

Part 2

I believe my research is about/is concerned with:

1 Describing – finding out information about an event, a   1 2 3 4 5
   set of relations between variables or a situation and
   carefully describing it/them in detail.
2 Exploring – look for reasons why certain things have   1 2 3 4 5
   happened and what might have caused problems/devel-
   opments/situations.
3 Right answers – if there is enough exploration and   1 2 3 4 5
   recording, there will be discoverable right answers to
   important questions which can then be recorded.
4 Experimenting – starting with a hypothesis and through   1 2 3 4 5
   trying out something, seeing what happens next, looking
   at the results and linking them back to the experiment.

5   Prediction – predicting the links from things, events and   1 2 3 4 5
    reactions in the past, similar to your area of research,
    or setting up conditions and activities and speculating
    and predicting about what could happen in the future.

6   Weaving, interrelating – believing that aspects of areas   1 2 3 4 5
    are related both distantly or closely to others, even
    across disciplines, and finding out about these links and
    overlaps.

7   Metaphorical links/leaps – using metaphors/creative   1 2 3 4 5
    comparisons between the imaginative and the real,
    across disciplines, in order to spot relations and simi-
    larities. Making often imaginative or philosophical
    mental leaps across areas which possibly seem logically
    unrelated.

8   Being creative – trying out a new activity or change   1 2 3 4 5
    mechanism, exploring 'what happens if . . . ?' and pro-
    ducing something original and creative/helping others
    to produce something original and creative. Pushing
    forward the boundaries of creativity and making some-
    thing new.

Is there anything else you would like to add about research?

Task

Now that you have completed the questionnaire, look back at the questions and the points posed above. What do the results tell you about
your conceptions of research, your approaches and any potential problems or clashes? If you do spot any difficulties, how might you now
overcome them? Look also at your research area, questions and
intended methods. You might find that you see research as leading to
changes and being creative and individual. You might see your own
research as numbers 6, 7 and 8 in Part 2, that is, interrelating areas and
disciplines, metaphysical and creative, but that you know you are
planning to use largely quantitative research methods. You might then
find that it is difficult to make the leap from the accumulation of data,
to creativity and change outcomes. There could be other dissonances,
contradictions or problems. What could you do to handle such a
discrepancy?

Conclusion

In relating learning to research we have looked at:

*   student learning approaches:
    deep
    surface
    strategic
*   student learning styles:
    activist
    reflective
    theorist
    pragmatist
*   reflective practice, self-directed learning, experiential learning –
    implementations for you
*   research as learning: identifying and seeking to overcome potential
    clashes or dissonances

These research-as-learning questionnaires have been a useful aid in
action research with groups of postgraduates (such as Israeli PhD
students at Anglia Polytechnic University).

Reflection on your own learning and research, as learning should feed
into your insights and practice

*   when planning and carrying out your research, analysing findings,
    and so on
*   when reflecting on the programme of the research
*   when diagnosing and coping with contradictions and problems –
    getting stuck in some parts of your research where this relates to
    how you go about it as a learning activity
*   when researching the learning of those you work with or teach

Some research into postgraduates' learning has been carried out and is
accessible in Wisker & Sutcliffe 1999. For international research students
it is also written up in Wisker 2000.

Further reading

Biggs, J. B. (1978). Individual and group differences in study processes and the
quality of learning outcomes. *British Journal of Educational Psychology* 48:
266–79.

Biggs, J. B., & Rihn, B. A. (1984). The effects of intervation on deep and surface approaches to learning. In J. R. Kirby, *Cognitive Strategies and Educational Performance*, pp. 279–93. London: Academic Press.

Brookfield, S. (ed.) (1986). *Self-Directed Learning: From Theory to Practice* (*New Directions for Continuing Education* 25). San Francisco: Jossey-Bass.

Dewey, J. (1963). *Experience and Education*. New York: Collier.

Entwistle, N. J., & Ramsden, P. (1983). *Understanding Student Learning*. London: Croom Helm.

Evans, P., & Varma, V. P. (1990). *Special Education*. London: Falmer.

Gibbs, G. (1981). *Teaching Students to Learn*. Buckingham: Open University Press.

Gordon, William J. J. (1961). *Synectics: The Development of Creative Capacity*. New York: Harper.

Hodge, B. (1995). Monstrous knowledge: doing PhDs in the new humanities. *Australian Universities' Review* 38 (2): 35–9.

Honey, P., & Mumford, A. (1986). *Using your Manual of Learning Styles*. Peter Honey Publications.

Kolb, D. A. (1984). *Experimental Learning: Experience as the Source of Learning and Development*. Englewood Cliffs, NJ: Prentice-Hall.

Marton, F., & Säljö, R. (1976). On qualitative differences in learning. I – Outcome and process. *British Journal of Educational Psychology* 46: 4–11.

Melamed, L. (1987). The role of play in adult learning. In D. Boud and V. Griffin (eds), *Appreciating Adults Learning: From the Learner's Perspective*. London: Kogan Page.

Meyer, J. H. F., & Boulton-Lewis, G. M. (1997). *Reflections on Learning Inventory*. Place: Publisher.

Meyer, J. H. F., & Kiley, M. (1998). An exploration of Indonesian postgraduate students' conceptions of learning. *Journal of Further and Higher Education* 22: 287–98.

Mezirow, J. (1985). A critical theory of self-directed learning. In S. Brookfield (ed.), *Self-Directed Learning: From Theory to Practice* (*New Directions for Continuing Education* 25). San Francisco: Jossey-Bass.

Ramsden, P. (1979). Student learning and the perception of the academic environment. *Higher Education* 8: 411–28.

Schmeck, R. R. (1988). *Learning Strategies and Learning Styles*. New York: Plenum Press.

Schön, D. (1983). *The Reflective Practitioner*. San Francisco: Jossey-Bass.

Svensson, L. G. (1987). *Higher Education and the State in Swedish History*. Stockholm: Almqvist & Wiksell.

Thomas, P. R., & Bain J. D. (1982). Consistency in learning strategies. *Higher Education* 11, 249–59.

Winter, J. (1995). *Skills for Graduates in the 21st Century*. London: Association of Graduate Recruiters.

Wisker, G. (1999). Learning conceptions and strategies of postgraduate students (Israeli PhD students) and some steps towards encouraging and enabling their learning. Paper presented to the 2nd Postgraduate Experience Conference: Developing Research.

Wisker, G. (2000). *Good Practice Working with International Students.* SEDA Occasional Paper 110. Birmingham: SEDA.

Wisker, G., & Sutcliffe, N. (eds.) (1999). *Good Practice in Postgraduate Supervision.* SEDA Occasional Paper 106. Birmingham: SEDA.

10 Developing a Supportive Research Culture Locally and at a Distance

> This chapter looks at:
>
> - Seeking support from colleagues and other researchers
> - Setting up support groups close by and at a distance
> - Work-in-progress and seminar presentations

Research students are expected to work largely autonomously, with supervision. One of the most helpful and supportive elements of this work is that of actually seeking support from colleagues who are other researchers. There are many queries that can be cleared up, much stress that can be relieved, and much clarification gained by working together in various supportive peer groups. Often, however, it is up to the research student, that is you, to set these groups up and maintain them, so it is important to look out for others who are working in similar fields to yourself and network with them. Some supportive groups develop because you are working together in a research team. More often, they develop because students decide to set up groups to exchange questions, developments and progress.

▶ Group/project team supervisions

In some subject areas, such as practical science or medicine, there are likely to be several students working on a related project. In these cases it would be useful to encourage your supervisors to organise regular group project supervisions at which you can share ideas, problems and questions, and the supervisor can say just once some of the things they would otherwise need to say to each individual – issues about learn-ing outcomes, length of the thesis, time, protocols, question framing, strategies, reading, and so on.

It is not merely the scientific researchers who work in research groups, however, although they are more likely to be working along-side each other, involved in the same experiments. Often there can be a social science or an educational research group with research stu-dents looking at different aspects of similar areas (housing, childcare, gender and schooling, and so on) in a research group. They too are easily brought together into regular work-in-progress meetings as a natural part of their research.

In other subject areas there might be only one student working in a specific area, but there will probably be a few working in cognate areas or areas which are otherwise related, whether in terms of methodol-ogy being used, or in terms of subject or discipline. It would be just as useful in these instances to bring these students together regularly or occasionally for group supervisions. This is not to substitute for individual supervisions but to augment them and provide a sense of sharing and support, and peer responsibility. It is important that research students take the initiative here. If it seems unlikely that a supervisor or group of supervisors will bring you and colleagues together, start a student research group of your own for mutual support and comment. You will get as much benefit (although perhaps a dif-ferent kind of benefit) out of sharing your own questions, ideas and work in progress with each other as in discussing it with the super-visor. Additionally, the group session enables you to keep updated on your progress, and gives you the opportunity to ask questions, make supportive suggestions to others which also feed into your own think-ing, and seek to develop ideas.

Often, initial methods training sessions or modules for MA students, and methods training programmes for MPhil and PhD students can be the basis for your groups. Ask at such a session if there is a group, or if anyone would like to help form one.

Task

Consider:

- Who would your natural supportive peer group be?
- How can you help set up a support group?
- Is there one you could join?

▶ Self-managed groups and networks

It is not only groups who are naturally working together on similar projects, perhaps with the same supervisor or close colleagues as supervisors, who can benefit from supportive group activities. All research students can benefit. If there is no natural grouping of research students around a project, then it is important that supervisors, you and other students work to bring about such a grouping. Meeting together in self-help peer-group sessions can provide support, give a social element to the work, and lead to a system of research-in-progress seminars. At these seminars you each share your research questions and development, and seek ideas, critical questions and suggestions about analysis or further reading from each other. When you present your work to the group it must be in a comprehensible shape, and this forces research students to start to organise and clarify their thoughts and order the kinds of data and results they are discovering. The presentation to peers is a marvellous opportunity to use the intelligent critical thinking of others who are working in similar areas or using similar methodologies. Their questions about questionnaire wording, the viability of research samples, how to interpret focus group and interview data, or whether some recent piece of writing on the subject is credible and important, all can help give you a clear focus. They will ease you out of any ruts in your thinking, and give you new angles and new ideas when you need them. Presentation at a work-in-progress seminar is also a practice or 'dry' run for later conference presentations. Working together in supportive peer groups, you can circulate information about conferences and publication opportunities to each other.

The sharing of key questions, about procedures, systems and ideas, depending on the context, can be immensely useful for students who might otherwise feel rather isolated. Not only does a group help students feel supported and discuss issues, developments, problems and breakthroughs, but it can also provide the perfect kind of opportunity for that very exploratory talk which we all value so much at undergraduate level, but which seems often sorely missing just when it is absolutely essential to the development of enquiry, the testing of hypotheses and the sharing of discoveries, at postgraduate level.

Self-managed groups can be immensely helpful in supporting each other, meeting regularly to discuss questions in each others' research, sharing skills in terms of how to do literature searches, pilot questionnaires and so on, and hear reports on each other's work in progress, providing useful feedback and sharing ideas.

Networks aid the dissemination of skills and information and keep students in touch with each other. With this kind of communication, not only can they support each other and discuss ideas and findings, and so on, but they can keep each other in touch on issues of dates, regulations, passing the hurdle of transfer to PhD from MPhil, and other such potentially threatening, often confused and ill-informed experiences.

For international students, such a group might well be set up initially by the international office. If not, you need to help set one up with your peers. Some international students could find research life very lonely and a support group is a social as well as an intellectual 'lifeline'.

Even if the supervisor plays a key role in setting up these self-managed groups and networks to begin with, the groups should then be able to run on their own, driven by the students, because they are useful to them. This is essential supportive networking and it is up to you as research students to work together to establish and continue it.

▶ Peer pairing

Supervisors can be asked to set up systems of peer pairing. In this system, research students are put in touch with each other to work together supportively in pairs. They do not have to be working on the same project, but should be involved in similar subject areas or using similar methodologies. They might both be students of the same supervisor or of her/his colleagues. For the new research student, actually being paired with another can be most helpful. You will, of course, make your own contacts and friends, but the supportive pairing ensures that you meet regularly and compare notes. Information can be shared regarding the way you can usefully work in the university on your research, issues to do with policies and practices, dates and availability of materials and resources, and so on. With a formalised peer-pairing system everyone has someone else to talk their work through with from the beginning. This relieves some of the initial burden of work from the supervisor, who can then concentrate on supervising the precise project and its needs rather than spending much of the time repetitively informing different students about policies, and so on.

Task

Consider:

- Do you have access to others who are working in the same subject area or using similar methodologies? Could you have?
- Are you already part of a research group that can develop further to support each of you in your research?
- What kinds of supportive systems and structures are present in your university or home base?
- Where, how and with whom could you set up supportive peer-pairing links, or groups, whether supervisor-led or peer-led?
- What would the specific benefits of such supportive peers or groups be for you?
- How can you set up self-help supportive groups and research groups?
- How will you use them?
- How can you keep in touch?
- What can you do immediately to help set up or maintain such supportive relationships?

▶ Peer support systems over a distance

An increasing number of research students are carrying out their studies in a country different from that of their supervisor. This is for a variety of reasons. Sometimes the expertise lies in another country and it is far too expensive and disruptive for the researcher to move to be able to work with the supervisor of their choice. Sometimes the second or third supervisor is external to the university home base of the student. Sometimes the student wishes to be registered with a distant university because there is nowhere locally with which to register, and they wish to study in a recognised and accredited university culture and context. Some students studying part-time will necessarily work away from the base of their supervisor. And sometimes supervisors move jobs, but wish to maintain supervisory contact with their students rather than passing the students on to someone else to supervise midway in their research. Many international students study at a distance for all or part of their MA, MPhil or PhD

Traditionally, contact with the supervisor will often be by visit and phone in this instance. However, with the advent of both e-mail and videoconferencing, it is possible for supervisor and research student, and for research students in a group, to be in contact over long distances, either on specifically arranged sessions by videoconference, or together through a chat room or a discussion list (Web CT, an online course management system, provides opportunities for this, for example), or at any time on demand, by e-mail. Both of these relatively hi-tech contacts can be used by the students wishing to maintain that necessary support and to further their studies.

If you are carrying out all or part of your research at a distance, do ensure that you stay in touch with others involved in MA, MPhil or PhD research at your university. Exchange e-mails and keep each other updated.

▶ Using electronic and video links to support research students in their work

Research supervision aided by e-mail and videoconferencing was explained in Chapter 6. With the use of videoconference links, groups of research students or individuals can become involved in a multimedia videoconference.

Videoconferencing links provide the opportunity for groups to work with their supervisor or for students in different locations to offer each other the kind of peer support and research in progress which has been described previously. In this instance, the kind of information and ideas exchanged will probably not be about local systems, but will concentrate on joint or individual research issues and problems and on trying out ideas and developed projects with each other. Here the peer comments and support can be invaluable, especially to the more remote or isolated student. The quality of comment from peers across the world cannot be underestimated, as there is a fascinating breadth of knowledge and approaches which spring from the different learning cultures of students of different nationalities. Students can put each other in touch with reading materials, resources and links in a number of countries, as well as keeping valuable contacts that could be most useful in the years after completion of the research.

Audioconferencing can fulfil many of these aims and objectives, both for supervisors and for groups of research students. With these practices research students can book audioconferences with each other to carry on work-in-progress discussions without the presence of the supervisor.

The third and possibly easiest contact is by e-mail. For groups of students, access to the e-mail can provide an invaluable discussion forum. The formal e-mail discussion group can be set up and joined by researchers around the world by their subscribing to be involved in it. As anyone who has used e-mail discussion groups will know, it is possible both to be involved in heated discussions with a group over a period of time, which is immensely profitable; on the spot; and useful and a slightly more distant involvement can also be maintained, where you read others' comments and only contribute if you have something to say, but remain in touch nonetheless. It is also possible if you have a specific request for ideas and information or solutions to a problem; an e-mail discussion group can be most useful for making specific suggestions to questions put out over the discussion group. Learning conversations of a high order can result and the research student can select the information they find useful, probe further and credit the provider. This takes place rapidly and over great distances. Subscription to specific mailgroups can also be a way of getting more information from a wide number of people, by sending out a request for information and ideas or describing a problem and asking for responses, over the broader e-mail mailgroup.

Another version of the e-mail discussion group is the 'chat room' or virtual tutorial discussion space. Students can post comments on work in progress and ask for support and tips from others in their research group or others engaged in similar kinds of research – whether on similar topics or using similar strategies. The supervisor of a group of students can occasionally join in and help solve some problem or provide tips, but the main discussion and support comes from the students themselves, to each other.

Task

Consider:

- Do you or could you have access to videoconferencing or audio-conferencing for distance tutorials and supervisions?
- Do you have or could you have access to these conferencing methods for discussion with other research students?

- Do you or could you use e-mail to discuss your work with your supervisor? How?
- Do you or could you become involved in an e-mail discussion group, or join a mail-base discussion group or Web CT (or other) chat room?
- If so, which ones are likely to be helpful and appropriate for you?

▶ Other peer-support systems – establishing a research culture

A key peer-support system and a very good one for developing the skill of research is the more formal research seminar series. During this both staff and students alike give research-in-progress seminar papers, followed by discussions. Here questions can be asked and methodology, practices, discoveries, theories and problems all aired and discussed, with a coherent base of a seminar paper upon which to build.

The establishment and maintenance of a research culture is a sensitive and complex issue. If you work in a learning environment which has always had a research culture, active research and the exchange and mutual respect of research ideas and findings, then you might take this culture for granted as a given. Do ensure that you discover its opportunities and make the most of them. If, on the other hand, you are starting to carry out your research in a university whose tradition of research is not as old as Oxbridge and some others, or you are researching part-time and only visiting the university, or are researching at a great distance from it, the existence of and your support and contribution to a research culture are essential. At its best a research culture is one which comprises respect, resources, activity, funding, mutual trust and sharing, and support for productive research (and occasionally, in the less successful moments, unproductive, frustrating research).

Some universities have research offices, postgraduate facilities and social activities, well-stocked research libraries and equipment, and a widely shared respect for the kinds of time demands, flexibility and pressures involved in carrying out successful research in all subject areas. Other universities need to develop these cultures. It is important that you work towards such development. Research is fundamental to the creation and development of knowledge and skills. It motivates those involved, and enables them and the subject area to move forward and develop. It provides a firm underpinning for what is taught in a university and also, often for how teaching takes place (depending on the area of the research – see, for example, action research). It contributes to our understanding of how others work, learn and behave, to our linking between knowledge, theory, experience and practice. Going outside the university, research contributes to moving forward human knowledge skills and development more generally.

Everyone benefits in the end from successful research that is shared and feeds into development and change. Clearly some subject areas can claim this direct relationship more obviously. Those working on Aids, cancer, and experiments to do with making aircraft safer, buildings stronger, TVs more hi–tech, are much more likely to be able to point to the direct effects of their work or work to which they have contributed. But even the most esoteric research contributes to the fund of human knowledge and development if it is shared and used. We need to ensure that other colleagues know we are involved in research and respect that, without arrogantly parading the fact. It is also our duty to ensure that the research findings are indeed shared and used eventually.

Conclusion

We have looked at:

- Support for a research locally and at a distance
- Peer-support groups and research methods groups
- Use of video links and e-mail
- Work-in-progress seminars and groups

---

11 Research Questions and Methods – the Processes of Research, Kinds of Research, Choosing Methodologies

This chapter looks at:

- *What type of research are you undertaking?*
- *Research processes – questions and hypotheses*
- *Kinds of research*
- *Ensuring research ethics are followed*

To qualify for the award of Doctor of Philosophy the candidate must:

a) Present a thesis on the subject of his or her advanced study and research and satisfy the examiners that it contains evidence of originality and independent critical ability and matter suitable for publication, and that it is of sufficient merit to qualify for the degree of doctor of philosophy.

b) Present him or herself for an oral examination and satisfy the examiners therein and in such other tests as the examiners may prescribe. (Extract from *Regulations for Higher Degrees* at a university, 1993, Anglia Polytechnic University)

When you begin to research you need to decide what kind of research you are involved in, which sort or sorts would best suit your aims and outcomes, and then how to acquire, handle and process the information produced in your research. You will, of course, need to ask the appropriate research questions first and interrogate the information as you acquire it.

The choice of methodologies for your research follows on naturally from the clear definition of a title and of the research questions which underpin your research. Different disciplines tend to favour different methodologies, but the choice is also dictated by the kind of information you wish to discover and the ultimate outcomes of the research. There are numerous weighty volumes and shelves full of journals and works which will take you through the stages of research using each of the methodologies outlined here. This is an introduction to some of the most popular methodologies used most commonly by those researching in the social sciences and humanities. There is a separate chapter on action-centred research which is used in health and social sciences, education and subject areas where practice is both the key concern and the source of the research data, and practice in the area into which the research results will feed, causing change.

▶ The research process

Research is about asking and beginning to answer questions, seeking knowledge and understanding of the world and its processes. Research is based on enquiry methods and hypotheses, and contributes to our fund of knowledge about the elements and areas of the world with which we are involved in the research. Other knowledge might well be produced during the course of the research, not least among which is self-knowledge on the part of the researcher.

The basic process of research is based on inquisitiveness. The cycle can start with either experience or a problem, a theory or hypothesis. The shape of a research process is:

- problem/experience/observation
- hypothesis
- investigation and experimentation to test the hypothesis
- data gathering
- data analysis and interpretation
- confirmation or disapproval of the hypothesis.

This leads on to further experimentation and data acquisition, or can feed directly into statements of findings, and practice change, depending on the kind, subject area and intended outcomes of the research.

▶ Stating your title

Choosing a title can be difficult. It is important that the title poses a question, suggests an area, an idea, a part of a field of study which can be questioned, makes a suggestion or proposes an innovation and suggests that you will check for its viability and success. It is not a 'say all you can find out about . . .' kind of title. It needs to excite, suggest scope for inquiry and reflection, and indicate that it is complex and 'meaty' or large enough for your exploration.

During the course of your preparation towards your research proposal submission you will find that you develop and refine your title, and you might even find that it changes during the research if the findings and focus of your work shift due to what you discover or how the field itself shifts. (This is especially likely with longer-term MPhil and PhD projects.)

Task

Note down the key terms of the area in which you want to work. What are the issues, questions and problems which interest you? Try to turn your notes into a question or an issue to be explained.

Some examples of titles:

The dysfunctional family as a vehicle for representation of social change in the work of Thomas Hardy

The relationship between religion and national identity of West Indian immigrants to Britain, 1948–1968

The professional socialisation of social work in Russia

These titles, by indicating relationships and developments in context, can easily develop into specific research questions which lead to research. A title which indicated the coverage of a huge area without any underpinning issue of question, relationship and time frame would produce work of a rather encyclopaedic nature, a great deal of information not easily organised into issues, questions, or findings, but just presented. For an MPhil and an MA it is more likely that the work will be restricted in terms of questions, area, depth and scope. Some MAs are asking complex questions, but answer them in a more restricted time frame than do MPhils or PhDs (a one-year project rather than a project of three or more years).

So that:

The experiences of mature students in higher education: a case study at one university

would be an MPhil proposal because of its scope – limited to one university, and because of its *descriptive* nature. It investigates, but doesn't pose a really deep question.

The history of GM fertilisers from 1950 to 1990

would also be at this level because it accounts for and documents rather than asking leading questions. Both are limited in different ways, and are possibly limited because of the nature of the area which the researcher seeks to study, rather than anything related to the researcher themselves.

▶ Key stages: developing a hypothesis and questions

During the research there are several key stages and issues which need addressing:

One of the first stages is that of planning the research. We will look at this in further detail in later chapters. But it is important to think about it generally now. Once you have decided on a title, you need to 'unpack' it and think about the questions and areas which need investigating in order to address the title:

- state the research problem or issue or question: introduction – nature of problem, why it is important, how research will contribute to its solution
- state the research question or hypothesis, in the form of an interrogative question asking the relationship between variables, phenomena, events, and definitions of terms
- decide on subsidiary questions.

Asking research questions – setting out to solve problems

Much research starts out from asking questions, considering and trying to solve problems, constructing a hypothesis about how someone or something behaves or could behave, and then testing out, trying out, working on these problems, hypotheses, and so on, using research methodologies and methods. It is essential when you go into research to decide exactly what your research questions are (or you will find that you could merely collect data).

One essential approach is to consider and break down a concept, asking questions about how it is constructed, how it works, what its implications are, what it affects. The research student is trying out ways of measuring aspects of the idea or concept, so they break it down into fundamental questions and aspects and ask questions about these.

'Operationalising' a concept

If we asked research questions about the concept of family, for example, we would ask questions about the number and ages of children, number of parents, whether it was an extended family, with grandparents, and so on, or a nuclear family with just parents and children. Operationalising a concept or idea means breaking it down into issues and questions about which one can then ask further questions and seek to research.

Asking questions about a concept or an idea – moving further: hypothesis and variables

You need to consider the research questions and assumptions of the concept or main question you are asking in your research, breaking it down into the fundamental issues and questions involved in it. You might ask more questions about these, pose research problems and use them as variables, elements of difference which are used as categories to show difference in gathering and interpreting data. Investigating and asking questions about the concept of higher education, for example, might include asking questions about numbers of students, their gender, age, class and ethnicity; kinds of different higher education institutions; the ways in which programmes of instruction are constructed, managed and advertised; the subject areas taught in higher education; the numbers of staff; locations around the country; admissions; quality assurance; qualifications; and so on. The researcher then moves further to construct hypotheses about the relationship between these aspects or different elements of the concept, or variables, as they are called. So a researcher might construct a hypothesis about the relationships between the variables of gender and subject choice, or between the location of universities and numbers of students attending what kinds of subject areas.

▶ Kinds of research and the questions they ask and answer

There are several different kinds of research, which can be classified as:

- descriptive
- exploratory
- predictive
- explanatory
- action.

These definitions provide researchers with a way of defining their aims and outcomes, and of clarifying their strategies. They help us to decide on the kinds of methodologies which are appropriate. Much, if not most, research will be a mixture of these kinds.

Task

Read on through the following descriptions and define *your* research type(s). What kind of research is yours? It will probably be a mixture of two or more of the following kinds of research.

Descriptive research

Descriptive research aims to find out more about a phenomenon and to capture it with detailed information. Often the capturing and description is only true for that moment in time, but it still helps us to understand and know more about the phenomenon. The description might have to be repeated several times and then further exploratory questions asked about the reasons for its change or stability. An example of (completed) descriptive research might be:

Achievement of pupils

> *... the Government released ratings for the achievement of GCSEs and A levels in schools in the UK which gives readers and parents an idea of the proportion of pupils who are entered for numbers of exams and the proportion who pass.*

Clearly this description would have to be repeated, probably yearly, so that stability or change could be noted. It tells us something about the achievements of pupils in schools and about schools who have low and high achievement rates. The research which led to the data collection and publication was not aimed at asking 'why?' questions but 'what?' questions, and so these tables and results tell us about a situation, but not its causes. This data does not tell us anything about why the schools have these rates of achievement, and so any reasons for choosing certain schools over each other or rewarding them with increased funding, or whatever might result from the publication of the list, would only truly be possible and fair when other questions had been asked of the reasons for the data. This questioning would lead us into exploratory research, which often goes alongside descriptive research.

Exploratory research

Exploratory research asks both 'what?' and 'why?' questions. It begins with the question 'does X happen?' and then 'why does X happen?' and sets out, using a variety of methods, to discover whether what is in question is true or not. Essentially it explores both simple and sometimes also complex issues. Sometimes the ostensibly simple issues turn out to be complex because a seemingly straightforward question such as:

> *Do women shop in supermarkets in the high streets more frequently than they shop in smaller shops specialising in meat, fruit and vegetables, and so on?*

has many underlying subsidiary questions and complex causes.

This might seem a straightforward question, but it is quite complex. Other factors than choice or availability are involved and these factors affect or bias the experiment you might carry out to explore your research question. For example, in this instance, the age, occupation, social class, culture and beliefs of the women might affect where they shop and why. They might be older, or single, and so perhaps prefer to shop for small items regularly and so choose small shops, or have large families and/or full-time jobs and find a large, weekly shop an easier option. An exploratory study which could gather information about these variables (and others) would be both more interesting and more useful for any further assumptions or action.

Exploratory research is commonly used when new knowledge is sought or certain behaviour and the causes for the presentation of symptoms, actions, or events need discovering. Returning to the published lists of achievements in schools, we might use exploratory research to ask more about the locations of the schools, their intake, class size, staff/pupil ratios, and so on. These variables will affect the achievement of pupils, it could be argued. The argument would need to be supported by the exploratory research. It could also be aided by explanatory research.

Explanatory research
Explanatory research also asks 'why?' questions. It specifically seeks to look at the cause/effect relationships between two or more phenomena. It can be immensely helpful when description and simple exploration have come up with a number of variables which confuse rather than clarify the assumptions and hypotheses. Explanatory research might, in the instance of the schoolchildren and school achievement rates, compare different sets of variables. It might, on the one hand, ask questions and collect data about the class size, school teaching and learning methods, qualifications of staff, quality assurance controls and the attainments of the children. On the other hand, additionally, it might ask questions about the class of pupils, their background in terms of income, location, housing and living space, the number of other children in the family, whether parents are in or out of work, on income support or not and the diet and health of the family. The one set of variables relates to quality in the school's delivery and the other to the background of the pupils. The two sets of variables need matching against each other before conclusions can begin to be drawn. Such research might be carried out to answer questions about:

Why women in some African countries find opportunities to publish fiction and poetry while there seem to be no publications by women from other African countries

Or, for example,

In the UK, why it seems that fee-paying public schools with largely middle- and upper-class children from the Home Counties gain better grades at GCSE and A level than comprehensive schools with large classes in, for example, the North-East, where there are high levels of unemployment, ill health and poverty.

This could try to determine, perhaps, something rather more subtle about the quality of teaching and learning being delivered in each of the schools, related to input and output. Clearly this kind of research could cause social and political argument! But it is certainly fascinating and much more complex than merely stating something about league tables of achievement on publication rates. It can also lead into or relate to predictive research.

Predictive research

Predictive research takes several variables and tries to predict an outcome. It asks 'what if?' questions. The hypothesis is based on data already collected and considered on knowledge and conceptualisation, as well as probably past experience. Predictive research is based on probability and can, for example, be used to predict: the likelihood in England, Europe or elsewhere in the world of seaside towns being full of day trippers on a hot summer bank holiday. It is based on predictions which themselves grow out of repeated actions and events which have been studied. Predictive research takes several variables into account. For example, as above, the proximity of a hot summer day to a holiday from work, and the attractions offered at holiday towns near the coast, plus the usual habits of English people (and other nationalities) to visit holiday destinations on hot summer days when they are themselves on holiday, act as variables which all add up to a predictable result. If the prediction, in the event, was unfulfilled, other variables would have to be questioned.

Predictive research works by using knowledge gained from past research and events. It is also possible in many instances to experiment with predictive research and to control some of the variables to test whether the results change. Predictive research is based on identification of relationships between variables, so changing one or more variables could, it is predicted, change the outcomes. You can then deduce the effect of that variable on the outcomes, to some extent.

Action research

Action research explores and informs practice. It also asks 'what if?' questions. It is experientially based and usually set up to try and solve a problem or try out a hypothesis which could improve a practical situation. Teachers, social workers, medical practitioners and other practitioners working with human subjects carry out versions of action research each time they try out an innovation in their work in order to solve a problem or develop a new and useful practice to achieve a developmental practical outcome. It involves collaboration with its subjects, and seeks to research practice. Action research focuses on bringing about the change process defined by Webb & Sherman (1991), 'doing research and working on solving a problem at the same time'.

A specific chapter is focused on action research.

Task

Take an area you might be interested in researching into, for example, divorce rates, drug abuse among the young, international students studying in the UK, religious worship, mature students, and so on.

1   How can you 'operationalise the concept' – that is, break it down into fundamental issues and underlying elements and questions?
2   How can you ask research questions and take the different research approaches which would produce data about this area of interest?
3   What would be the questions you would ask, what variables might you take into account, how might you gather information and data using:
    • descriptive research
    • exploratory research
    • predictive research
    • explanatory research
    • action research?

Now look at research methods, as described in Chapter 11. This identifies dimensions of research. Complete the sheet in this section.

Completing the sheet helps you to identify where in your research you are, for example, measuring, and where you are speculating and defining meaning – how much your research concentrates on information gathering and how much it concentrates or perhaps *should* concentrate on asking questions, criticising and analysing, generalising and coming to (tentative) conclusions.

The exercise aims to make you think about clarifying the dimensions of your research, and probably also extending them – research in the UK tends to ask questions and critique as well as, rather than merely, detail, record and inform.

▶ Research paradigms

What are the major paradigms and perspectives driving the research?

We have looked at the kinds of research you might be involved in and how it is useful to consider research *paradigms*. A research paradigm or perspective is the underlying set of beliefs about how the elements of the research area fit together and how we can enquire of it and make meaning of our discoveries. Do we believe things, events and people interact and link logically (positivist), and logical conclusions can be determined through our study of this? Or do we believe that the way we see the world, our beliefs, affect how we interpret our research field and items within it, and that we are studying and interpreting interactions between people, things and relationships (relativist).

A particularly lucid explanation of different research paradigms is offered by Denzin and Lincoln (1998: 185–93): the *positivist and postpositivist* paradigms, for example, which focus on *internal validity*, *external validity*, *reliability* and *objectivity*. These approaches cannot fully take account of the ways in which inquiry is interactive, and sets of facts can be read in different ways, and are value-laden, not value-free. By contrast, *constructivism and critical theory* use a *relativist ontology*, *transactional epistemology*, and *hermeneutic*, *dialectical methodology*. What this means is that the research based on this paradigm aims at the production of reconstructed understandings. It is not as focused on validity but concentrates instead on trustworthiness and authenticity. It looks for the ways in which meanings are made through relationships – people and things, or events and events, through the ways discourse deals with, controls and represents events, facts, and so on. How do we construct and interpret knowledge? Critical theorists of the Marxist and feminist modes have given us new insights into the different ways in which versions, values and knowledge are produced. Their knowledge of the world (epistemology) is transactional (recognising that one set of actions causes other interactions and responses), and the methodology is dialectical and dialogic, recognising that as different readings and arguments are presented and set up against each other, knowledge and versions of the world move on through this interaction and *dialogue*, producing different understandings and expressions. Poststructural, postmodernist feminist and cultural studies theories spring from and are attached to these methodologies and epistemologies. Much of their tasks aim to show that constructions of knowledge and of value, representations of versions of readings of the world, lives, are relative to who is doing the constructing and representing, where and when. This construction and representation have particularly focused on any group defined by the dominant normalised group as 'other' – women, black people, the working class, gays and lesbians, and so on. Critical theorists seek to produce transformations in the social order, in the way things are in society, and produce knowledge which is situated historically. It is both historical and structural and relates to the possibility of causing change. Many feminist theorists and ethnic theorists grow from these constructivist and critical theory bases, some developing an *interpretive perspective* examining ways in which gender, race, sexuality, and so on are repressively inscribed in everyday life and everyday representations. This is done in order to critique and expose these inscriptions as not 'normal' and 'essential', that is, the way reality *is*, but as interpretations, as constructions which could be interpreted and constructed differently (because they are relative – to time, place, paradigm, the interpreter and their cultural group and positions) (Denzin and Lincoln 1998: 191).

Task

Consider:

- Is your research *positivist*, that is, has it an underlying positivist paradigm which suggests that people/events/things are logical, linked and predictable? Or is it, for example, based on a paradigm or underlying belief/knowledge-constructed theory that meaning is created through relating things (that is, it is interpretative – interpreting events and relations – or dialogic – showing a debate between different interpretations.

▶ Ethics in research

You will need to take into account your university's statements on ethics. When you complete your research proposal for the research degrees committee it will need to contain a specific statement about taking ethics into consideration.

Whatever kind of research you are involved in, you will need to ensure that you take ethics into account. Research ethics have been a major issue since the Second World War, which triggered off insistence that all research should be ethical. Since scientific research has always claimed to be free from any issue of morality or amorality, and 'pure' in its concentration on pushing forward the frontiers of knowledge, whatever the issue and subsequent cost (think of the development of the atom bomb and germ warfare, for example), the introduction and maintenance of ethical watchdogs has been a key factor in regulating research. Ethical guidelines insist that researchers should do no physical or psychological harm and that when people are involved the participants should give their fully informed consent before taking part. Other areas involving animal research also raise issues of ethics, although clearly here the animal cannot give or withhold consent, and so an appeal to a broader concept of ethics is needed. It is also essential if ethics are really taken into consideration, to think of the longer-term effects of the research. Even if the actual experimentation seems to harm no one (this would apply to the development of bombs and warfare instruments not actually tested on people), the results of the experiments must be fully considered.

Task

Look back at your research area and the questions you are asking:

- What ethical considerations do you need to take account of in your research?
- Are you using people in your research?
- Are they in any kind of work relationship to you?
- How and why would this matter?
- What would you need to take into consideration?
- If they are already dead – that is, historical research – are ethics and permission still involved?
- What if the data people presented is very old? Are ethics still involved?
- Are animals involved in your research?
- What else might relate to ethics in your research?

*You will need to make quite a full statement about having taken ethics into consideration when writing your proposal.

Conclusion

We have looked at:

- Different kinds of research
- Different kinds of research paradigms and how to determine what *your* research could be
- Ethics and how to ensure that your work is conforming to the ethical guidelines

---

Further reading

Denzin, N. K., & Lincoln, Y. S. (1998). *The Landscape of Qualitative Research, Theories and Issues*. Thousand Oaks, CA: Sage.

12 Carrying out a Literature Review

> This chapter looks at:
>
> - *What is a literature review?*
> - *How does it differ in different fields of study?*
> - *How to go about a literature review*
> - *The ongoing literature review*
> - *Engaging your own work with the literature – summarising, analysing, contributing and engaging in dialogue*

Your research is seen as a contribution to knowledge in the field and it needs to indicate, therefore, that there is an awareness of what that knowledge comprises. The reasons for literature reviews are twofold. You need to read yourself into the field of study in order to gauge where your own ideas fit, what can inform them, what others think and have discovered, and to define where/in what ways your area of questioning, your research and your findings could contribute to existing knowledge. Your own work both engages with the known literature and adds something else. This might seem a tall order, because you cannot possibly read everything that has been written about your field of study, nor everything about your particular area, unless it is very specialised. By searching out the literature to which your own work will contribute, you are not trying to cover and summarise everything. This would be an endless, daunting and ultimately pointless task. Yours is not a role of summariser of everyone else's thoughts and discoveries, but an engagement in *dialogue* with what has been written and what is to be written and discovered by others. You need to read the background literature to contextualise and underpin your own work rather than substitute for it. This indicates to readers and examiners that you know the field and know also that you have something to contribute to it.

Literature reviews depend upon extensive literature searching. This is (a) undertaken before the research question is posed and the purpose written then (b) ongoing, taking place alongside the research throughout. Literature reviews do not usually appear as a separate chapter as such, but form a considerable part of the introduction *because* they indicate previous work in the field, the context into which your own work fits and the different *theses* from which your own work springs, which inform it. You will be reading in areas of the field, of related fields, of critical and theoretical questioning and approaches to properly inform and drive your own work.

While the literature review you do is largely written up in the introduction, you continue to refer to key themes, texts, writers and experts as and when their work informs and relates to yours throughout the thesis or dissertation.

If you are an international student you will most probably find that you need either to seek a translation of the work of international theorists, critics or experts you hope to use in your own arguments and research, or provide your *own* translation of the quotations you use if they do not publish in English. If your university allows you to present your work in your own language and assumes that it can be examined in your own language, you will clearly not have to do this (but you would probably be translating the work you find into English!). However, most UK, Australian and US and other English-speaking universities do expect the dissertation or thesis to be presented entirely in English.

This introduction sets the scene for the research questions, the major arguments of the research and thesis and then throughout the work itself, taking different elements of the thesis argument on in different places and providing a coherent thread of reference for key arguments and ideas. In both kinds of literature review activity it is sensible to keep reading throughout the research. There could be really important new discoveries or key texts which appear even quite close to the end of your own work, and you will need to acknowledge these, even to say that they could not be incorporated into the research design because of when they were produced. This shows that you have an awareness of the field, and of the learning conversations taking place within it, and can see what your own work contributes.

> The process of the literature review involves the researcher in exploring the literature to establish the status quo, formulate a problem or research enquiry, define the value of pursuing the line of enquiry established, and

compare the findings and ideas with his or her own. The product involves the synthesis of the work of others in a form that demonstrates the accomplishment of the exploratory process. (Andresen 1997, adapted from Bruce 1994)

Literature reviews establish the background and the context, and involve consulting and engaging with primary sources of all sorts, and secondary sources too, or rather other researchers and academics' contributions to the field of discussion. They involve reflection and analysis and comment on contributions to the field of study, recognising that you are aware of what has been found, the methods of research, and the underpinning arguments in your field:

> A literature review uses as its database reports of primary or original scholarship, and does not report new primary scholarship itself. The primary reports used in the literature may be verbal, but in the vast majority of cases are written documents. The types of scholarship might be empirical theoretical, critical/analytical, or methodological in nature. Second, a literature review seeks to describe, summarise, evaluate, clarify and/or integrate the content of primary reports. (Cooper 1985: 8)

The purposes of literature review, according to Andresen, are:

- becoming familiar with the 'conversation' in the subject area of interest
- identifying an appropriate research question
- ascertaining the nature of previous research and issues surrounding the research question
- finding evidence in the academic discourse to establish a need for the proposed research
- keeping abreast of ongoing work in the area of interest. (Andresen 1997, part 3: 48)

The literature review is an essential part of planning your research and helps you to develop your own line of thought. As an ongoing process it also helps you to keep abreast of developments in your subject and field and possibly enables you to get in touch with others working in the same field (you can contact other researchers and discuss work with them). Your examiners will be looking for how far your thesis contributes to knowledge in the field, to which the literature review element of your work is central.

▶ Carrying out the literature review

There are several activities associated with handling a literature review.

You need to scour the library and associated libraries, probably using a computer to help in your search, but not substituting it completely for looking around the shelves in the area where you find a useful book. We often find other related texts in close proximity. Look in the reference sections of key books and articles you are using and of other's theses on similar topics. Here you will find what might be minor references for others' work but possibly either background or really key references for your own, depending on the different slants and lines of argument taken in these sources.

Literature searches: using the library and the Internet – a brief introduction

Every researcher needs to become familiar with the use of the libraries available to them – not always your local library, but often a specialist library, perhaps at a distance – and to make good use of the information available on the Internet also. Using e-mail and the Web to keep in touch with other researchers and your supervisor is important (see groups/support materials in Chapter 10).

Trawling for information is fascinating when you know how – and many of us do this every day. However, there is often too much information, and on the Internet it is not likely to be organised in the way you need it, so be careful with copying it. Do manage it, organise and sift it. There is a real concern with students at all levels merely downloading topical material from the Net. This is plagiarism as serious as merely copying from a book. The other problem with material on the Net is that it is put there without any quality control checks, and some of it is incorrect and poorly written. You have been warned!

You will also need to consider how to handle the information you gain in your literature searching throughout the research. One model suggests that you acquire a great deal of information, summarise the key points, keep careful references, and write the introductory literature review from this. Another suggests that, as the literature review process is ongoing throughout your work, you will need to keep returning to the field and reviewing and rereading, certainly catching up on new texts and new areas of study which become more obviously

Task

Consider:

- When have you used libraries, CD-ROMs and the Internet for research?
- Which libraries will you use?
- Which ones might you need to join?
- Will you need to develop skills using the Internet?
- Will you need to update these skills?
- What experience do you have of accessing subject indexes and abstracting databases?
- Do you have good access and if so, where?

In considering these questions, note down an action plan for:

- improving your library access – will you need to ask for a letter of reference signed by your supervisor in order to gain access to another local university library, for example, in your home town?
- improving your Internet access – will you need to take a brief training course to use the Internet for literature searching/to use the online access computers in the library?
- finding the subject indexes and the abstracting databases and conducting a trial search – do you have experience in this? Or can you conduct a trial search to give you an idea of advice you need to seek?

Action points

-
-

relevant as your work proceeds. A reflective approach to literature searching is the most useful, that is, one which enables you to go through a cyclical model, searching, recording, processing and researching as new sources or new ideas and developments become clear (see Figure 12.1).

Your literature searching leads to the incorporation of ideas, quotations, arguments and references into your own work. You will need to establish a sound set of study and working strategies to make full use of this. Try the skills audit on the next page.

Task

What skills needs do you have?

For example:	Good	quite good	needs practice
quick and effective reading	1	2	3
• note taking	1	2	3
• summarising	1	2	3
• finding and using subject indexes and abstracting databases	1	2	3
• reference keeping	1	2	3
• interweaving your reading into your arguments and discussions.	1	2	3

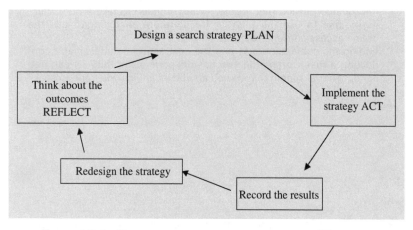

FIGURE 12.1 REFLECTIVE LITERATURE SEARCHING MODEL (BRUCE, IN ANDRESEN 1997: 16)

Abstracting, noting and summarising

You can usually take one photocopy of a journal article under copyright law. You will need, however, to take notes from and 'process' both journal articles and books, chapters and other sources. Try the 'SQ3R' method for rapid and effective notetaking:

- Survey – quick read through
- Question – what was that about?

- Read/reread – look through it all/read it carefully and reread, but only if necessary
- Record
- Take notes under main key headings (having identified these main points in your survey). Take full quotations and full citations of other references you will need to follow up.
- Summarise major arguments and quote to refer. Always indicate with references where the ideas and the quotations come from.
- Make some sub-notes and discussion points alongside your notes. Underline in colour the main ideas and arguments.
- Start to structure your notes and process the arguments.
- Review – quickly look back at the chapter/article, and so on. Have you caught the most important points, the main arguments, all you need for your own work? Have you recorded the references appropriately? Are the quotations correct? What have you missed?
- Consult some of the good study guides available to remind you of these effective practices (Cottrell 1999 or Dunleaky 1986).

Filing and retaining
You need to keep full, informative notes in card-indexes or on your computer of all the sources you consult, your contacts and correspondences. See below for comments on computer or card-index storage.

Learning journals and logs
You could also write up the ideas, arguments, findings, and so on of your ongoing literature search in a *learning journal* or learning log. This helps to show the shaping of your arguments and the shaping of your use of your reading, how it informs your investigations, research questioning and interpretation. If you are a part-time student, it also helps you to return to the key questions and findings after periods away from your study (for example, on work projects, family holidays, house moves, new babies, and so on).

Good research habits
You need to ask yourself regularly:

- Have I updated my literature search and review?
- Have I returned to key sources to investigate further what emerged as important issues?
- Have I fully recorded the reference I have found?

- Have I been writing up and using what I have found? Have I been using the ideas and spurring on more of my own ideas?
- Or have I been leaving it to stockpile (and possibly go stale)?

Management on a computer

Programmes for management of literature include Procit, Notebook and Reference Manager, among others.

Establish a list of headings that fits your research – subjects, questions, methodology, methods, and so on.

Read papers and parts of books as soon as you get them and assign headings to the material so that you can record these and later access the reference from those several appropriate headings. Consider headings of:

- author
- title
- methods
- key words and areas
- date of publication.

You need to link these headings and areas to the file management system so that when the system is interrogated it indicates work collected under the appropriate heading/author/date, and so on, as required.

This is obviously more sophisticated than a card-index which tends to force you to keep information under author in alphabetical order so that you are not immediately able to go to the repository of information on a subject area. Card-indexes, however, are portable, cheap and can be marvellously idiosyncratic. You will need to find the system that suits you and which you can manage. The most important element of each kind of storage system is that you have the information you need to retrieve. So ensure that you have:

- author
- title
- place of publication, publisher, date (the citation format which is required by your university) and page numbers, if appropriate
- areas of interest and importance – subject headings
- some key quotations
- where the source came from, for example, library, inter-library loan, the Internet, a friend's collection.

Are all recorded. Otherwise you will find that towards the middle of the thesis you cannot locate those wonderful early pieces of reading, and at the end you will have to spend days in libraries trying to track down the books and the journals with the full references in them. This is a frustrating waste of time.

For sophisticated computer users, Carol Tenopir and Gerald Lundeen's *Managing your Information* (1988) is a full source of how to create your own database and which systems to use.

Task

- Select a journal article that relates to your area of research.
- Process it using the SQ3R methods (see above).
- Now write down the key points, the full citation details, the author, subject, and so on, *on an index card.*
- decide where/under what headings, for example, author, key words, area of argument, methods, and so on you would want to store the information so that it can be retrieved when writing chapters.

Conclusion

We have looked at:

- The function of literature reviewing to form the introductory context and theoretical underpinning and to integrate with your own research throughout
- How to carry out literature searching
- How to take notes, process and make the information and ideas your own
- Storage and retrieval.

Further reading

Andresen, L.W. (1997). *Highways to Postgraduate Supervision*. Sydney: University of Western Sydney.

Cooper, H.M. (1985). *The Integrative Research Review: A Systematic Approach*. London: Sage.

Cottrell, S. (1999). *The Study Skills Handbook*. Basingstoke: Macmillan Press – now Palgrave.

Dunleaky, Patrick (1986). *Studying for a Degree*. Basingstoke: Macmillan Press – now Palgrave.

Tenopir, C., & Lundeen, G. (1988). *Managing your Information*. New York: Neal Schuman.

13 Choosing Appropriate Research Methodologies and Methods

This chapter looks at:

- *Introduction to different methodologies in research*
- *Qualitative and/or quantitative methods*
- *Qualitative methods, for example, focus groups*
- *Quantitative methods, for example, questionnaires, structured observations*

▶ Choosing qualitative or quantitative research methodologies

Your research will dictate the kinds of research methodologies you use to underpin your work and methods you use in order to collect data. If you wish to collect quantitative data you are probably measuring variables and verifying existing theories or hypotheses or questioning them. Data is often used to generate new hypotheses based on the results of data collected about different variables. One's colleagues are often much happier about the ability to verify qualitative data as many people feel safe only with numbers and statistics. However, often collections of statistics and number crunching are not the answers to understanding meanings, beliefs and experience, which are better understood through qualitative data. And quantitative data, it must be remembered, are also collected in accordance with certain research vehicles and underlying research questions. Even the production of numbers is guided at base by the kinds of questions asked of the subjects, so it is essentially subjective, although it appears less so than qualitative research data.

Qualitative research is carried out when we wish to understand meanings, or look at, describe and understand experience, ideas, beliefs and values – intangibles such as these. *Example*: an area of study that would benefit from qualitative research would be that of students' learning styles and approaches to study, which are described and understood subjectively by students (see Chapter 8).

► Using qualitative and quantitative research methods together

This is a common approach. The results of qualitative research into students' learning, as described above, can be measured to some extent in quantitative data too, as the numbers of students choosing certain closed responses in a questionnaire or survey about their approaches can be set against the results they achieve in assessment tests, and the numbers produced can be quantified. The statistics produced do not, however, tell us all about *how* and *why* students succeed in their learning. There are so many variables, such as the kind of teaching and learning methods, types of assessment methods, timing, student ability, and so on that it is difficult to make assumptions that some kinds of learning approach lead inevitably to success or failure in higher education assessment tests.

Subjectivity exists in both kinds of research methods, as it does also in what could be termed 'pure', scientific research where scientists carry out well-managed and well-documented experiments. Their choice of experiments and, to some extent, the questions they ask of the data in order to interpret it are based on essentially subjective research questions, a need to know some things rather than others. This can be determined by different times and places, different needs and abilities, the opportunities for different kinds of study, and different subjects.

► Sampling

A sample is a selected and chosen group upon which you carry out your research. As a sample they are chosen to *indicate* the larger whole of which they are but a small part. Any research method will depend initially on your ability to find and work on a sample. Sampling is an important research step. If you cannot find ways of discovering a sample on which to test your hypothesis you will have no data. If you choose too small a sample size the data will be invalid, and if you sample only from a small, unrepresentative proportion of the population (whether it be a human, animal, or object population) your results will be affected by the influence of this skewed sample. You will need to decide, then, how to find and take a sample, what to take into consideration and what to acknowledge as affecting the data when using the results from this sample. You could decide to sample a percentage or proportion of the whole population/group. You could decide to use an entirely *random* sample, which might mean looking at the responses of, for example, every tenth person, every tenth antelope or every tenth cream cake (whatever you are studying). A random sample is chosen just at random – not selected along any specific rules for any specific reason. It is one which is a proportion, or percentage of the total population and other variables are not taken into consideration in selecting the sample. You could instead take a *stratified sample*, which means initially being able to describe your population in strata or layers of types, of differentials in terms of, for example, age differentials, old and new universities, economic classes, and so on. Once you have divided the whole population into strata, either using your own definitions which you must explain and defend, or using established definitions, for example, the division of people in the UK into economic and social classes in relation to their jobs, ranging from 'A' downwards. You then take a sample from each of the strata, and decide whether to take the same number from each, or the same percentage or proportion from each (if, as with social class, for instance, each stratum is of a very different size to the rest, this can be an important deciding factor which will affect the results you obtain). It is also possible to take a random stratified sample. In doing so you would first stratify or used recognised stratification, then randomly sample every tenth (for example) in each of the strata. The reason for this sampling is to get a fair spread and to reduce bias of choice.

Once you have your sample you will gather research data from them using one or more methodologies. With action research in particular, it is important to use several methodologies and to compare the results they produce in order to better authenticate your results.

Task

Consider:

- Where are you taking your sample from?
- How will you find them?
- Can you foresee any problems or difficulties in your sampling?

Further details about both quantitative and qualitative research methods follow in forthcoming chapters.

▶ Kinds of research methods in brief: introduction

Please look at the very brief outlines of different methods, below. Consider which you intend using and whether you could also find it more useful to combine the *quantitative* with the *qualitative.* You will be familiar with many of these methods from your work and from MA and M.Sc. or BA study.

▶ Qualitative research methods include

Interviews

Interviews enable face-to-face discussion with human subjects. If you are going to use interviews you will have to decide whether you will take notes (distracting), tape the interview (accurate but time-consuming), rely on your memory (foolish) or write in their answers (this can lead to closed questioning owing to pressure of time). If you decide to interview you will need to draw up a schedule of questions which can be either *closed* or *open*, or a mixture of these. Closed questions tend to be used for asking for and receiving answers about fixed facts such as name, numbers, and so on. They do not require speculation and they tend to produce short answers. With closed questions you could even give your interviewees a small selection of possible answers from which to choose. If you do this you will be able to manage the data and quantify the responses quite easily. (The

Household Survey and Census ask closed questions, and often market researchers who stop you in the street do too.) You might ask them to indicate how true they feel a certain statement to be, and this too can provide both a closed response, and one which can be quantified (30 per cent of those asked said they never ate rice, while 45 per cent said they did so regularly at least once a week . . . , and so on).

The problem with closed questions is that they limit the response the interviewee can give and do not enable them to think deeply or test their real feelings or values.

If you ask open questions such as 'what do you think about the increase in traffic?' you could elicit an almost endless number of responses. This would give you a very good idea of the variety of ideas and feelings people have, and it would enable them to think and talk for longer and so show their feelings and views more fully. But it is very difficult to quantify these results. You will find that you will need to read all the comments through and to categorise them after you have received them, or merely report them in their diversity and make general statements, or pick out particular comments if they seem to fit your purpose. If you decide to use interviews, draw up a set of questions that seem appropriate and try them out with a colleague before you pilot them, then refine the questions so that they are genuinely engaged with your research object.

Focus groups

Focus groups are small groups brought together specifically to focus on certain issues, for example, the uses of the library and how library facilities might be improved, or how international students' learning is aided (or not) by teaching and learning strategies and resources, or how a group of people respond over time to a *particular* project, or TV show. Focus groups enable close scrutiny and lengthy discussion. They can be repeated over time and used to test out ideas. Like any other research sample, if studied over time, they will actually change in responses and attitudes and so this will affect any random sample quality they initially had. The focus group is also constantly affected by the presence of the researcher, and this will need to be taken into consideration. Discussions can, as with interviews, be either noted down or recorded and transcribed. They are very useful indeed for capturing people's responses and feelings, their records of experiences, and so on. With several people present in a focus group, ideas and issues tend to shape themselves as people speak, and the subjects start to form an understanding as participants debate certain points. This is really helpful as you deal with different areas and issues in your research.

Participant observation

In participant observation the researcher joins the group they are studying. This is much more straightforward if the group is similar in kind to the researcher as the researcher will stand out less, and so affect the responses and results less. However, this is essentially a very subjective form of research and great care has to be taken in recognising what is subjective, and what is objective fact, when considering data and responses. Historically, various sociologists have joined biker gangs and lumber camps, mixed with hardened criminals, changed their skin colour to experience what it is like to be on the receiving end of racism, and so on. It is clearly not so easy to be involved fully in participant observation if you are of a very different ethnic group, age, class or gender to your subjects. It is rather like 'going undercover'.

Personal learning logs

The researcher using a personal learning log is using their own experiences and responses as research data. They are also recording their observations. The log is a forum for recording response moment by moment, so tracking changing attitudes and the build-up of knowledge and understanding. It can be used as a research vehicle in itself to record, for example, how the researcher is feeling about undertaking the research, and is here it is especially helpful if the research is very personally related and ethically testing, involves emotions, and so on. It can also be used like a captain's log to record what is experienced and what effects noted, and what data is collected. Usually it is a mixture of discovered detail and personal response.

▶ Quantitative research methods include

Questionnaires

Questionnaires often seem a logical and easy option as a way of collecting information from people. They are actually rather difficult to design, and because of the frequency of their use in all contexts in the modern world, the response rate is nearly always going to be a problem (low) unless you have ways of making people complete them and hand them in on the spot (and this of course limits your sample, how long the questionnaire can be, and the kinds of questions asked). As with interviews, you can decide to use closed or open questions, and can also offer respondents multiple-choice questions from which to choose the statement which most nearly describes their response. Their lay-out is an art form in itself, because in poorly laid-out questionnaires respondents tend, for example, to repeat their ticking of boxes in the same pattern. If they are given a choice of response on a scale 1 to 5, they will usually opt for the middle point, and often tend to miss out sub-sections to questions. You need to take expert advice in setting up a questionnaire, check that all the information about the respondents which you need is included and filled in, and ensure that you actually get them returned. Expecting people to pay to return postal question-naires is sheer folly, and drawing up a really lengthy questionnaire will also inhibit response rates. You will need to ensure that the questions are clear, and that you have reliable ways of collecting and managing the data. Setting up a questionnaire that can be read by an optical mark reader is an excellent idea if you wish to collect large numbers of responses and analyse them statistically rather than reading each ques-tionnaire and entering data manually.

While research methods you use, you will probably need to pilot them first and then refine the research vehicles and change your format, questions, and so on, as needed.

While further chapters explore research methods in greater detail, you would find it useful to consult the range of full and excellent research books available. These will deal in much greater depth with the reasons for, processes of holding, and processes of analysing data from the variety of research methods available to you.

Task

What kind of research methods are you going to use? Are they mostly:

- quantitative, or
- qualitative, or
- a mixture of both?
- What do you think your methods will enable you to discover?
- What might they prevent you from discovering?
- What kinds of research methods would be best suited to the kind of research you are undertaking and the research questions you are pursuing?
- What sort of problems do you envisage in setting up these methods?
- What are their benefits?
- What will you need to do to ensure they gather useful data?

Conclusion

We have looked at:

- The choice of research type and methodologies
- The choice of research methods

Further reading

Miles, M., & Huberman, M. (1994) *Qualitative Data Analysis*. London: Sage.
Robson, C. (1993) *Real World Research*. Oxford: Blackwell.

Stage 3

More Detailed Research Methods – Maintaining Momentum

14 Designing and Using Questionnaires

This chapter looks at

- *Why use questionnaires?*
- *What are their pros and cons?*
- *How can you use them?*
- *Analysing questionnaires*
- *Managing and presenting data from questionnaires*

Questionnaires gather information directly by asking people questions and using them as data for analysis. They are often used to gather information about attitudes, behaviours, activities, and responses to events and usually consist of a list of written questions. Respondents can complete questionnaires in timed circumstances, by post, or by responding to researchers directly who, armed with the questionnaire, can actually *ask* them the questions directly. It is a method of gathering large numbers of responses, although the response rates are quite frequently not high because so many people become rather irritated by questionnaires and refuse to fill them out. You need to ensure that your questionnaire is perfect when you use it with your sample, so it is important to take advice, pilot questions thoroughly and then use the questionnaire with your samples. It is not usually possible to return to the sample with a further developed version of a questionnaire, not least because having completed it once they will not be able to respond in a natural and genuine manner.

You need to ensure that your questionnaire is:

- kept confidential
- trialled, piloted and refined
- really able to ask the questions you want

- avoids ambiguities and multiple questions
- has entirely clear questions.

When setting out a questionnaire you need to:

- clear the use of it with your sponsor or whoever is allowing you to use it
- ensure you can code up the questions after the response has been collected so that you can analyse the data. Yes/no and Lickert scale-type questions (on a range of 1–5, where for example 1 = strongly agree and 5 = strongly disagree) are easier to code up. While open-ended questions produce fuller responses, you will need to have an idea of the trends for which you are looking and to develop a code to deal with expected areas of answers so that when the open ended question responses come in, you can code them up. The coding is so that you can handle the amount of data and carry out some statistical analysis since questionnaires are most often used to suggest the response of a significant number of people in terms of percentage and proportions.

When sending out questionnaires you need to:

- Explain what the purpose is and guarantee confidentiality
- Explain who the sponsor is/who it is for
- Provide a return address and a time for the return (if it is posted)
- Explain that the responses are voluntary
- Thank the respondents for their time in completing the questionnaire.

▶ Layout

This is a complicated science! Questionnaires should not be too long or they will get a lower response rate because people become bored and irritated and fail to complete them. Use single-sided paper and quality production, do not crowd the questionnaire, and try not to repeat questions too often (although this is useful for cross-checking, it irritates respondents).

- Number your pages as well as your questions.
- Whatever kind of questions you pose, you need to include a coding

box, probably on the right-hand side, so that you can code up the responses when you have gathered all the questions together. Make sure this is an integral part of the questionnaire as you develop and then pilot and print it, or there will be a lot of tedious work inscribing boxes and coding them afterwards.

- Make sure your questions are very clear and unambiguous. Respondents should be willing and able to answer the questions so that they are properly targeted, are not insulting, not vague, and avoid unnecessary assumptions.

- If you provide consistent kinds of questions with a consistent scale, for example, 1–4, your respondents will be more able to focus on the questions without worrying about the format. They are also more likely to coast along on the columns, ticking the same response for several questions, so beware of and spot respondent boredom.

- Do put the most simple and obvious questions at the beginning and make them more complicated, if necessary, as the questionnaire proceeds. This keeps your respondent with you and does not confuse them at the start.

▶ Examples of kinds of questions

(A)   Closed questions – these are easier to code

1   Yes/no answers

Q. Have you travelled abroad in the last year?
A. Yes/no

2   Agree/disagree answers
Please indicate whether you agree or disagree with the following statements:

Q. Travel by plane is always preferable to travel by land
A. Agree/disagree

3   Choosing from options
Please indicate your chosen option by circling the item which relates to your choice:

Q. Which country do you feel has the best provision for holiday-
makers?
A. Cyprus Spain France Italy Australia USA

4   Putting items in order
Please place the following items of food in order of your choice, using
1 for the most preferred, and so on, down to 6 as the least preferred:

paella lasagne spaghetti fish and chips moussaka chilli con carne

5   Rating responses
Please rate the following responses on a scale of 1 to 5 where 1 is
'strongly agree' and 5 is 'strongly disagree':

(a)	Housework is a natural activity for women.	1 2 3 4 5
(b)	Domestic work should be shared by all members of the family.	1 2 3 4 5
(c)	It is quite normal for women to be involved in paid work outside the home.	1 2 3 4 5
(d)	The man of the house ought to earn more than the woman for paid work outside the home.	1 2 3 4 5

(B)   Open-ended questions

6   The relatively simple answer

Q. What has been your preferred module this year?
A. ....

7   The longer, more complex, more varied answer

Q. For what reasons has this been your preferred module?
A. ....
....
....

Question types 6 and 7 will also need coding, or there is no way in
a long questionnaire that you can draw any conclusions and sum
anything up.

Once you have gathered in and labelled up your questionnaires, coding them and removing those which are incomplete, you will need to analyse them. You can do this by counting responses and coding the open-ended response and quoting from them wherever appropriate. Alternatively, you can enter the coded and numerical responses into the computer using statistical packages such as SPSS, which then work to produce a frequency analysis for you. The next stage in a frequency analysis is to ask the package to produce responses in relation to variables and to produce responses which relate variables. This is so that you can match up, for example, the frequency of holiday trips abroad and the frequency of which of those are to a particular country.

Task

Decide on a topic which is related to your research or one which is not, such as student responses to the facilities provided for post-graduates around the university campus. Draw up a questionnaire which has at least one question of each of the seven kinds illustrated above.

Consider how to word these questions very carefully and which ones would be better as closed choices or open choices, on a scale, yes/no, and so on. Defend your reasons for those choices. Try the questionnaire out on yourself or preferably on a friend/colleague/relative, and ask them:

- Can you actually answer these questions? Are they clear? Ambiguous? Leading? Insulting? Irrelevant?
- Do you think that they enable the researcher to approach information on the object of their study?
- Are some of the questions going to be unhelpful because the wrong questions were asked?
- How would you code up, analyse and then present the data?

As with interviewing (see Chapter 15), you will soon discover that there are questions you employ that cannot be asked directly, such as those about personal hygiene, sexual relations, spending habits, and bad habits. This is because people will not want to be entirely honest and will boast or lie to some extent. Some questionnaires are considered too insulting or awkward.

▶ Laying out the information from the data

There are many different ways to treat the data. One thing to remember is that the presentation must be appropriate, useful and accessible to readers. It must also be translated for them, in a way that is interesting, not merely laid out.

Bar charts

See the examples of bar charts in Figures 14.1 and 14.2.

The results presented in Figures 14.1 and 14.2 relate to the researcher's learning questionnaire in Chapter 9, which was given to 25 Israeli PhD students in 2000. Initially the results were represented as a sample frequency table, then converted into this bar chart in order to visualise the different kinds of responses produced by the different questions. The bar chart in itself is useless unless we match it with the questions, so that some sense of what these choices mean can be produced. (Note: The first part of the questionnaire is not included in full in Chapter 9.)

Information can be presented in a number of ways. The bar chart enables us to compare single items of clusters of items against each other, which is useful if there are a couple of variables involved.

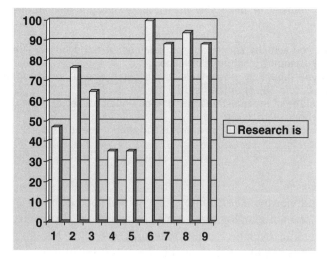

FIGURE **14.1** RESEARCH-AS-LEARNING, PART 1. 'RESEARCH IS . . .' (WISKER 2000)

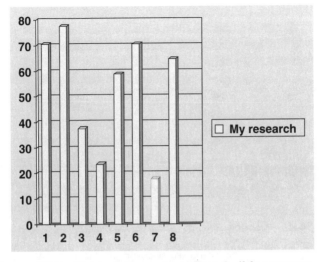

FIGURE 14.2 RESEARCH-AS-LEARNING, PART 2. 'MY RESEARCH ...' (WISKER 2000)

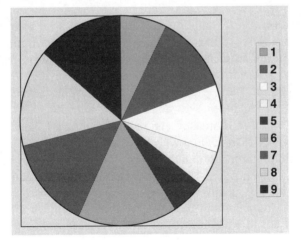

FIGURE 14.3 PIE CHART: PROPORTIONS OF STUDENTS STUDYING IN DIFFERENT SUBJECT AREAS IN THE FACULTY OF APPLIED SCIENCE

Key: 1 = Biology 2 = Chemistry 3 = Physics 4 = Forensic Science
5 = Radiography 6 = Animal Sciences 7 = General Science 8 = Biochemistry
9 = Opthalmics

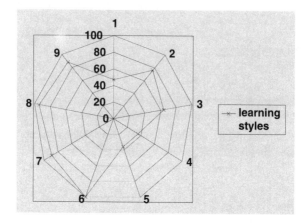

FIGURE 14.4 RADAR CHART WITH MARKERS: ANALYSIS OF THE RESPONSE TO A QUESTIONNAIRE ON LEARNING STYLES, SHOWING THE PATTERN OF RESPONSE ACROSS THE PREFERRED LEARNING STYLES

Pie charts
A pie chart, on the other hand, shows the proportion of a whole which the item or question selected relates to (see Figure 14.3).

Radar charts
Radar charts indicate patterns of choices and behaviours for individuals or groups in relation to the categories of answers chosen (see Figure 14.4).

Styles
Each of the numbered areas in Figure 14.4 relates to a specific kind of learning style. The individual who has been analysed has a variety of leanings and preferences, and the radar chart enables us to see the use in relation to each other. There are many different kinds of layout of your results and you will need to choose the most visually suitable.

Task

Consider:
  What kind of layout would suit the kinds of questioning you are carrying out and the kinds of questions underpinning your work? And in your sample? Are you looking for percentages, proportions in relation to the whole, comparative samples, variables in operation?

Conclusion

We have looked at:

- The reasons for using questionnaires
- The kinds of questions to ask
- Organising and laying out questionnaires
- Analysing questionnaire results and laying them out visually

15 Action Research and Phenomenography

Many people choose action research because it enables us to work in partnership with the people on whom/with whom we are carrying out the research. It enables ownership and change to result alongside and after the research. It is particularly useful in practitioner-based research as it is likely to combine quantitative with qualitative methods.

Consider:

- *What is action research?*
- *Have you carried out any action research?*
- *Do you intend to carry out any?*
- *Have you read or heard of any?*
- *If so, what are the characteristics of action research projects as you understand them?*
- *What is action research?*
- *What are the advantages of practitioner action research?*
- *Setting up and running action research in your own work*

▶ Action research

Action research is research that we carry out with our students in order to try out an idea or an innovation, test a hypothesis about their learning and to see what would happen if. . . . However, the process is actually more rigorous than this, which is merely a description of the ordinary kinds of innovations we carry out as teachers. Using the principles and practices of action research, we can try out an innovation with students and assess and evaluate its effects, then move on to apply it further. We need to have an initial hypothesis, a plan, probably a pilot stage and one or several methodologies, and then to try out this innovation, measuring and carefully observing its effects. As much of the research is qualitative rather than quantitative, we will be involved in interviews, participant observation, and so on, as much as or instead of the more calculable methodological forms, for example, questionnaires.

When we have come to some conclusions, we need to test these in relation to other methodological strategies and see if the same kinds of results are produced. In terms of our work, educational or practioner enquiry is another descriptor for the research we do. It is essential that it is practice based and aims to enhance the learning of our students, rather than merely collect information. Action research depends on working with other people to discuss, plan, test, retry, ensure validity, and so on. It is research related to our teaching and to our students.

Key features

- The researcher and those being researched are in partnership. The aims, practices, strategies and findings of the research are shared at each stage.
- The research often aims to develop those researched through their involvement and through their subsequent reflection.

Tendencies

- use triangulation, that is, information is thought through two or more research methods and strategies
- share the research and findings with colleagues who were helpful or made formative comments
- lend itself to reflection by the researcher and researched
- feed into change.

Advantages

- It is *based* in practice and thus avoids the problem of needing to be 'implemented'.
- It enhances morale (individual and collective) because it encourages practitioners to recollect and use their strengths.

- It uses validity criteria and validation processes based on involvement in the practices situation.

Many MAs, MPhils, and PhDs use action research strategies or are totally action research-based. If you want to be involved with your students, clients, customers or patients and to make changes, try out models and programmes, and trial developments, you are probably going to be involved in action research.

The action research process

> PLAN → ACT → OBSERVE → REFLECT → REVISED PLAN → ACT → OBSERVE → and so on.

How is this different from practice? Essentially it isn't, it is *based* in practice but it requires and establishes a more sustained and explicit examination of:

- decisions
- relationships
- the knowledge base for decisions
- the critical interpretation of evidence/data
- the learning that can be derived from practice.

Resources for 'reflection' within practitioner action research

- *collaborative* working with clients (challenging power relationships) and colleagues (challenging personal assumptions)
- awareness of emotions – one's own and others'
- evaluation of dilemmas within values and commitments
- drawing together the implications of *varied* bodies of knowledge (e.g. theory, research, law and regulations)
- comparison between current and previous experience.

In other words, '**critical analysis**' – that is, awareness of a varied *context* and its *contradictions*, leading to a sense of *alternative possibilities* both in practice and in one's understanding of practice.
   In this sense, the basis for action research is similar to the basis for the role of the 'reflective' professional practitioner.
   This in turn suggests a form of 'research' that is best undertaken by the practitioners themselves.

Action research plans

Task

Consider:

- What parts of the work, if any, that you do with students/clients/customers/patients, and so on would be appropriate for action research?
- Why would you want to carry out action research on these concerns, developments and issues?
- What would you hope to find out?
- What are your research questions?
- What kinds of methods could you use?
- What might the perils and pitfalls be?

'Action research is not only a possible alternative to advancing knowledge in higher education; it is also a more effective and immediate way of improving learning and teaching practice' (Zuber Skerritt 1992).

Action and research are two sides of the same coin.

Academics are in an ideal position; on the one side they can create and advance knowledge in higher education on the basis of their concrete, practical experience; on the other side, they can actively improve practice on the basis of their 'grounded theory'. The ultimate aim should be to improve practice in a systematic way and, if warranted, to suggest and make changes to the environment, context or conditions in which that practice takes place. The assumptions are that people can learn and create knowledge on the basis of their concrete experience through (i) observing and reflecting on that experience by forming abstract concepts and generalisations, and (ii) by testing the implications of these concepts, in new situations, which will lead to new concrete experience and hence to the beginning of a new cycle.

Action research is an alternative approach to traditional research. It is:

- practical
- participative
- emancipatory
- interpretative
- critical

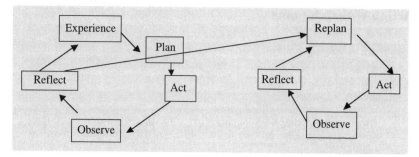

FIGURE 15.1 A SPIRAL OF CYCLES OF ACTION AND RESEARCH

It operates using:

- a critical attitude
- research into teaching
- accountability
- self-evaluation
- professionalism

and it entails:

- critical and self-critical collaborative enquiry by reflective practitioners:
- being accountable and making the results of their enquiry public
- self-evaluating their practice and being engaged in parcipitative problem-solving and continuing professional development.

Steps in action research

- focus on the problem
- produce a general plan of action
- action step
- monitoring step
- collect the data
- evaluate the results
- reformulate plans.

A few tips

- For action research, we have to have outcomes and criteria against which to measure plans and actions, developments and results.

- You don't undertake action research alone. It is collaborative and involves testing your ideas and results against others and against several tests: triangulation (helps check results using one measure, and back up results using a couple of others).
- Rigour is different in qualitative research from that found in quantitative research – but it is still immensely important.
- Action research involves researcher and researched in a shared activity that usually leads to change.

Much action research takes place within the methodological framework of phenomenography, which recognises an overall picture of expectations and behaviour in context (see Zuber Skerritt 1992).

▶ Phenomenography

Phenomenography is a theoretical framework that relates to being in the world (phenomenology) and so, in terms of research, enables us to focus our feelings, interactions and experiences of our subjects *in context*. This sounds both highly subjective and very broad. In fact, phenomenography, by encouraging us to track, focus and capture experience, between people and people, people and things, and people in events *in context*, enables us to recognise more clearly all the influences and interpretations which affect our research. We also become aware of the need to concentrate on one small segment of interactions in context, rather than trying to capture the whole.

Phenomenography began as a theory that focused on student learning.

In this model (see Figure 15.2) we recognise that we can say something about how student learning takes place by looking at the interaction between student conceptions of learning, student learning styles, learning approaches, strategies, the object of study (learning outcome in the subject) and the way it is being taught and assessed. It also enables us to consider these interactions more broadly in context. For example, the learning experience of a group of Israeli PhD students working intensively in a badly ventilated room on a cold day, in a summer school in the UK, would be recognised as quite a different learning experience from that experienced by a small group of UK managers in a plush conference suite on a weekend residential course, or on an adult evening class in a schoolroom in Norfolk in November, studying for 'pleasure'.

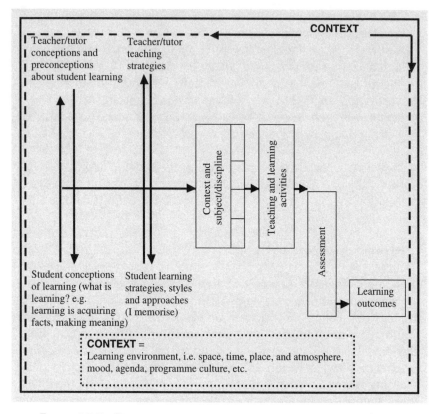

FIGURE 15.2 PHENOMENOGRAPHICAL MODEL OF STUDENT LEARNING (AFTER PROSSER & TRIGWELL 1999)

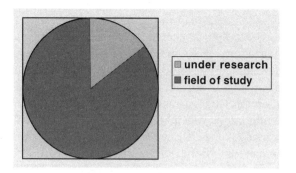

FIGURE 15.3 CHOOSING A MANAGEABLE PIECE OF RESEARCH

Should a researcher be trying to *study* any of these situational inter-actions and experiences, they would need to take a number (not all – impossible) of the factors into account and focus in their study on an *element* of the whole field of study. This is of course true of all research to some extent, for we only ever take a focused 'slice' of the whole field (see Figure 15.3).

Both interviews and observations can be vehicles for phenomeno-graphical research, although phenomenography often operates by inviting researchers to combine quantitative and qualitative methods. The next chapter focuses more specifically on both interviews and observations.

Conclusion

We have looked at:

* Action research – practices and planning
* Advantages, resources and outcomes of practioner action research
* Phenomenography – a study of interactions in context

How might any of these ideas and practices fit in with your *own* research?

Further reading

Biggs, J. B. (1999) *Teaching for Quality Learning at University: What the Student Does*. Buckingham: Open University Press.

Prosser, M., & Trigwell, K. (eds.) (1999) *Understanding Learning and Teaching: The Experience in Higher Education*. Buckingham: Open University Press.

Zuber Skerritt, O. (1992) *Action Research in Higher Education*. London: Kogan Page.

16 Qualitative Research Methods: Interviews, Focus Groups and Observation

> *This chapter looks at:*
>
> - *Developing, carrying out, writing up and analysing interviews*
> - *When and how to use focus groups, running them, writing up and analysing*
> - *Kinds of observation – planning, managing, analysing and writing up*
> - *Ethical issues*

If some or all of your research methods involve capturing people's opinions, feelings and practice, their experience and the kind of atmosphere and context in which they act and respond, then qualitative research methods are likely to form a large part of your exploration and your research. Previous chapters gave a brief introduction to interviews, observation and focus groups. There are some more in-depth explorations of each of these in various books devoted to research methods (see the Bibliography).

▶ Interviews

You need to decide whether the outcomes you seek for your research would be better served by going directly to people you can access, who could give you in-depth comments. Decide how you can select who to interview and how to gain access to them. You need to ask their permission to be interviewed, whether you approach them in the street with a clipboard (a rather accidental sample) or visit them at home (a more controlled sample).

Why decide to interview?

Interviews give you the opportunity to meet the subjects of your research. They can provide both the detailed information you set out to collect and some fascinating contextual or other information (not all of which you can use). But they are certainly time-consuming. You need to consider that should you decide to tape an interview, it is likely to take six hours or more to transcribe what you have taped, and a great deal more time besides to analyse and then use what was said. Not all interviews are either worth such an expense of time (and perhaps money, if someone else is transcribing for you). You might decide to interview if you are looking for:

* information based on emotions, feelings, experiences
* information based on sensitive issues
* information based on insider experience, privileged insights and experiences.

They can be used to gather information:

* to supplement information provided in a questionnaire
* to help pilot a questionnaire, interview a few people to test out the areas and questions
* to follow up a questionnaire – select who to interview for in-depth or variety of responses following the broader information produced in a questionnaire
* to add to a variety of other methods such as questionnaires, observation and documentary analysis, by closing in on a smaller sample dealt with in depth.

Processes

* Decide on an interview as a method – why?
* How would you find your sample?
* Decide on your sample and if and how you can gain access to them – do not try to do too many interviews, as they are very time-consuming. You might want to gather a variety of responses from very different kinds of people within your strata or a number of interviews with the same kind of interviewees.

For example:

- A selection of external examiners in a variety of different subjects and different universities; or
- Three external examiners who have indicated previously that they support the role staying as it is, and three who would wish to change it in line with the Quality Assurance Agency recommendations.

These two kinds of samples would clearly yield very different sorts of information, so you need to be clear from the outset what it is you wish to enquire about in order to get the right sample (and ask the right questions). Do be careful to ensure that you can locate your sample and gain access to it.

Case study

For example, Sarah wished to find out about the attitudes and professional development of educated Greek Cypriot women in Cyprus. Her work, she decided, would be based initially, upon a questionnaire, and then on in-depth interviews with a few women. Her first problem was finding the sample – how could she have access to a list which would give her 'educated Greek Cypriot women', and what definitions would be used? The second difficulty was to decide who to interview from the sample who completed the questionnaire. This would inevitably be (a) already self-selected (they chose to complete the questionnaire) and/or (b) people she already knew – a skewed group. For Sarah, a chance loss of access to the list (loss of a contact person) meant that she lost her sample.

Sensitivities

One thing to keep in mind is that behaviour and wording are culturally inflected. If you are interviewing someone from a different cultural, gendered or class background, and so on, you will need to be careful to observe their rules of behaviour, check out their context, check out the meanings of what you ask and what you are hearing, to avoid cultural confusions. You will also find that where the interview takes place, how you dress and sit, are affected by cultural differences. Do some research into this before setting up and running an interview – you do

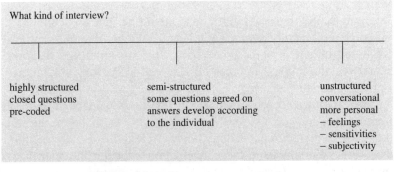

What kind of interview?

highly structured	semi-structured	unstructured
closed questions	some questions agreed on	conversational
pre-coded	answers develop according	more personal
	to the individual	– feelings
		– sensitivities
		– subjectivity

FIGURE 16.1   THE INTERVIEW CONTINUUM

not want your interviewee to be awkward or embarrassed and you do not want to be awkward or embarrassed yourself. Equally, you do not want cultural misunderstanding to either limit what is discussed, or cause misinterpretation.

Go on to explore the needs in terms of setting up and running these chosen interviews.

Kinds of interview

There is a continuum of interviews, which ranges from the informal and conversational interaction which flows with the thoughts and feelings of both interviewer and interviewee, and the much tighter, more structured interview. There are pluses and minuses to all kinds of interviews along the continuum.

What kind of interview do you have in mind? Would you want interviewees to give yes/no or Lickert scale 1–5 answers, which you fill in yourself? Or would you want to collect all that they say, and code afterwards the kinds of answers you get? The first kind of interview questions produce results very like a questionnaire – they can even be quantitative (although you are unlikely to be able to carry out quite the number of interviews as you would be able to send questionnaires), or they can be highly qualitative, conversations between yourself and the interviewee which, as they go on, reveal interesting new insights into the topic. These latter tend to be used later on and returned to. In the latter instance you read through transcripts/listen carefully to tapes/read through your notes, and decide on the themes and issues that are emerging in relation to your area of enquiry and your questions, and code the responses accordingly.

Structured interviews rely upon the interviewer completing a set of structured questions with answers of choice, and asking questions according to the order of these questions (rather like a questionnaire, but completed by the interviewer after questioning the interviewee). A structured interview with closed questions can guide the responses clearly, making analysis simpler, *but* can be too guiding and limiting – it might not gather feelings.

Semi-structured, open-ended interviews manage to both address the need for comparable responses – that is, there are the same questions being asked of each interviewee – and the need for the interview to be developed by the conversation between interviewer and interviewee – which is often very rich and rewarding. With a semi-structured, open-ended interview there are a series of set questions to be asked and space for some divergence, with the interviewer then returning to the structured interview questions.

The unstructured interview

The unstructured interview has been variously described as naturalistic, autobiographical, in-depth, narrative or non-directive. Whatever the label used, the informal interview is modelled on a conversation and, like a conversation, is a social event with, in this instance, two participants. As a social event it has its own set of interactional rules which may be more or less recognised by the participants (Holland and Ramazanoglu 1994: 135).

An open-ended, conversational interview may be rich in gathering feelings, following the thought and discussion processes of the interviewee, but could go very much off the point and be difficult either to transcribe or to analyse and compare with other interviews. You might find you have incomparable data that is rich in itself but not easy to start to draw conclusions from in relation to your project.

Interviews may seem like conversations, but in fact they are more complex, structured, interactive and controlled. Some interviews develop a strange kind of antagonism between interviewer and interviewed, probably due to the power invested in either side, and to the prying which an interview seems to suggest. Others make the interviewee feel flattered; their opinions are being sought, and these matter. In both unstructured and more structured interviews the real words of the interviewee are used, rather than just their responses to closed questions.

Ethics

You need to explain carefully to anyone you intend to interview exactly what you will do with the interview material. While some short interviews of the Yes/No clipboard variety are unlikely to yield very sensitive material, others are more personal. It is assumed that what is said in an interview is 'on the record' but some participants may choose to remain anonymous or to vet the script of the interview before you use it. This is something that should be offered to them – agree to send the transcript to them before you use it.

Organising the interview
Interviewing itself needs to be as carefully thought out and structured as any questionnaire, even if it does sometimes appear to be rather like a conversation.

Contact
Contact your interviewee in advance and introduce yourself by letter, following up with a phone call. Explain the reason for the research and what your aims are in interviewing them (but don't give all the questions away).

Time and place
You need to agree on a time and place that is mutually suitable, and indicate how long the interview is likely to last. Try to ensure that the place will be interference free. Since the interviewee is giving you their time, it is a good idea to fit in with their plans. This can involve awkward hours and travelling. In interviewing external examiners I travelled all over the country and met them when it suited. One met me in the early evening, just before he boarded a train, another in the early morning before he started teaching. Both required my travelling at difficult times. Do avoid interviewing someone when they are walking somewhere else or not fully concentrating.

Recording the interview
A small, sensitive tape recorder is necessary, but the most expensive tape recorders are not always the best, so try them out first. Don't forget to have enough tapes ready, and to ensure the batteries are fully charged (sometimes there is a battery in the tape recorder and a separate one in the microphone, so check this). Place the tape recorder somewhere unobtrusive but point it out. Your respondents will soon ignore it (hopefully – sometimes they seem to speak directly to the tape in a rather stilted fashion. Do discourage this!).

You might feel happier taking notes – but this is also rather obtrusive. Do not rely on memory alone. Do write up either notes or tape (transcribe) as soon as possible after the interview so that you can contextualise and make sense of the responses.

Asking interview questions

Open-ended questions can enable the interviewee to expand with prompting and follow up with questions which refine an area if there are misunderstandings – but they can also be misleading and provide a large amount of information you cannot then use. Closed questions can limit interaction and the creative exploration, as well as the opening up of the interview, and hence its richness.

Some questions are more sensitive than others. The framing of all questions should be carried out very carefully.

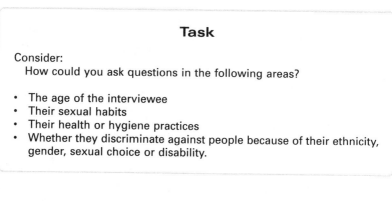

Task

Consider:
  How could you ask questions in the following areas?

- The age of the interviewee
- Their sexual habits
- Their health or hygiene practices
- Whether they discriminate against people because of their ethnicity, gender, sexual choice or disability.

You could try some of the following methods:

1 Ask them when they left school for the first time. Ask them when they started their first school/primary school (at the age of 5).
2 Ask them to choose between a set of statements that describe habits.
3 Ask them to agree or disagree with a range of statements, such as, 'Do you shower or bath (A) once a day; (B) twice a day or more; (C) once a week; or (D) less frequently?'
4 Describe some case-study scenarios and ask for responses on a scale such as, 'A student in a wheelchair arrives at an interview for your school/college. Would you:
    (A) Explain that there is no disabled access so they will have difficulty attending?
    (B) Explain and apologise for the lack of disabled access, but put in motion the plans that could improve access for them?

(C)   Explain the current lack of access, and the plans to improve it, and ask them about their specific needs – then take these to whoever can make the necessary arrangements?

With (4) you could not ask a direct question about attitudes to disability and student access, so you give choices. It is then a subjective interpretation as to what attitudes are revealed by the choices. (C), for example, seems to indicate greater willingness to look at the individual's needs. However, you would need to contextualise the answers and your interpretation of them in relation to college resources. Again, do take cultural differences into account and try and avoid questions that can be embarrassing, awkward or produce misleading responses.

What's said and what's not said
In an interview there are areas which people are prepared to discuss, and those they won't discuss, areas they are aware of, and areas they hide or are not aware of. Think of what can be discovered as lying somewhere along the axes in the boxes shown in Figure 16.2.

For example, X is an area you and the interviewee can discuss openly, they know about and can reveal, for example, 'Where do you live?', while XX is an area they probably are unaware of or are repressing, and

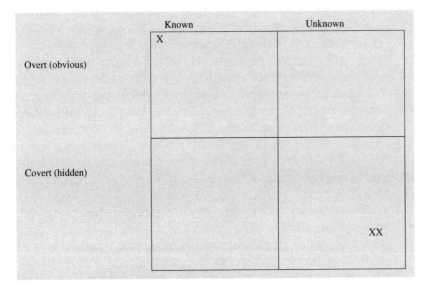

FIGURE 16.2 INTERVIEW INTERACTIONS

which they won't directly reveal, for example, psychological or behavioural disturbance due to traumatic experience. You might suspect it, but you can't *ask* about it and would need to use 'what if?' questions, choices between scenarios, and other methods of information gathering to really find out (if you can).

Honesty

Don't make any promises you cannot keep, and do not mislead the interviewee about how the information will be used, when or where. Agree to let them see a transcript if this suits you. Sum up your notes and check them periodically with the interviewee if you have been talking for a while about something complex.

Be polite and pleasant and thank the interviewee for their time.

Questions and behaviours to avoid

- *Don't* appear threatened or bored.
- *Don't* ask:
  - Excessively long questions – they may only remember part of the question.
  - Multiple questions packed into one – this will confuse them and they might answer only one part or run several together in a way you cannot use later.
  - Questions using excessive jargon or technical terms – explain what you seek in ordinary language.
  - Questions which lead or suggest bias and prejudice, such as, 'Why have you chosen to retire?' (It may be they have not *chosen* to retire!) or 'Don't you agree that mobile phones are a nuisance in the street and on trains?' Rephrase these to capture a range of possible responses and not just to gain yes/no answers (which actually halt the thought and interview processes).

Questions and behaviours to use

- *Do* stay in control and appear friendly and responsive.
- *Do* use prompts and probes.
- Probing questions or behaviours can be as simple as smiling and nodding, with an indication that the interviewee should go on and say more, or 'mmmn?' or repeating back part of what they said, which usually makes them carry on (the Queen is said to do this when interviewing, for example, 'What is your occupation?' 'I am a

greengrocer.' 'Oh, so you are a greengrocer?' 'Yes, and I sell vegetables and fruit.' 'You sell vegetables and fruit?' 'Yes, and . . .')

All of these are affected by age, gender, ability, ethnicity, religion, class
and a number of cultural differences, so do be careful. If in doubt,
consult sensitive others from a similar cultural background to your
interviewees.

The shape of interviews

Interviews are interactions, whether they are open, semi-open or fairly
closed. There will be a momentum and rhythm to them, as with any
other interaction. You need to manage this well. They often run along
the following lines:

- Introductions.
- Social comments about time and place.
- Background information to the interview and explanation of how it
  will be conducted, what you are seeking, and so on.
- The interview itself:
  - variety of appropriate questions and some space to let answers
    develop
  - ways of prompting and probing to expand, if the answers seem
    to be leading in an interesting and useful direction
  - a way of closing down and moving on if the answers are ram-
    bling or not focused
  - more formal movements to and from necessary questions to
    ensure they are not missed out and are fully answered
  - perhaps even rephrasing questions if they seem misunderstood
    or ignored, or returning to them if ignored.
- Winding down.
- A few straightforward questions to finish the interview off and some
  information about use and contacts.
- Closing down – thanks and goodbyes.

Task

Mock interview

- Choose a colleague to interview. Decide why you want to interview
  them, what you want to find out about, and decide on the schedule
  of questions and the setting.

Continued

- Develop your interview schedule and compare it against the checklist below. Think through your responses to the items in this list and share them with your colleague.
- Develop some questions you could ask.
- Ask your colleague the chosen questions.
- Collect the responses in notes or tape them.
- Reflect on the process – how successful was it? What worked and what went wrong?
- What would you do differently next time?
- Debrief and evaluate what you did, what you discussed, what worked well and what didn't. Discuss with each other how you might improve the interview.

Checklist of questions to support your interview development

- Why do you want to use interviews?
- Is this the best method to gather the kind of information you need?
- How will an interview fit in with the rest of your research methods?
- What kind of sample would best suit your needs?
- What kind of an interview is it to be? How structured, free-flowing or semi-structured do you want your interviews to be and why?
- Are there any cultural sensitivities you will need to take into account? How can you do this? What should you avoid or ensure happens?
- Are there any sensitive areas of questioning you need to use? How will you ask these sensitive questions?
- Will you need to tape the interview, transcribe or analyse it, and tape it to use as back-up for notes? Will you take notes while you interview, read them through and firm them up afterwards, then analyse them? And
- How will you analyse them? Will you listen and annotate a transcript? Will you use a computer programme such as Nvivo or Nudist (programmes which thematically analyse qualitative data)?
- How will you analyse the data you acquire?
- Decide on your questions, trial run them with a colleague or friend, refine them and collect them on a clipboard, cards or in some other useful form – what will you do?
- Prepare an interview schedule: consider the order of the questions, especially those which must be answered. Prepare some prompts such as photographs, other questions, samples or examples, in case your interview does not move from one point to another as expected. Which questions and which prompts?

- Pilot your question schedule: does it work with a friend? Do the questions seem to flow more smoothly in a different order? Have you been able to overcome the problems associated with those more sensitive questions? Are you missing some of the sensitive questions? What can you do to make them more accessible?

Can you now start to draw up a series of questions that you could use for the body of your own interview *for your own research*? Try out a couple of key questions.
 Pilot them with a colleague and ask:

- Are these too vague?
- Too probing?
- Embarrassing?
- Closed?
- Will they cause the interviewee to ramble?
- Are they clear?
- Do they follow on from the questions already asked?
- Can they really give me the information I am after?
- Are they not really going to capture that information?
- Are they misleading?

Discuss and advise each other on exact wording.

Creative interviewing
Areas of feelings, interactions, emotions, deeply hidden fears and desires, and so on, are very difficult to discover through straightforward interviewing. You could try to use creative interviewing. This involves using interview techniques and a creative visualising exercise. To gain a response about traumatic experiences, a sensitive emotional development or a feeling, for example, about someone's relationship to a group or organisation, asking them to draw, point or act out can release creative energies. This is termed 'synectics' and is the use of creative metaphors or imaginative comparisons to capture sensitive responses. For example, someone trying to describe how they feel they are being ostracised in an organisation could visualise themselves as a weed in a flower patch. You can then discuss with them how they (or others) might move towards a more positive image. In this way a creative interview captures feelings and can also start to effect change (if that is one of your research areas).

▶ Focus groups as group interviews

Focus groups can be a good way to capture the responses of a small group of people. One method is to ask to meet a selection of students/clients/interviewees several times over a certain period to gauge their responses to a changing situation. In this way, they become familiar with the research, with yourself as a researcher, with the context and with each other. They often feel valued because their views are being sought in relation to a development or change, and they often also change and become more self-aware and reflective because of being involved in the focus group. This latter point could affect the kind of information you acquire, but could also be very developmental for those involved in the focus group.

If you use focus groups, you need to follow all the guidelines also suited to an interview, that is:

1 Decide if it is open-ended, semi-structured or structured. It is unlikely that a fully structured interview will work over time with a focus group because it is too closed. However, the use of some structured and clear questions in a schedule does help the group to stay on the point and to focus clearly and specifically. The main problem with a focus group is that, like any other social group, it can dissolve into social discussion or go off the point, and it does need to be *focused*. If you are meeting the group over time, you will also need to prepare questions which match the developments over time, rather than asking the same questions over and over again, or just letting them talk.

2 Take cultural context and difference into account in what you ask, where you ask it, how you ask it and how you respond.

3 Ensure you have a suitable method of recording the focus group interviews, such as a tape recorder in the middle of the table with the group clustered around. They will need to say their names when they speak, certainly until you are familiar with their voices (on the tape). Videoing the discussion is another option. Both methods could inhibit the group initially, but as a group they are more likely to ignore the methods after a few sentences and get on with the discussion and answering questions.

Unlike individual one-to-one interviews, focus groups need firmer or clearer 'ground rules' such as:

- taking some responses in turn so that one person does not dominate
- prompting each other to speak
- being polite, as in conversation people tend to cut in on each other
- remembering to let the other person finish what they were saying (without cutting off the creative interaction that could lead to development, exploration and a higher level of thinking and articulating, as with group work with students).

Focus groups with undergraduates working on identifying how they learn and what teaching and learning activities enable them in their learning have, in the past, dissolved into a discussion about 'horrible' rooms, the modular system and how much they hate a particular subject. Other focus groups, nurtured and prompted to stick to the questions while developing their answers, have built up sensitive responses over time to the same set of questions and their belonging in the group has in itself caused these students to be more aware of how they learn – that is, it has developed their 'metacognitive' skills. If the focus group work is part of an action research project, this development of the students will be a very valuable product.

Focus groups have been used by market researchers and housing groups, people seeking responses to building and social changes, to media developments and so on – anything where the responses of a group interacting with each other can provide a rich sense of people shaping feelings. However, because they are a group activity, they need managing in terms of group dynamics – and there is a special value placed on the collective responses and views. In order to manage this, it is important to set the group up carefully and to agree ground rules about behaviour. Silence and dominance are two behaviours that could inhibit general discussion. The researcher can act as a facilitator to the group and use triggers, prompts or specific questions to develop the discussion. One set of focus groups has revolved around the use of 'trigger tapes', which are short video extracts, to prompt responses to areas in relation to discrimination and attitude. Managing these has helped to discover both attitudes and help attitudinal change. They can enable the more silent participants to say more because, as with other group activities, they are prompted by the contributions of others. They are better managed over non-sensitive issues but, as is suggested by the trigger tapes, they can also be used to gauge responses to sensitive issues. Set them up with clear channels of communication over time.

▶ Observation

Observation can be a rich source of information for the researcher. It enables you to capture what people actually do rather than what they say they do. You can observe them in context and relate to your research questions while you observe.

There are two main sorts of observation, defined by Lacey – *participant observation* and *non-participant* observation (1976: 65).

Participant observation involves the researcher becoming a part of the group they observe. As Lacey notes, it involves 'the transfer of the whole person into an imaginative and emotional experience in which the fieldworker learned to live in and understand the new world'. In *The Organisation and Practice of Social Research* (Shipman 1976), he explores his experiences of working for three years observing classes and talking with teachers and pupils at Hightown Grammar (quoted by Judith Bell). The author Zora Neale Hurston worked with Frederick Boas, the anthropologist, and lived with loggers in a camp, getting herself beaten up by a jealous logger woman who thought Zora's interviewing of her partner was too intrusive. There are dangers to participant observation.

Non-participant observation is less intrusive but involves observing the actions of others. Both require careful planning, determining what exactly is going to be observed and what fundamental or underlying issues and questions are going to be addressed by the observation. They require parameters to be set – observing others is so rich that an enormous amount of unusable data can be collected and be of no use at all to the study. On the other hand, collecting data and making field notes sometimes produces results that are unexpected, so being too rigid and structured in your approach might limit you. You might miss something surprising that could be revelatory in your research.

Direct observation is a key to both kinds of observation. You, as researcher, directly observe what your subjects are doing and saying. You can collect real-life data that becomes part of your *fieldwork*. You are conducting first-hand research from empirical data, that is, data that comes immediately from experience rather than books or notes made by other people. However, your own experience and perception will colour what you observe. Your previous experience of observation and of observing something similar will affect how you 'read' situations and behaviours, and while this can lead to insights, it can also skew or affect what you see in an unhelpful manner. As it is unavoidable, you need to reflect on it and take it into account, when you describe and defend your research methods, and when you analyse and make inferences from your analyses.

Both structured and unstructured observation requires careful planning. Your role is to observe rather than intrude, to decide on time, place and who to observe, under what conditions, and to take these conditions into account:

- Limit the events and people.
- Decide on what you want to observe so that you narrow the field.
- Take careful field notes.
- Find ways of testing out assumptions about context and observation to help interpret these field notes.

If you carry out observations of a series of people or events over time, be careful to have a structured observation checklist – what you are looking for, the time and place, and ways of collecting data so that you can match your samples. If someone else is helping you with your data collection, you will need to work closely together not only to collect information to the same schedule but to discuss your framing and interpretation of what you find, since this will inevitably be affected by experience and feelings.

Organisation and use of observation
You might find the following useful:

- Develop an observation schedule that enables you to record certain things and the time you notice them, their frequency, and so on.
- If you precategorise and prestructure your observation you will not be overwhelmed with too much information, but it would be useful to observe first in a more general manner and see what kinds of behaviours or responses appear, then develop your structure and categories.
- Find a way to be unobtrusive, to not join in fully and change the behaviour of those you observe. With participant observation this is very nearly impossible, so you will need to find ways to take into account the changes your presence could cause.
- You need to concentrate on observing.

Observation schedule

An observation schedule should include:

- Events, actions and responses which are noticeable and recorded, the times, frequency and duration of the events.
- Practices, issues, events and actions that are clear, relevant and recordable. You cannot jump to conclusions and record what you do not observe, although you will need to analyse what you observe afterwards and can record also your thoughts and concerns about what you see.
- If you are keeping a very systematic observation schedule, you might like to keep a separate *research diary* which collects your hunches and thoughts about what you see to help you monitor your own responses and to manage the data from the observation later, when analysing it.

Non-participant observation

In order to carry this out you will need to:

- be unobtrusive – do not make your presence obvious or you will alter what happens
- be aware of the full context
- be able to sift out irrelevant data. Do not record everything – record what you are looking for, and the context
- ensure you carry out your observation over a reasonable period of time, and preferably repeat it several times to ensure that the data is relatively stable.

Task

Look at this example of a non-participant observation schedule and discuss/think

- why it might have been set up and what it might help us to discover
- what else would need to be taken into consideration in starting to interpret the data.

Behaviours of colleagues arriving at work in the morning

What might this observation schedule be seeking to discover? What

Colleague	Arrival time at car park	Parking space found?	Arrival at desk
A. Wendy	8.10 a.m.	Yes	8.20 a.m.
B. Steve	8.20 a.m.	Yes	8.25 a.m.
C. Ann	8.35 a.m.	Yes	9.00 a.m.
D. Alan	8.40 a.m.	Yes	8.50 a.m.
E. Angela	8.50 a.m.	No	9.30 a.m.
F. Andrew	9.00 a.m.	No	9.35 a.m.

FIGURE 16.3 OBSERVATION SCHEDULE

can we deduce from analysing this data? What else would we need to know about the context in order to interpret the data?

In this instance, the decision has been made to observe arrival at the car park in order to work out at what kind of peak time it becomes impossible to find a car parking space on a normal morning, and how long it then takes people to get to work if they have to park elsewhere. In order for this schedule to be useful, the observation would have to be performed over several 'normal' days since the time in question (seen above) might well be either a day in the middle of the holidays or one when there are many visitor spaces booked, or some other factor might affect the parking.

Interpretations – some thoughts and problems
With this car parking study you need to know more about those you observe, and the context in order to interpret what you have observed. At first glance you could deduce that Wendy is punctual and efficient while Angela is disorganised (she doesn't park, she gets to her desk late). However, it could be that Wendy has no dependants and lives close by so minimises possible traffic congestion hold-ups. Angela might have to drop children at school, a partner at the station and drive in from the countryside. You will need to find out more in order to use what you have observed, and more still before making decisions about, for example, extending or cutting car parking. Having special places for longer-distance commuters with dependants might make Angela's 'efficiency' soar!

Observation – a continuum
As with interviewing, observation practices can be seen along a continuum from the highly regularised, factual and scientific to the more sensitive and subjective (Figure 16.4).

Where along this continuum might your intended observation take place?

Factual, timed collection of observed actions

Observation of interactions and feelings, awareness of body language and context as much as what is said or done

FIGURE **16.4** OBSERVATION CONTINUUM

Task – your own observation schedule

On your own, or with a colleague, decide on:

- A topic/subject – something you might like to observe such as shopping behaviour, car parking, people eating, children playing, the number of people coming through the front door, in whatever way, at work, or some other such easily observed activity.
- Decide what you would like to ask the subjects and what questions you might ask about the activity.
- Draw up an observation schedule that will let you observe the behaviour of several people over time, possibly (preferably) several times.
- What are you looking for and why?
- How will you observe it?
- How will you take notes and of what? Don't forget to keep a time log if this is appropriate.
- Do you need a diary for comments, too?
- Carry out the observation and then discuss your findings, how you might analyse them and what kind of deductions you might come to, once the analysis is concluded.

Participant observation

There are several types of participant observation which spring from different levels of involvement on the part of the observer.

Some observers choose to immerse themselves completely in the activities of those they observe.

Benefits: you use yourself as the equipment for this research. You are fully involved and taking part, and can register the experiences and behaviours at first hand from the inside.

Problems: it can be quite dangerous, depending on who you are observing. Lee (1995: 1) comments: 'Researchers often work in settings made dangerous by violent conflict or in situations where interpersonal violence and risk are commonplace.' Lee also notes that it is often the violence that the researcher is observing. This can be risky. One social scientist carried out participant observation with a biker gang. Clearly not all of us could fit in here, so participant observation depends on not sticking out as too different from the group you are observing. It also requires that you do not become a thoroughgoing member of the group. This is particularly important if you are observing criminal behaviour or dangerous activities (as undercover cops have found out, to their disadvantage!). It could seriously disturb and even invalidate your findings, and could be dangerous.

You could be semi-immersed – if some of the group know you are an observer, and therefore are a part of the 'secret'.

Or you could be *accepted by the group as an observer*, who does not become part of the group itself but is tolerated. The different levels of immersion affect the kinds of information you can collect, as they affect the context and personal influence on the events.

In all three kinds of participant observation:

- You will need to win the trust and confidence of those with whom you are working.
- You will need an observation schedule which records not only actions but your personal responses to them, your feelings and changes, because you are part of the equipment and also part of the subject matter.
- You will need to keep careful field notes, probably after events.
- You need to work out how much your presence affects the events and people with whom you are being involved in the observation.
- Do make sure you are observing for long enough, not capturing a biased snapshot of activities.
- You might well find it useful to keep a diary, log or journal of your experiences and responses to what you see, so that you can chart changing interpretations and separate out what you see, what you seek and what you interpret.

Recording interactions among people in groups

Some students studying social interactions between members of groups could find the published observation schedules and categories developed by Bales (1950), or Flanders (1970) or the Open University (OU) D101 course's simplified version (see Bell 1993) most useful. The problem with both Bales and Flanders is that there are many complex categories and sub-sections in which to record different behaviours and personal choices about what and how to categorise affects the recording. The OU example follows the Huthwaite Research group which builds up a system to study management skills and behaviours.

Task

In your group, observe the behaviour of the group over a particular period of the day during an activity or exercise. Using a record sheet, note the numbers and kinds of interactions. Indicate the number of interactions with a line, one for each interaction, and if you want to find out how long particular interactions last, to see who says most of what kind of interaction, then put a line for each minute. This tells you something about the kinds of interactions each group member favours, their behaviour, and possibly provides information about how and in what ways some dominate and prevent others from talking: some lead, some try and ensure that the interaction is pleasant and positive, and so on. You can draw some tentative conclusions about gendered behaviours, power and personality from these interactions but you would be advised to back the conclusions up with other information from other data-gathering sources. Prior observation and background reading should help you to decide on your categories. Note the responses and interactions in each category.

What might this tell us about interactions in this group (see Figure 16.5)? I have deliberately made it non-stereotypical so that you can see Avi and Roger proposing, disagreeing and giving information, while Ruth is very supportive and nurturing, not leading. Now draw up a schedule for the interactions of your own group/a group you are involved in, over a short period of time.

You will also need to keep field notes about who is sitting where, what the activity is and how long it lasts, and what the room and atmosphere are like. If you are recording verbal responses, you might also need to keep notes about non-verbal behaviour and body language.

Discuss your findings with a colleague. What can be deduced from these findings? From these research data?

Example group member	Kind of interaction and time spent					
	Proposing	Supporting	Disagreeing	Giving information	Seeking information	Team-building
Avi	11	11	111	11		
Ruth		111		11	1111	1111
Anya	1	1	11	11		
Gill					1111	11
Roger	111		1	111	11	

FIGURE 16.5 GROUP INTERACTION SCHEDULE (1)

Group member	Kind of interaction and time spent					
	Proposing	Supporting	Disagreeing	Giving information	Seeking information	Team building
A B C D E						

FIGURE 16.6 GROUP INTERACTION SCHEDULE (2)

Remember

If setting up an observation:

- decide what you wish to find out
- are you going to be a participant observer or not?
- gain the consent of those you are to observe (unless you are a participant observer and wish to remain anonymous)
- establish a system for keeping field notes and recording behaviours
- establish a system of observation over time, repeating actions
- collect detailed notes about context, other people's actions, atmosphere, and so on, to contextualise what you observe
- if you need to tape or video record, ensure the equipment is working and that you have consent

- record meticulously
- look through your records – are the event and notes, diary/log entries of your *own* feelings?
- analyse in relation to the categories of areas you decided to observe
- come to some initial conclusions or deductions
- and, if you have agreed to do so, share the findings with those you have observed
- interviews and observations both involve interactions in context
- they can both be quite structured, factual and formal or quite (or very) involved with feelings and emotions, capturing attitudes and 'hidden' behaviours (through body language and what's not said, for example)
- gaining consent, keeping confidentiality and respecting individuals' rights are all very important, as these are quite intrusive research methods.

Conclusion

We have looked at:

- Varieties of interviews – focus group, individuals – the pros and cons
- Varieties of observations – participant, non-participant – the pros and cons

---

Further reading

Bales, R. F. (1950). *Interaction Process Analysis: A Method for the Study of Small Groups*. Cambridge, MA: Addison-Wesley.

Bell, Judith (1993). *Doing your Research Project*. Buckingham: Open University Press.

Flanders, N. A. (1970). *Analysing Teacher Behaviour*. Reading, MA: Addison-Wesley.

Holland, J., & Ramazanoglu, C. (1994). Coming to Conclusions: Power and Interpretation in Researching Young Women's Sexuality. In M. Maynard & J. Purvis (eds.), *Researching Women's Lives from a Feminist Perspective*, pp. 125–48. London: Taylor & Francis.

Lacey, C. (1976). Problems of sociological fieldwork: a review of the methodology of 'Hightown Grammar'. In Shipman, M. (ed.), *The Organisation and Impact of Social Research*. London: Routledge & Kegan Paul.

Lee, R. (1995). *Dangerous Fieldwork*. Thousand Oaks, CA: Sage.

17 Using Grounded Theory, Case Studies, Journals and Synectics

This chapter concentrates on the reflective qualitative research methods of and methodology of grounded theory, case studies, the use of personal learning journals – both to record your own experiences and decisions as a researcher – and the use of journals as research material. It also looks at the use of synectics or creative metaphors.

This chapter looks at:

- *What is grounded theory and how to use it*
- *How and why to use case studies*
- *The use of personal learning journals for reflection and as part of the research*
- *Using synectics*

▶ Grounded theory

Grounded theory is really what it says it is – theory grounded in experience(s). However, it is often cited as a rather loose and unstructured way of approaching observed experience, which then provides the grounding for the development of theories. This approach would be a rather slapdash use of grounded theory, however, since its real reason for use and use in practice is to ground the theory (small-scale rather than large-scale theories) in experience, observation and practice, probably in small samples, and build up some theoretical concepts and hypotheses from there. In 1967, Glaser and Strauss published *The Discovery of Grounded Theory*, which lies behind current use of the term. This book provided a sound basis and framework for years of qualitative research. The authors offer an approach which has space for the different personal and professional perceptions and strategies of different social science researchers, and suggest that a rigid set of rules for approaching social science research would hamper and constrain the discovery and focus on the object of the research, which is often itself shifting and being transmuted because it is based in human interactions and behaviours. The authors argue that 'a standardisation of methods (swallowed whole, taken seriously) would only constrain and stifle social science researchers' best efforts' (Strauss 1987: 7). Theories are generated empirically, from the data, and constantly checked and tested against that data. 'Good qualitative social science research, according to the principles of grounded theory, involves a constant checking of the analysis (theories, concepts) against the findings and a constant *refinement* of the concepts during the process of research' (Denscombe 1998: 215).

> A grounded theory is one which is inductively derived from the study of the phenomenon it represents. That is, it is discovered, developed and provisionally verified through statistic data collection and analysis of data pertaining to that phenomenon. Therefore, data collection analysis and theory stand in reciprocal relationships with each other. One does not begin with a theory, then prove it, rather one begins with an area of study and what is relevant to that is allowed to emerge. (Strauss and Corbin 1990: 23)

The researcher using grounded theory begins with a fresh perspective and some insights, but a willingness to develop and change their views and understanding of the research produces new evidence and information, feeding into theories. Because the situation they are researching is constantly evolving, they cannot usually say how large their sample will be and need to set out with 'theoretical sampling' in mind – a sampling of incidents, actions and events directed by the theory as it evolves. However, this does not mean the research goes on forever, since once the information seems to continue to confirm the analysis, to repeat, then the sample can be closed as it has reached the point of 'theoretical saturation' – rather than real exhaustion. It is theory that is not suited to the study of evolving situations and people and as such it is:

- based in fieldwork observations
- produces explanations suitable for those carrying out the research, or from whom it is directed
- produces limited explanations based on immediate evidence
- works from an evolving design which adapts to suit the situation as it develops – but appropriately.

Strauss and Corbin (1990) suggest it is:

- a scientific method of investigation used by researchers
- inductively derived from the study of the phenomenon it represents
- discovered, developed and provisionally verified through systematic data collection and analysis
- representative of the reality that has been researched
- comprehensible to the persons who were studied
- comprehensible to those who inhabit the area that was studied
- specific to the phenomenon that has been studied
- capable of providing in generalisation when the validity of the theory has been established.

Grounded theory is not an excuse for laziness or vague interpretations; the data needs to be substantiated and argued in terms of reading meanings from them. But as the basis for much qualitative research, it offers the opportunity to enquire that the data and analysis can be rich, even richer than the particular area under research at any one moment, for any one project, and that it can enable the exploration of contested readings and interpretations. It does tend, however, to be rather more selective, localised, and perhaps not as generalisable as strict scientific experimentation could be. Research findings 'constitute a theoretical formulation of the reality under investigation, rather than consisting of a series of numbers, or a group of loosely related themes' (Strauss and Corbin 1990: 24). Concepts and relations are generated and then tested as well. It is very related to the subject or self who directs it, decides on its aims and focus, its use and methods, and its interpretations. It is a flexible, sensitive approach, which needs to be very clearly set out and explained at each stage of the research so that limitations and constraints are expressed, and findings seen in context.

Task

Consider

- Is your own research based in grounded theory?
- How might grounded theory help you in your research?
- If you are going to use it, what is the situation in which you will use it?
- What kind of theory do you think might be generated from your research? (You cannot be exact, of course, as yet, but you might be able to say, 'I aim to be able to develop a theory about how people in failing organisations . . .' or 'The theory I wish to develop concerns how those suffering trauma after war incidents could engage with and deal with the trauma and carry on with normal life . . .'.)
- How can you use grounded theory to explore contextualised meanings?
- Where are *you* in the research?
- How will you carry out your fieldwork?
- What kinds of methods do you think would be suitable at the outset of your research?
- Can you foresee any problems?

▶ Case studies

Some of the origins of case study methods lie in health, others in social work or in the law. Case study as a method has been around for a long time and offers an opportunity to consider a situation, individual, event, group, organisation, or whatever is appropriate as the object of study. One of the pluses of using case study methodology and methods is that an in-depth situation/individual, and so on, can be explored fully. One of the issues is that you cannot easily generalise from one case, so either the case needs to be contextualised and carefully described and then others can consider its usefulness in other contexts and examples, or it is better to take a few cases, to establish a range of examples and interpretations of a situation, event or development. It is essential throughout the use of a case-study method (as any other research method) that you insist on rigour in the methods of data collection and analysis, acknowledging the subjectivity of the researcher, the limitations of generalising from individual cases. You also need to defend the kinds of implications and shapes of the cases chosen.

Robson (1993) defines case study methodology as follows: 'case study is a strategy for doing research which involves an empirical investigation of a particular contemporary phenomenon in its real life context using multiple sources of evidence' (1993: 52). It is a research strategy based in empirical research which focuses on the particular, in context and, like action research, involves using a variety of methods of data collection.

Task

Consider:

- Why might you choose to use a case study method?
- What could you use as a case?
- Could you use several cases?
- Could you generalise for your case(s) (you do not *need* to)?

Often consultants are used to using case study methods to find out about a development, a problem, or an interaction within an organisation, and to point out difficulties and/or suggest changes.

When you have gained your evidence and explored, discussed, problematised and written it up, your case study could be useful as:

- a consultancy
- an example of particular practices in operation from the point of view of a single set of examples
- an example which others can use to transfer/translate into their own context.

A couple of examples follow and might indicate situations in which case study method is appropriate:

Case Study 1: Alan and the external examiner system

In his work on the use of the external examiner system, Alan focused on the practices, problems, benefits and limitations of quality assurance of the external examiner system as it operated in his own college, taking

Continued

that college as a case study. A simple description of activities would not have been appropriate, although description formed part of his case.

Description and documentary evidence

He described the system of use of the external examiner within his college, set this in the context of the external examiner system (a system where an examiner from another institution works with your own examiners and moderates or agrees/queries the way assessment works, and assures the justice of the marks awarded to students). He also set these practices against documentary evidence, provided by his college, about the way the system was meant to work there, as part of the overall quality assurance.

Use of observation and interview

As a field researcher, Alan established how the system was working through observation of external examiners in practice at award boards and through interviews with both examiners internal to the college and the external examiners. He asked both groups some overlapping questions and some questions which were specific to the two different groups, about how the role in practice was seen to help quality assurance and justice to students, how it helped assure the appropriateness of the teaching, the assessment and the version of the subject taught. Finally he asked how the various systems and practices of meetings, papers exchanged, results, consultation, and so on, actually operated.

He was using multiple methods of enquiry to establish a single case, and to fit that case into an overall context, asking questions about the situation and practices that could be used by/transferred to others in similar situations. But, since he was looking at a single case, he expressed the note of caution that not all would be transferable, and that anyone using his methods or seeking similar outcomes would need to take their own context and position, as well as their aims and outcomes, into consideration. As a insider of the college, Alan was aware that his role might affect what he asked, what he saw, how he was treated, the answers given, and his interpretations of all of this evidence, and so he described his own role, and explored and expressed his position and concerns about that position. This element of self or subjectivity does not invalidate the case study – researchers are always involved in their research to some greater or lesser extent – but did need to be taken into consideration because it would certainly affect what was recorded, how it was interpreted and presented, and the generalisability or transferability of what was found, to other instances.

Some researchers will find it useful to work with the single case study, and others to select several cases, the commonality or variety of interpretations which they produce providing a greater claim for generalisability, and perhaps setting a range of versions and interpretations which others would find useful to look at. This could be interpreting a set of examples, instances, events, behaviours, roles, or whatever is the subject of their own case study. The use of multiple cases helps to establish a range and to increase the likelihood of generalisability. However, it must always be recognised that any experiment or survey, any study, takes place in the context of a specific time and place, with specific events or individual or groups involved, and also taking you as the researcher into the equation. As such, then, anyone seeking to generalise from or replicate your work that used case study methods (and actually, any other methods, however scientific they seem), would need to take such differences into consideration and acknowledge their potential effects. Using action research, which involves a variety of research methods and bases itself on changing the research with the participants/those researched, in a collaborative manner (see Chapter 14), you might use case study method to explore behaviours in an organisation, for example. In such a situation you would need to:

- establish the aims and outcomes of the research
- establish the context
- probably set the scene of the issue in hand with the use of documentary evidence – so you need to carry out both exploratory and descriptive research using documents
- set the scene through asking insiders and outsiders for their views and experiences
- decide on a sample, who will act as your case studies
- set up a research schedule which enables you to collect data from a variety of appropriate research methods such as observation, focus groups, interviews, and so on
- possibly ask those who form your case study to themselves carry out enquiries with others, and become field researchers carrying out what can be called 'appreciative enquiry' (Cooperrider and Srivastra 1987)
- involve those with whom you are collaborating in this research in interviews, observations, focus groups, or whatever is appropriate.

In some instances, the researcher themselves can actually be used as a single case study, if their own situation and experiences are an example of what is being studied. Clearly, in this instance, the context, the description of self as set against other cases, and the particular issue of unavoidable subjectivity will need to be considered. But using the self as a case can be a very rich source of insider information. The case of the individual self as subject can be set alongside other cases, but should not really be included in as just one of the samples. It provides a chance of an insightful source for a case study.

Case study 2: Florence and women working in the Chinese takeaway industry

Florence was a Women's Studies Master's student who used the case studies method for the MA Women's Studies dissertation. Florence, working on the experiences of immigrated Chinese women (her term) in the Chinese takeaway industry in the UK, decided, on advice from her supervisor, to use herself as one of the case studies. She also worked with three other women who provided other examples of case studies. In the use of herself as a case study she recorded her own experience and her reflections, and systematically addressed the questions about isolation, amount of work, social interaction, rewards, and so on, which were the same questioning areas she applied to the other women. The example of her own experience used a storytelling format set alongside the more formal self-interview and written questions. With the other women she asked for an oral storytelling response and the answers to the same set of questions. In this instance she was able to both expertly use the richness of her own experience (which would have looked costly otherwise) and base her interactive insights and her rapport with her subjects partly on this experience, and also to collect information in a very systematic way.

Task

Think of a problem, development, experience, or situation you would like to explore as part of your research or, separate from your research, another interest and set of questions. Decide on using either yourself or someone with whom you work/a friend/a relative to act as a case study sample for you. Can you develop a brief case study outline that will enable you to use them as a case study, in context?

Ask yourself:

- What? How? What are my aims and questions? What am I trying to find out?
- Who might benefit from this case study? What fund of knowledge and understanding, problematising arguments/debates might it contribute to?
- Who else has written in this area? Can I use them/what they have written, as part of my theoretical context?
- Who am I using as a case study/in my case study? You need to develop a short rationale about why this is the appropriate method to use.
- What else do I need to set up as the context? The specific context of the research (location, people, and so on, rather than theory). Can I describe it from observation, or do I need to use documentary evidence of a recorded/written form as background and context?
- What research techniques can I use to enable me to gain the information I need from this person? For example: questionnaires, interviews, storytelling, a written account, an observation schedule, or a mixture of these.
- When could I have access to the subject of my case study? What barriers and difficulties could there be to prevent me from finding out what I need to find out?
- For example, attitude, access, prior experiences, wrong questions, and so on.
- How might I overcome these barriers?
- Carry out your first case study – sketch in the background and context, interview/observe/use questionnaires/ask for all storytelling evidence, and so on.

Writing up case studies

Now you have your material – how can you write it up as a case study?

As with writing up any piece of research, a standard format can be adhered to which resembles a scientific report. However, at the other end of the spectrum, case studies can be more descriptive and can follow the discourse and development of those observed or interviewed. For further details of different ways of writing up case studies, see Robson (1993: 415).

Lincoln and Guba (1985: 3, 62, cited in Robson 1993: 416) suggest that bringing the more technical and scientific report format into the qualitative method of a case study helps to mitigate against any questions over rigorous subjectivity and focus. Robson lists the following formats:

- **scientific journal** – focus, context for enquiry, description and analysis for data, discussion of outcomes
- **suspense structure** – findings, faults and reports on investigation and context flows afterwards
- **narrative** – a story told in continuous prose, or following question-and-answer sequence
- **comparative** – two or more examples compared throughout
- **chronological** – evidence presented in a chronological sequence – useful to show cause and effect
- **theory-generating** – sections establishing further elements feeding into the support (or underpinning of a theory)
- **unsequenced** – descriptive, but sometimes it is difficult to see what has been missed out and what is important.

When you write up your case study, you will have to decide what goes in the body of the text and what goes in the appendices, and whether tables, and so on, in an appendix actually serve any purpose. You also need to decide whether a descriptive narrative gives a flavour of the response in a more sensitive manner – each case will be different, and the reason for developing the case study will also contribute to the choice of the appropriate format for writing it up.

▶ Journals

Journals are a very useful way of capturing the changing decisions and reflections involved in carrying out research. They can help to capture things that would otherwise disappear from memory, or, because they are not committed to paper or tape, might fail to be clearly articulated. They can capture:

- moments when you are asking questions
- showing engagement with problems and issues
- developing solutions
- showing moments of decision about research design or analysis, and so on
- developing reflections about experiences.

They tend to be used in two ways:

(1) For the researcher to develop and keep a reflective account of their research, and (2) as part of the research itself, when the subjects

of the research keep journals, which can be used as documentary evidence, back-up for interviews and observations, examples of their experiences and analyses and reflections on these, and so on. If you the researcher are part of, or all of, the research sample itself, then your own journal can form part of the material for the research, rather than being a reflective journal kept alongside the research to help you articulate, clarify, reflect and record, alone.

You could ask your subjects to keep journals as part of the research matter, the material you use. If you do this you will need to ensure that they are aware of what kind of journals are needed, that is, not just a diary record of what is done, unless that is the kind you seek (a blow-by-blow account), but a reflective and analytical piece, completed regularly, that enables engagement with issues and decisions. They also need to know that your sampling of the journal will not infringe their confidentiality or their liberties, and they will need to 'clear' with you which elements of the journal you use on the research.

Task

Consider:

- Could you use a journal yourself?
- What could it help you do?
- Could you use journals with your subjects?
- What would it help you and them to do?

▶ Synectics

Synectics are creative metaphors that enable the opening up of creative and imaginative comparisons from which decisions and arguments can then be created and developed. They can be used either as ways of gaining information, getting close to the subject of study, and opening it up and out for rich responses and subjective understandings. For yourself, they can open up your own creativity and/or serve as a method or vehicle to engage your subjects of study, in order to enable them to be creative, imaginative, sensitive and responsive, and to respond to the metaphor, opening up as a result.

- For yourself: as you start to develop research questions and areas of study, the creative technique of synectics can sometimes help you to visualise the area of study more fully and imaginatively, so that you can then consider how to approach it more fully.
- People: clients, practitioners, students, colleagues, whoever is the focus of the research, frequently find it difficult to engage with problems, cases or issues which require creative thinking when they are in classroom situations. Synectics involves the use of creative metaphors with which students can engage. They might be asked, for example, to compare a particular problem position to a fruit, flower, or supermarket – and the elements of the comparison free up their thoughts. Similarities and differences between each half of the comparison can be collected and problems or issues addressed.

For example:

- If I wished to research how, why, and in what ways the organisation and practices of staff development had changed over a period of time, within a university, I might find it useful to compare the situation and practices of staff development at the beginning of the researched period with that at the end, and to use the creative metaphor of a garden to do so.

An example of the use of synectics:

- Staff development is the focus of this study. Staff development is a system of development, support and training in universities which helps and enables lecturers and/or administrative staff to engage with professional practice issues and develop their skills and knowledge in these. It involves both formal training activities and courses, and less formal individual support or workshop activities, and sometimes consultancy with departments or heads, or other university staff.
- In using synectics you need to define the metaphor or comparison (or get the subjects to define it) and pose the comparative question, for example: (a) Five years ago, staff development was like a cottage garden – in what ways? (b) Creative brainstorming and thinking then follows, and individuals or groups can start to engage with the comparison. They might think it through like this: 'Well, there would be a single developer like an individual gardener, operating in a

small patch, weeding out the problem weeds and tending the growing plants, but the effect would be limited, it would not grow much. What it could grow could be hardy annual, some solid crops (vegetables?) and the odd rare plant, maybe in a greenhouse. It could be killed off by freak weather or lack of care, and maybe no one would notice? They could set up another garden – although much of value would be lost. It could also be a focus for pride and joy, like the gardener who grows huge vegetables or wonderful strains of flowers and wins prizes for them.'

- Why is this like staff development?
  (a) Because often there is a lone developer or small unit without much support from the university, which works with individuals or small groups and nurtures innovations, enables people to tackle some of the problems of their work, helps to develop and train in a regular way – but is also rather vulnerable or overlooked.
- Now – since staff development has institutional support and national funding – what is it like? What can it be compared to in terms of gardens and growing things?

As those involved in the research engage in the comparison, they start to tease out different elements, sort problems, see trends and decisions, clarify their thoughts and get the change to causes and effects and its potential opportunities and problems in focus. They could use a SWOT analysis on the overall situation when they have spotted, defined and clarified these elements in comparison with the metaphor (identifying strengths, weaknesses, opportunities and threats). In this way the creative metaphor releases energy.

Synectic tactics enable articulation of issues, practices and problems through the comparison. Other synectic tactics involve separating approaches and issues out by listing them under different headings on a flip chart and asking for different kinds of comment, information and contributions under each heading. Students can be asked to give information, and suggest areas in which they need help, under separate headings, on the flip chart. They are then enabled to offer information or help, out of the main group, and their offers or points are collected on the flip chart. By dividing up elements of interest and information it acts as an enabling device.

When the strengths, weaknesses, opportunities and threats have been clarified those involved can look at how to overcome or avoid potential problems, and how to capitalise on and benefit from potential or real opportunities and strengths. Furthermore, they need to draw up a point-by-point development plan to do so. In this way the creativity moves you on to planning and action.

This can be used to help you, as the researcher, to focus on problems in research, and can help you to express your ideas and the shape of the work when you write it up. If your research is into, for example, how people process ideas, deal with issues and problems, and plan, being involved in a problem-solving exercise with your subjects, the people, can provide you with information on *how* they deal with problems, etc.

Task

Take a problem situation or issue either in your professional/personal life or in your research. Can you compare this to a food or a holiday?

- How does the comparison tease out different elements?
- How do the different elements compare?
- How do they enable you to focus on the specifics of the problem when you look clearly at them?

Now do a SWOT (Strengths, Weaknesses, Opportunities, Threats) analysis and decide what to do work on, how to sort out the problem areas, how to avoid problems by prior planning and action, and how to capitalise on the opportunities.

Conclusion

We have looked at:

- Grounded theory, what it is and why and when to use it – fieldwork, development, and so on
- Case studies – shaping them and using them
- Journals – for you as a researcher and for the subjects of our research
- Synectics, to enable you to clarify and focus on issues and problems in the research, or as a vehicle to enable your subjects for research to engage

Further reading

Cooperrider, D. L., & Srivastra, S. (1987) Appreciative Inquiry into Organizational Life. In W. A. Pasmore & R. W. Woodman (eds.), *Research into Organizational Change and Development*, vol. 1. Greenwich, CT: JAI.

Denscombe, M. (1998) *The Good Research Guide*. Buckingham: Open University Press.

Glaser, B. & Strauss, A. (1967) *The Discovery of Grounded Theory*. Chicago: Aldine.

Robson, C. (1993) *Real World Research*. Oxford: Blackwell.

Strauss, A. (1987) *Qualitative Analysis for Social Scientists*. Cambridge: Cambridge University Press.

Strauss, A. & Corbin, J. (1990) *Basics of Qualitative Research: Grounded Theory Procedures and Techniques*. London: Sage.

18 Research Methods for the Arts and Humanities

Some arts and humanities research uses social science strategies, particularly in subjects close to the social sciences, such as history, and cultural studies. However, much of the research in the arts and humanities uses quite different strategies, and when presented in a thesis, is of quite a different shape to that of a social science thesis. In terms of both research methods and overall final shape, some arts and humanities research can tend to seem amorphous, or even highly subjective, when it needs to be just as conceptually clearly organised and managed as any other research in any other field.

This chapter looks at:

- *Strategies of arts and humanities research*
- *Conceptual framework and research methods*
- *Self-reflection, linking theory and practice, relating the creative to the analytical*

To the uninitiated, and particularly to the highly structured social scientist, research in the arts and humanities often seems to be simply a matter of reading and responding, even responding from a subjective and personal case. This is because the object of study is itself likely to be seemingly imaginative, creative, not as tangible and situated or grounded in the real world as the objects of social science or health practice research are. What kind of change can analysis of literary texts possibly produce? How does this relate to the real world, if at all? Is it merely self-indulgence, or is there rigour involved in this kind of research also? Actually, much literary and arts research is concerned with exploring critical questions in the material, in the same way as social science- and health-related research. It can be more overtly engaged with the researcher, perhaps, than some social science research, although a personal connection between an author, a performance artist, or an oral history context is not necessarily part of the research, and most arts and humanities work does not directly involve the researcher reporting in person, except critically and analytically. What is rarely asked for is a personal emotional response; instead, a critical and analytical response is expected. Arts and humanities researchers are perhaps more honest than others since they clearly acknowledge their own directness and involvement in the work. A literature researcher, for example, might be relating personal critical responses to a group of writers, a writer, a group of texts, or a phenomenon, theme, or issue in texts, to those of established critics, and weaving something new out of this mixture of the personal and the established. Or it can be much less personal. The research can be carried out in quite a theoretical manner, with the debates between schools of critical thought in terms of artistic product. This is much as a scientific or social science researcher measures different theories and theoretical or conceptual frameworks up against their objects of study to evaluate the appropriateness and validity of the interpretations these frameworks offer.

What are the objects of study? And how might the research be carried out? Much arts and humanities research relies upon the analysis of documents, both primary and secondary sources (primary sources are those produced at the time, and by the originator – while secondary are works about the time or the originator, about others). It is not merely personal response, and it is not merely documents that you read or see. Such a simplifying of the arts and humanities research processes could lead to a sense of amorphousness and a lack of direction. However, a possibility of charting, recording and narrating what is there rather than delving into the personal, concentrating instead on the ways in which the form can articulate any message, makes a major contribution. This latter definition of research in the arts begins to pinpoint the crucial elements. Arts research needs to ask questions of its subject matter like any other research area; just like the scientist, the artist cannot afford to be merely descriptive or narrative in his or her research recording mode. Arts and humanities research often integrates theory and practice, as do social science research areas, such as a performance artist researching their own or others' individual relationship to, and interpretation of, the world in the context of the underpinning theories. They would probably ask themselves to what extent, and in what ways at what times, do theories underpin their personal and professional practices? And how do these practices engage with, contribute to and further the development of theory? Literature theses have underpinning theories, just like any others, and many arts and humanities research areas are interdisciplinary by the time they get to Master's or doctoral research stage.

▶ What are the major paradigms and perspectives driving the research?

A particularly lucid explanation of different research paradigms is offered by Denzin and Lincoln (1998: 185–93), some of which appeared in Chapter 10 of this book where we looked at the *positivist and post-positivist* paradigms, for example. These focus on *internal validity, external validity, reliability* and *objectivity*, and cannot fully take account of the ways in which inquiry is interactive, sets of facts can be read in different ways, and are value-laden, not value-free. *Constructivism and critical theory* use a *relativist ontology, transactional epistemology, hermeneutic, and dialectical methodology.*

These interpretative perspectives enable an examination of relationships and values in context. While these are applied/social science- and cultural studies-oriented research paradigms and strategies, they can also be widely used by arts and humanities researchers who examine texts of whatever kind – literary, popular, film, media, documents, diaries, the personal record. They can also look at other sites for the dialogic and interactive – such as the individual in a performative space in a cultural context, the literary text in a cultural and critical context, or making a variety of cases about a cultural phenomenon. For example, Norman Mailer's semi-fictionalised autobiographical text, *Why are we in Vietnam?*, questions the political positioning and actions of others during the historical moment of the Vietnam War through a personal, critical and semi-fictional response. It sets up a dialogue which researchers can use to focus on how individuals construct meaning in a context. Many texts and performances themselves question such interactions, set up such dialectic, and encourage a postmodern approach. Others do not in themselves encourage such approaches but the researcher and critic can use all texts and performances as examples of contextualised products which say something about their times, origins and construction as part of a cultural discussion. Within this research paradigm some researchers' research is driven by investigation into interactions, and cultural and social reproduction of meaning in and through texts and their readership/audiences/performers/producers. Much feminist research, as well as ethnic research and cultural research, is informed by these paradigms.

▶ An arts example: women's writing

A student engaged in exploring the development of women's writing since the second wave of feminism, for example, would need to involve research methods more usually found in research focused on history and on culture and society, as well as literature, in their work. They would also have to engage with some key questions in their exploration rather than merely delineating an area. Their exploration is likely to be dialogic and interpretative, looking at how at different points in time, different constructions and representations have been produced and why, and why and how these might be critiques, and might change. Some underpinning questions might include, for example, asking: In what ways do women authors of the period engage with the developing issues of feminism? How do they challenge representations of women and their role? What kinds of writing strategies, themes, characterisation, style, and so on do they use to help them in this engagement? The development of these questions has already teased out a range of issues from the bald statement of the period and the area of study – and this suggests some underlying assumptions which will need establishing, checking out and exploring through the object of study, the texts themselves in context. Assumptions include the thought that women's writing in this period will involve itself with issues to do with the representation of women's roles, and so be aware of and to some extent enact or mediate feminist criticisms and feminist theory as it develops. Methods used would spring from these questions. Some would need to be largely documentary and to include analysis of the kind of themes and variation of the arguments in these themes in the texts, which deal with representations of women, and comments which critique the established versions of women. Some researchers have chosen to count the times that such themes emerge and so to indicate patterns and frequencies. This rather scientific approach is not so popular in the end of the twentieth and beginning of the twenty-first century. Equally unpopular is the merely personal response of enjoyment or empathy. There needs to be a middle way between recognising and characterising themes, patterns and language and indicating how these serve as vehicles for argument, how language affects emotions and responses, as well as how the text is structured. The personal integrates with the analytical at every stage but both are clearly defined. And the dialogic is a key here – meanings, representations and interpretations are relative, are produced through interactions between people, events, events and people, and so on, and they change as they interact with each other. This is explored in such research even when it captures a very narrowly defined moment and set of texts or text, because it situates such moments and such expressions and texts/within a constructed and interpreted frame. The researcher is always part of the research project, though not necessarily its focus.

It is important to take a critical and analytical approach to reading and artistic practices. A typical literature research project would set out to critique, explore, analyse and evaluate a body of work – that of one author or of several authors, of several texts on a specific theme or issue, texts in context in relation to the cultural context, texts in a theoretical framework, and so on. It would bring to bear specified theoretical and critical frameworks – such as historical/Marxist, psychological, linguistic, biographical, feminist, structuralist, deconstructionist, poststructuralist, postmodernist, and so on. It would need to define and defend the theoretical frameworks and the bodies of knowledge/approaches and to situate the investigation in the context of their work and other writing with similar and opposing frames and views, so that this new piece of research contributes to a *debate*. The variables as such are likely to be relationships between, for example, the author in historical context and their work – so, for example, how Thomas Hardy's novels engage with explorations of the changing experiences of families in the nineteenth century. This is a historical literary perspective. Another thesis might look at the works of African women writers' representation of women's lives in Africa and the UK. So they might compare, contrast and explore representations of women's lives in Africa and in Britain, establishing and relating with contexts both of everyday life, cultural practices, and literary or artistic expression practices, defining the particular version of these their chosen authors develop. This latter would involve cultural context, the texts, the writers, feminist criticism, awareness of debates about culture, gender and ethnicity, and also an exploration of the literary in that the work would involve the imagery, characters, themes, language and shape of the novels themselves. The 'what' of the text is added to by 'in what way?' and 'how?', as well as 'in what theoretical and cultural context?' and 'Through what approaches?' The approaches question is one which substitutes for questions about qualitative and quantitative methods, although literary research can use the social science strategies when it is interdisciplinary in nature, and could, for example, in one version, look as much at audience response (using statistics as at the way in which texts and writers represented things and events and people) as at the texts themselves.

Task

Choose one or more of the humanities and/or arts titles which could underpin a dissertation or thesis:

- What mini-questions and subsidiary questions are involved in approaching this title?
- What theoretical frameworks, what theories could you use to help you to approach the asking of these questions?
- What material could you use to drive the asking of the questions? For example, what literary texts, what artistic products, what mixture of documents from different sources – historical, diary, and so on, could you use? Could you use media texts? Would you need to use social cultural and historical information, and where might you get this from?
- Which theories are you using to develop and underpin your own? What critical, contextual, interactive and personal elements are involved in your research and how do these all fit together in your work? How can you argue that the mixture of theories and other elements fit into a cohesive, directed, *whole* piece of research?
- Why do your questions matter, and are you sure/how could you argue that your explorations and theories underpinning and driving these can really help you answer your questions? What are the tasks involved here?
- Why does your research matter? Will it affect others? Cause change? Contribute to knowledge and argument? What will it do?

Examples of titles:

- *The treatment of relationships as an index of cultural change in the work of Elaine Feinstein.*
- *Kennedy's political strategies and the Cuban crisis: a turning point of American political response to Communism.*
- *Techniques of confessional poetry and the explorations of self and the body in the work of Sylvia Plath and Robert Lowell.*

Continued

- Star Trek *and beyond: how TV science fiction negotiates and represents versions of cultural imperialism.*
- *Thomas Hardy's dysfunctional families as an index of the historical change in the nineteenth century.* (Chosen example.*)

Questions:

▶ How can texts represent versions of historical change?
▶ What were the historical changes to the family and to people's lives as a whole – key points – during Hardy's period?
▶ What specific texts act as examples of representations of historical change in the family in the period?
▶ What kinds of families does Hardy deal with? What might they represent? Is there any argument developing over time in his work in relation to dealing with the changing family in history?

▶ The critical approaches

This work integrates the historical, the cultural and the political as well as the textual area or materials, and it also asks for a dialogue and interpretations – a dialogue between the historical change and the texts which represent it through the fictional families, and which charts events, images, and so on. How can you defend the work at the intersection of these different theoretical approaches? This would be a key question here.

Some critical approaches and theories we will need:

- Marxist historical criticism – this enables us to look at the relationship between textual examples, their production and the historical moments in a politically aware sense. Seeing the people's lives as produced by the political and historical moment, and seeing textual representations as ways of exploring, arguing and debating things about how people lived.
- Literary critical analysis of language, image, symbol, characterisation, the narrative, and so on.
- Some historical approaches to document analysis, acquisition of historical data through other means (Archives? Testimony?)
- Some feminist critical approaches – because this deals with families it will be saying something about women's roles and mothering, motherhood and the upbringing of children. This will be usefully interpreted through feminist critical approaches since that will allow for the recognition of stereotyping, impression, original-

ity, argument, interactions between representations of women and children and families and the questions of role and opportunities for women at this time – especially as represented by a male author.

▶ How would you write up your methods?

You would not detail what you did step by step as you would in social science methods. Having set out the theories which underpin your exploration you would then engage in exploring and pulling together the context and the material, and using the secondary critical theoretical material (the Marxist or feminist critics, for example) to bounce off/underpin/inform/guide your analyses of the texts. In a theoretical context, you would be establishing and developing your *own* readings, but using the critics to establish, back up or disagree with – so your own contribution is engaged in an informed dialogue with them. If there are critics with whom you disagree, have a dialogue with them. It is also important that you do not spend all your time arguing with them. You have you own case to establish and critics to use to back this up and inform it. You would use evidence from the texts and other appropriate documents themselves, quoting and analysing, synthesising from different parts of the texts and different critical or theoretical areas and comments. This is so that your synthesis and analysis are your own, your choice of quotation is your own and used at different times in different places in different ways to variously illustrate, exemplify and explore (through close critical analysis of the images and language, and so on) the arguments.

Different chapters could segment the material and the approaches to the questions differently, depending upon your choice. You could:

- Deal with an underlying set of questions as explored systematically through different texts and cover one per chapter, possibly in chronological order, possibly as they exemplify different angles or answers to the questions.
- Or scrutinise your area of questions further. Are there themes emerging? For example, in Hardy's work names, titles and events or elements set up an argument that because of the changing employment conditions and economic situation of the rural poor, families were less likely to be cohesive and able, caring and nur-

turing, and so there were many broken families, and feckless fathers who sacrificed or harmed or abandoned children.
- Hardy explores the ways in which the middle classes started to develop, with education and economic growth and he worries that this could be a problem. Some novels reflect on the many scenarios in families where education was sought, but leads to suffering and lack of economic growth, broken families and unhappiness.

Either the themes or the critical arguments could head the chapters – the choice is yours and depends on the overall direction of the research.

▶ The form and shape of arts and humanities theses

Students undertaking literary and arts research need to discover and defend their critical approaches and frameworks probably rather more than defending their research methods, unless these are unusual. The theoretical frameworks and literature review chapter will explore the critical and theoretical approaches used, while a methods chapter will possibly not be part of the thesis. It would also be unusual to describe the research activities and analysis. The findings of literary research theses are more likely to contain chapters on exploring themes, angles and arguments through contexts, and interweaving the debates by leading from one chapter to another and referring back and forth. They do not necessarily move in a chronological sequence through one piece of research followed by another followed by findings – the 'findings' or point of argument as such is led into at the beginning of the chapter, and the exploration flows on within the chapter. This is more of a journalistic than a scientific report writing method (see Chapter 23 on writing up). Chapters might follow developments within research, deal with periods of change, or deal with grouped themes in an author's work.

Thesis – possible shape

Abstract
Laying out the questions which underpin the thesis, the conceptual framework which allows the questions to be asked and tracking

through the different kinds, stages or focal points of the different chapters which are asking and addressing the questions through the material.

Introduction (and sometimes a separate theory chapter)
This acts as a chapter to both situate the enquiry and its theoretical and conceptual location and framework. Unlike a social science thesis there is not usually a separate theoretical chapter – although there could be. It should be written in the third person, and in the past tense.

The Introduction concentrates on situating the arguments and questions in theories, context and background, the work of those interested in, and working in the context of the questions and ideas, even one's own practices, and establishing a critical, theoretic frame and focus for the work. Here the researcher is explicit about the research paradigms and key theories, and the researchers whose views and approaches are being used and why. If it is an interdisciplinary research work, the integration of, relations between and use of different theoretical and conceptual approaches and contexts would be outlined, and an argument put forward for integrating them into or relating them to the inquiry.

Case study 1

For instance, in a performance arts PhD, MPhil or MA, which includes the self as an artist, a researcher might:

- Establish the theories of the key performance arts and arts critics and theorists, and stake a position in relation to them.
- Set up a position for integrating their own performance work in this critical and theoretical context, reading it through the theory, and reading the practice through the theory.
- Establish the critical distance and objectivity and the issue of subjectivity because of personal invention – using the self as the case study. This is really very similar to many other dissertations or theses which would here establish the position of the researcher involved in addressing these specific questions. A separate theory or methodology chapter would be unlikely, but possible.

Case study 2

A researcher writing on gay male writing since Stonewall charting the different themes which run through this writing, its relationship to the cultural and historical contexts of the times, and its historical development for a few key writers would need to:

- Define the underlying questions and make some assertions about the field of study.
- Clarify the theories and critical approaches being used in the context of 'queer theory' (which would need explaining). A cultural theory 'take' on this would need to be established, as well as a discourse analysis-based critical way through.
- Establish the reasons for the choice of themes and texts. This would form the focus of the beginning of each of the chapters. Establishing themes, clear approaches and text choices would provide a good lead-in paragraph or two to direct the reader in each chapter.

For both theses:

The ensuing chapters would focus upon the themes and the texts/artists performances/artworks/cultural products and interactions with self, in context (as appropriate to the dissertation or thesis) choices, developing the arguments through each chapter, linking the chapters. There could be a dialogue between the texts and the researcher, especially if they are using themselves as a case study. There could also be a dialogue between different interpretations offered by different critics or by the writers/artists and their works and the critics, so that meaning is made through a dialogue, a dialectical approach, and the argument is seen as an interpretation which is situated.

The conclusion would establish the significance overall for the arguments, explorations and discussions as developed through the dissertation or thesis, and could point towards cultural or social change. It could establish a new take on the theory/theories which have been underpinning the work, or it could bring opposing views together into a new synthesis through the interpretations of the texts/artefacts/ actions, as appropriate.

▶ Researching your own creative work/using the creative in your research work

Many students are involved in the kinds of critical approach we have discussed, at all levels. However, many engage in literary, artistic, musical or performance work directly, rather than through the lens of a critic as such. So their research is not merely in the arts and humanities but in relating their own performance and production, their own creative practices to these areas, seeing their creative work as a product of the theories and critical contexts and being fed by them. Technically, they are therefore exploring their *own* work as if it were a large-scale case study in the social science sense, analysed critically and contextualised. They could study their own experience, as well as the product itself. At undergraduate level, those who have already been involved in creative work – art, creative writing, video production, and so on, will be familiar with the issues of relating the actual texts, artworks or creative products and activities to an analytical framework. There are a set of theories which help engage the work with concepts and argument, and which enable a link between the theory and practice to be established.

Critical approaches and theoretical frameworks, as well as the basis of the dissertation or thesis, can be very much the same as those already discussed. Much creative work takes place in the intersection of critical perspectives, cultural contexts and the personal. Its main difference from more standard arts and humanities research is the inclusion of the creative work as part of the research object explored by the theories and critical perspectives, and the involvement (here appropriate) of the self as a research object, because the self is a vehicle for the creative work if it is a performance, or if the self is partly the topic of the research.

Some students choose to carry out this kind of research through the use of artwork itself. Where does the personal and developmental work go? Some work needs to capture the personal as part of the critical element of the thesis, focusing on the personal/critical/developmental choices and responses, the critical decisions made in the performance or artwork and integrating theses, and what the theoretical and critical perspectives and arguments in the context of which other work has developed. One student involved in a piece of performance art developed her performance work out of her own theories – about the relationships between the virtual (technology, media representations) and the visceral (the real person, the body in the space). This student then acted out the performance, which she had videoed and included on CD-ROM, as well as videoing each element in the appropriate technological format. She then accompanied the work with a standard thesis, which explores decisions made about and the theoretical underpinnings to the performance and the ways in which it acts as a vehicle for explorations and discussions about the critical theories between them. She comments on the way it contributes to the thesis, using both personal comment, critical comment on personal performance work – which has been made objective because it has been shared with an audience – and the comments from the theorists, moving in a dialogue between them. Programme notes linking the performances themselves with the thesis are a great help here, as readers are not so used to making the links between performance in space, and its theoretical explanations.

Another student chose to explore her own relationship with her own history of artistic and personal response to her memory of life in South Africa as a woman in her family, now that she has moved to live in the UK. She is a visual artist working in installations, and she videoed and produced several linked pieces:

- A thesis which set out the drift and theoretical frameworks and explored and explained the video and all her critical points about self, memory, place and artistic response.
- A log or journal of her developing personal explorations and critical choices about the thesis – issues to do with the difficulty of capturing the feelings and experiences about decisions concerning visual representation. This includes actual videoing questions, problems such as fading, using sound on, over or off. It also involves looking at the visit back to South Africa, the shooting and the planning or accident involved in this. It notes what could or could not be caught on film and how.
- The video itself and accompanying notes, explaining and exploring its links with the arguments of the thesis and explaining also how its shape and form enable the arguments to be developed.

These examples of creative products, including videos, have involved the construction of sculptures, a dress, objects in installation, and creative pieces of writing. They need also some form of accompanying work for an exploration of the critical and theoretical engagement. This should lead to and enable the production of comment and analysis of themes and issues of the work itself. A log and analytical, critical piece are the natural accompanying pieces of work.

A more standard thesis piece which uses the theoretical and critical to establish arguments and explorations and place this work within the context is additional. This serves to establish its contribution to critical debates in which it is placed.

Task

- Think of a text or texts, and/or a personal experience, which you would like to explore using artistic forms.
- Which forms will suit your exploration and research? Could it become a video? Are some forms art or media products? Creative writing? Technology? Sculpture?
- How can you use this creative piece to explore the arguments and issues rather than merely reflect or be a creative piece?
- What kinds of underpinning theories and critical approaches inform your work?
- What forms can you use to record the reflective critical, personal process? Why?
- How might you also produce an analytical and critical connecting commentary between the creative, personal, critical works and the thesis itself?

Conclusion

We have looked at:

- Arts and humanities research integrating the critical and the creative, interdisciplinary approaches
- Creative performance and critical work using the creative and the personal
- The specific form and shape appropriate for arts and humanities research and the thesis itself

---

Further reading

Denzin, N. K., & Lincoln, Y. S. (1998). *The Landscape of Qualitative Research, Theories and Issues*. Thousand Oaks, CA: Sage.

19 Problem-based or Inquiry-based Research and Problem Solving

Problem-based learning places the student at the centre of the learning process and is aimed at integrating learning with practice (Ross 1995).

This chapter looks at:

- *Problem-based learning and problem-based research – the essential underpinning for research*
- *Using problem-based learning strategies and techniques to release creative energy at different stages in the research*
- *Creative problem-solving techniques*
- *Negative brainstorming*
- *Force-field analysis*

Many dissertations and theses develop out of a concern with real-life problems, which spring from practice. This is particularly so in the area of health and social sciences. There are an increasing number of practice-related, problem-based or inquiry-based research projects and products and if you are considering embarking on one of these, it is useful to look at some of the strategies and stages involved. See Chapter 3, which mentions practice-based research degrees, and Chapter 15, which describes action research. For students involved in an MA, MPhil, PhD or an EdD, the education doctorate, often a practice-based piece of research which will contribute to your professional practice is the best choice. Sometimes it is even possible to obtain employer funding for such research.

All research involves the posing of problems or the positioning of ideas, innovations or questions of some form or another. This happens at the start of the research and often during it at different stages, sometimes following revelations or disappointments, successes and failures, or even the necessary stages of different elements of the research. Problem-based learning (or inquiry-based learning) is the basis for whole curricula in health subjects in particular. We are considering it here as a structural element, at key moments in the research or as underpinning the whole research project itself.

Essentially, problem-based or inquiry-based learning, or research, in this case, involves the researcher conceptualising the problem or underpinning question, and then all literature searches, experimental work, questionnaires, and so on, and other methods of finding out and scrutinising data and information, spring from there. Everything that you set out to discover springs from the problem or question posed. Some of the strategies of problem-based learning, which release creative energy in the learner, can usefully be transferred to and engaged with in research. Indeed, if they are not used, often the research itself becomes quite dull and merely descriptive, rather than exploratory in even the most basic way. It can be argued that problem-based research is the stimulus for creative research, and a strategy for going about that lively and necessary release of creative energy which makes for a quality piece of research.

Some of the key features of problem-based or inquiry-based learning and research at any level are that it starts with the needs, interests and goals:

- of the learner
- of the work team/research group
- and of their subject/discipline/interdisciplinary area.

Also:

- it is centred around a real concern, development, problem or issue in relation to their research/the real world/the context of the research
- it is both sufficiently challenging and realistically solvable/ achievable
- it encourages the acquisition and organisation of information
- it encourages the development of appropriate skills and behaviours/ attitudes

- it helps develop transferable skills useful in the thesis, further research, the workplace and in the future (and in the learner's work/life)
- it helps to encourage individual skills and teamwork skills.

▶ Stages of problem-based or inquiry-based research or learning

Problem focus

A problem/development/innovation/issue lies at the centre of all the learning and research that takes place. It sparks off that learning which is necessary to tackle the problem/issue.

All teaching and learning sessions or activities relate to the problem or project and spring from the kinds of questions and needs you have to help you to solve it.

Case study

For example, *How to overcome non-compliance with procedures for ensuring precautions are taken by nurses for health reasons*. This problem is central to a thesis and needs approaching with the nurses and the researcher (and their access to the nurses and the problem) in mind.

Initial enquiry

Initial enquiry into the nature and scope of the problem/issue/innovation is undertaken by the researcher, eventually involving all the stakeholders, that is, all those involved in the actual situation who stand to be related to it or to gain by its solution. There might be a problem in carrying out your research – you have hit a block, for instance – and you and the rest of any research group could benefit by solving it. For example, one student came up against the following problem or question in their research sampling: *How do I gain access to information about statistics related to disaster survivors?* Or you could identify one of the essential issues or problems you are researching, as you see it, and as you research, you could share this with those involved. The problem is contextualised as a question, which is then structured into a project to be tackled. Sharing essential inquiries and ongoing problems often leads to a group employing problem-solving strategies to help tackle the problem, and so solve it.

Planning a course of action

1 The problem/inquiry is identified and broken down. Using problem-solving strategies (force-field analysis), the various elements – people, context and resources – involved in the problem are discussed and analysed, objectified on a diagram and then broken down and considered to make each manageable.

2 The outcomes sought are identified, and when planning and actions are considered, they are checked against the sought-for outcomes. Will research activities, vehicles and strategies really help achieve these outcomes?

3 Strategies, people, resources, and so on, and plans of action, are discussed in relation to each aspect of the problem/project defined, and a list of action points drawn up to help tackle the problem/engage with the project.

Case study
For example:

If nurses seem to be non-compliant with procedures for precautions and you want them to *be* compliant, you first need to identify:

- who is involved (nurses, doctors, patients)
- what is going wrong, for example precautions not taken
- what results in reality or possibly from not taking precautions (illness, health hazards or danger, spreading bad practice)
- what is blocking the taking of precautions:
  - attitudes
  - analysis
  - time
  - experience
  - fears
- what is working against your success in persuading nurses to take precautions:
  - attitudes
  - power
  - time
  - access
  - your position

Are there any hidden areas of nurses' responses or reasons that could be a problem? Consider these, then look at what could be used to help or cause change.

- who or what could help you change the nurses' behaviours:
  people:
  - immediate managers
  - nurses themselves
  - top managers
  - patients
  - doctors
  practices:
  - developing good practice through modelling
  - developing good practice through training
  - visible and discussed policies for compliance

Then you will need to ask what you can actually *do* to engage the nurses in following established compliance behaviours and in over-turning bad practices. You look back at people, practices and policies which cause problems and consider strategies to cause change, and strategies to encourage and enable that help.

Then turn the strategies into an action plan with outcomes and a timeline to help you see what needs to happen first, and when, and what needs to happen next.

The actions and strategies need to be identified and costed in terms of time. Plan the time to fit in each stage of the research, activities, reflection/evaluation, replanning, and so on, to conclusion and writing up/presentation of results (a critical path/time planning exercise is often carried out here).

Consulting resources
Identifications of resources and skills, strengths and needs are established to carry out a project which is based on problem solving. If you are engaged in your own individual research, you will need to look at how you fit into the research groups/company/team/situations appropriate to the kind of research in which you are involved, and in relation to the knowledge base and conceptual structures of the subject/discipline.

- You need to decide what skills you have, what skills you need, what knowledge you have, what knowledge you need to acquire and what kinds of energies, people, powers, practices and policies are there to help you with your work, or seem to hinder you or simply do not relate. You will need to identify the problem and project, those things which can help you, how to overcome contradictions and problems and negative responses. Then consider tackling the problem. You will also need to consider acquiring the skills and knowledge to tackle it (and to determine if you need new skills and knowledge).

• How are you going to write the problem up? Is it a whole process or element of your research, or will it be one which has invisibly been solved so that your research can proceed – in this case, it might only appear in your journal.

Do not forget that you are working on two different activities at least here, depending on how many different problem stages you find in the research: (1) the problem, (2) the thesis. When the problem is solved or the project completed, the thesis still needs writing.

Your whole thesis might concentrate on solving a problem, or part of one. A thesis, dissertation or a write-up are a snapshot in the life of *some* ongoing projects or problems. They are not merely self-indulgent activities because of this, however. They help capture the difficulties, and the energies and activities spent engaging actively with these difficulties to achieve a positive solution, so they form a kind of interim report. An interim report is not enough for a PhD, however. If your work merely reports rather than engages with the concepts and the literature, it will not be of a sufficient standard to gain a PhD – and this could be of concern if that is the level of award you are seeking. So ensure you have a big enough issue or inquiry problem to solve or inquiry to pursue (if it is your main research area), and ensure you engage with the necessary theory, literature and concepts as you tackle it.

Putting resources into action

Once you have identified, clarified and strategically planned to solve your problem or carry over or pursue your inquiry, you need to set about acquiring the information, using the resources and seeking help from people, carrying out experiments and assessing results, collating data, interacting with samples or materials and transferring information to presentational formats (as appropriate to the problem-solving activity).

Examples of problem-solving activities and strategies: force-field analysis

You might find it useful to carry out a brief problem-solving exercise as part of problem-based or inquiry-based learning.

Task

Picking a problem-solving/inquiry case study:

- If you pick a manageable problem for your re-search, such as *'matching learning activities to tutees/students/trainees with a variety of learning styles'*, in order to enable different students to learn, you would find it a useful exercise to feed into your own course/ programme planning.
- When planning your course/sessions/programme and fitting problem solving into it, you could decide to develop a problem-based learning programme, as above. This involves a thorough, problem-based approach to the whole programme, or it could include problem-solving exercises, as:
  - Identify the problem/inquiry issue as you see it, or the *development* you wish to ensure, and think carefully about the preferred outcome(s). What do you ideally want to happen – or to avoid? For example, what kind of learning needs to take place for the variety of learners involved?
  - Next, identify the various forces (people, practices, policies, contexts, resources, rules, crises, and so on) that are causing the problem or are working *against* you and which could cause problems in a development or changes. Fill these in on the diagram below.
  - The object of the exercise is to *objectify* and to *visualise in a diagram* these various forces and then to look at what forces (people, contexts, policies, decisions, and so on) you have working *for* you in your planned change/development/problem solving.

Weigh up precisely what could be difficult for you and consider the worst that could happen.

Now consider:

- systems, plans and actions which need putting in place
- what actions you need to take, the research needed – how and where to go about it
- who you can work with, tasks to be started, actioned and completed

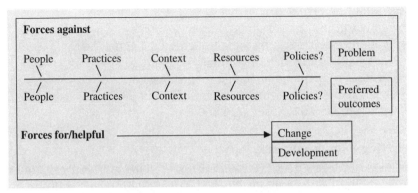

FIGURE **19.1** PROBLEM SOLVING

- who can help you in your work, people to be persuaded and negotiated with
- what policies, resources and practices can help, working systems to be set up with the team
- you to achieve your outcomes, team roles and responsibilities negotiated
- plan the activities on a timescale related to your plans:

ANALYSE – PLAN – ACT – EVALUATE AND REFLECT – REPLAN

Reflection, refinement and development

As a researcher, you will probably find it useful to keep a journal or learning log of the plans, thoughts and learning activities you undertake in relation to the problem, and to reflect on the things or ideas, and so on, you feel you are learning as you go along. This is particularly necessary if the problem forms the bulk of your research. It is also necessary if it is a small problem you have overcome or faced along the way. Record the stages. You will need to note other skills and knowledge which you acquire as the result of more conventional training and development activities (for example, you might find that in order to tackle the problem, you will need to update your IT skills or undertake other research methods courses).

In our case study, suggested above, of developing a learning programme *making learning activities to further students/trainees with a variety of learning styles* you might find that you need to:

- identify student learning styles
- gather resources to help develop those styles
- gain further skills in learning to better enable that learning
- develop and trial the programme
- reflect on the programme and then change it
- outline the final programme so it can be put into practice to benefit your studies and those of others.

Findings and analysis

At different stages in the problem-solving work/the project/the research you will need to sum up, review and assess your findings and decide whether you have achieved your intended outcomes – and if not, what to do next to further your work. If you are reviewing stages of problem solving/projects as parts of the research you will need to review what these findings mean and how you can refocus and structure your future work.

Conclusion

Depending on what was being studied and the nature of the problem, this is the moment to review what has been achieved and what learned. For example, in health subjects, an appropriate solution might be the diagnosis of a problem situation, a plan of action to deal with it and a specified means of evaluating whether the plan of action was successful, how far it was successful and how it might have been improved.

▶ Some points about problem-based or inquiry-based research for practice-based doctorates

Problem-based research and learning are action learning-based and often, therefore, related to the workplace. They:

- enable continuous engagement and improvement
- encourage self-reflective researchers/learners who can continue to learn
- encourage learners to transfer the learning from the problem-based project/case to their work with the organisation and the various problems and projects which emerge during the course of this work – that is, it is transferable and practice-based

- encourage teamwork, goal analysis, action planning, time management, evaluation and presentation of results to others.

This is why students studying for EdD programmes or for MPhils and PhDs related to their practice frequently adopt a problem- or inquiry-based approach.

▶ Choice of problems in relation to goals and needs

Problems/projects chosen for practice-based research should be topical, useful, relevant and in alignment with the work in the company/workplace carried out by the learners and with the development needs of the institution/company, the department/section and the learner, as recognised in appraisal and other goal- and need-identification scenarios, as appropriate.

Problems should be real, big and rich enough, but not too big, and should have achievable enough outcomes so that learners can use the problem as a jumping-off point to:

- relate to their own goals and needs
- identify and develop team and individual roles, where appropriate
- acquire important knowledge and information
- develop skills
- develop ideas and thoughts
- discuss and share progress and achievements with others in the workplace who relate to the problem or inquiry in which you are involved
- consider difficulties with team members.

▶ Problem-based learning can use project and case-study approaches involving individuals, teams and managers

After the problem
If and when the problem is solved, ask:

1 If it is a problem about the process, can you now carry on with your research? For example, if you were trying to gain access to some

sample, what do you do if you can't gain that access? Implement changes, develop, change direction . . .

2 If the problem is the core of your research, will you be able to take forward any insights or changes your research has produced? What needs to be done beyond the thesis?

Conclusion

We have looked at:

- Carrying out problem-based or inquiry-based research
- Solving problems which form the main question or focus of your thesis or dissertation
- Solving problems which provide difficulties along the way, as part of the research process
- How you might identify, tackle and action problem solving, and record your activities
- What you might do to ensure appropriate change after you have solved the problem and even after you have written up the dissertation/thesis

---

Further reading

Rossi, C. (1995) *Problem Based Learning in a Health Sciences Curriculum.* London: Routledge.

Stage 4

Support, Progress, Analysis, Writing Up, the Viva, Presentations and Afterwards

20 Being Organised, Keeping Records, 'Writing up', Stage by Stage

This chapter looks at:

- *Planning your study – time plans and critical path analysis*
- *Planning the stages of the thesis and the chapters*
- *Getting into good habits – recording references, colour coding, keeping files and cataloguing research activities and results*
- *Organising your findings and your draft writing up*
- *Writing each chapter – what each can contain, coherence and so on*
- *Structure of a chapter*
- *Language – 'fog', technical terms and accessibility*

Here we consider 'writing up' as an ongoing activity rather than something which happens in a rush at the end of the year. You should find it useful throughout your MA, MPhil, EdD or PhD and particularly useful as you start to produce drafts, then final versions of your dissertation or thesis. *Read it* as you *start* to work *and* as you continue.

It is important to get into good habits in your research, using your time fruitfully in a planned way, and to get into good habits in writing up. Look back at the section on managing your time. This will be particularly important for you if you are also balancing paid or unpaid work and domestic responsibilities, but strangely (perhaps), it is often those engaged only in full-time research who lose track of their time in relation to their research plan and fail to complete. They might have become overwhelmed with other activities, or have lost their way in the research and the thesis. Do be careful to keep a clear idea of your way. This is not a blueprint for rigidity and being closed to new ideas: being open to surprises and needing to change as a result of findings as you go is not the same thing as having no real plan in the first place.

Task

Look back at your draft plan of the study.

- Have you clearly and carefully plotted each stage of the research?
- Have you ensured that some activities, such as the literature search-ing, continue alongside other research activities all the way through your research?
- Have you written in enough time for each stage of the activity?
- Have you considered what (technology, equipment, and so on) and who (subjects, helpers and advisers) can help you at which points in the research? Where, when and why might you meet difficulties?
- How can you overcome these difficulties with good practice, rescheduling and the help of others?
- Do you intend to give presentations, work-in-progress seminars, con-ference presentations, or write papers along the way? If so, when might you plan these in?

Look at Chapter 5 on time management, consider the example of a time plan or critical path analysis and map your own plan of study in a similar way, or in overlapping lines to indicate different coincidental elements of your work as you have proceeded. Right now, as you are proceeding with parts of your work, consider and review in brief the whole process for the next few years. Use the space below to map out your time and task plan of study, briefly spotting difficulties. You will need to add in the dates against which you are plotting your work and you will also need to add in the clashes and difficulties which emerge in your other life, that is, work and home.

Discuss the plan with a colleague. Can you spot any difficulties? Explain how it will work, how it has worked *so far* and where there might have been stressful moments, clashes of work and other inter-ests, a need to rely on others, possible delays, and so on.

Look back at Chapter 5 to consider how you have been:

Time and task plan – key stages and obvious potentially difficult moments

1 Research question, choosing your university and supervisor. Interviews and house moves? Job changes?
2 Refining questions and sub-questions, defining methodology and methods. Meeting supervisor to clarify.
3 Ongoing literature searching, craft submission – meet supervisor.
4 Submit/revise/meet supervisor – resubmit. Carry on with the research.
5 The business of the research – using pilots, refining methods, gathering data, continuing to read, *starting to write up each tentative part of the work*, meeting supervisor to check ideas, arguments and findings.
6 Carry on as above, for the bulk of the time, and continue to write up drafts and discuss with supervisor.
7 Progress reports/transfer documents.
8 Work-in-progress presentations with other researchers, some publications, continue to work as above – drafting and redrafting as you go and seeing supervisor.
9 Organise charts, diagrams, produce them, refine write-ups, produce final versions and discuss them.
10 Edit and re-edit, check rules for layout and presentation again, ensure bibliographies are in correct format and that nothing is missing.
11 Submit (unbound, in case of revisions).
12 Viva and success or viva, some rewriting, resubmission/sending in of rewrites and success.
13 Celebrations, conferment of degree, publications and different work.

- keeping good notes of sources, methods, results and data
- talking and thinking through drafts of chapters
- writing up drafts of chapters
- altering your work in the light of comments from your supervisor(s).

Have you had any difficulties in writing up? In keeping good records? As you start to write up into your final version of the thesis or dissertation or, for EdD, your *final* progress report/thesis, you will start to revise your record keeping and update it, and start to rewrite previous chapters to make them fit into an overall cohesive work.

▶ Developing the framework of different chapters

Areas you will have considered when writing your proposal provide a key to the main areas of the developing thesis. Look at these again now and ensure that your proposal is aligned with the developing work. Ask yourself whether it really addresses each of these areas. You will find that the areas of the proposal that you address will form important beginnings for your chapters.

In your proposal you will have thought of (a reminder):

(1) **Indicative title** – What will you call the dissertation/thesis? It is better to pose a question and to make a suggestion about links in argument rather than to give a single word or area of study.

(2) **Aim and focus of the study** – This should suggest the underlying research area and your main question and sub-questions. Eventually it helps to form the abstract of your thesis, so think about it carefully. What are you really exploring, arguing or trying to find out, hoping to find out, then suggest? What links with what in your mind?

(3) **Context for the research** – What issues, problems, history, background and others' questions provide a context, an academic culture and ongoing set of questions, thoughts and discoveries for your own work? How is it contributing to academic work in this area? *As you start to write up (2) and (3), these form part of your Introduction where you lay out your main arguments driving the thesis.*

(4) **Theoretical perspectives and interpretations** – Where have you taken your theories from – what kind of framework? What are the underpinning theoretical perspectives informing your ideas, for example, feminist theory or Marxist theory? *As you start to write up (4), this will go into your Introduction and into your literature review chapter, if you have one, or probably into your theory chapter.*

(5) **Research design** – How will you go about collecting information, carrying out literature searches, and so on? Provide an outline of the different activities you will undertake at what points in your research and do a critical path analysis of this.

(6) **Research methodology and methods** – What is the research methodology underpinning your research and what methods or vehicles and strategies are you going to use? Why? How do they link with and help inform and develop each other?

(7) **Ethical considerations** – Many dissertations and theses have

ethical considerations and these will be particularly complex when you are using human subjects. Obviously if you are involved in medical research this would be so but it is also true of protecting the identities of those who give you information through questionnaires, focus groups or interviews. You will need to take care when asking certain sorts of personal questions or using documents which refer to people alive or dead – and so on. *(5), (6) and (7) form the basis of your methodology and methods chapter.*

(8) **Outline plan of study** – This part of the proposal asks you to indicate what you thought would be the main features of each of your chapters, and it would be useful to revisit this at different points in your ongoing research and consider how they are developing, if any early findings are changing these.

(9) **Justification for level of award** – An MPhil, EdD or PhD usually involves answering this question – you will need to describe and discuss what you feel your research will contribute to the field of knowledge, the development of arguments, and the research culture. What kinds of practices, thoughts and arguments cannot move forward? How can it make a difference? Why does it matter? And why is it obviously at this level? Is it serious, broad, deep-questioning and original enough? Primary references – 10 or 12 of these will be in your submission. *(9) partly ends up in your **abstract** and also in your concluding chapter.*

Of course, much of your thesis goes way beyond the original proposal because it is all about *what* you find and how you place it in your conceptual framework, what it means and what sorts of analyses are made. The conclusions will be what you draw from what you find.

▶ The shape of the thesis as it develops

When you come to think about the actual shape of your thesis you can bear several models in mind. A thesis often has a narrative or storyline running through it and some secondary storylines – these are the trains of thought or argument in which your investigations, readings and findings all fit. Start by thinking what case or major argument you want to make and then consider the questions you need to ask, where and how you might ask them, the research methods and vehicles you will use, and the way the main reading and theories informing your work all fit together. Broadly speaking you are considering:

1 Your research area and how you have defined your topic and your questions – and how you are defining these.

2 Your thoughts and arguments exploring why you are asking certain questions using certain methods and vehicles in certain ways to help you explore your research area.

3 Discussion, analyses and reports on the work you have done, your discoveries and arguments, the way some information leads to other thoughts and links to other information and ideas and helps develop arguments further. This involves looking at the data which you are producing and analysing it, asking it further questions, speculating, making creative leaps of ideas and pulling ideas and findings together.

4 Some of your solutions and conclusions and further thoughts on future work – recommendations for developments, actions and explorations beyond the scope of your thesis here.

There are differences between theses in different fields of study. Arts and humanities theses tend to concentrate on exploration of arguments in a storyline throughout the thesis, rather than in methods sections, findings and conclusions (often there are no conclusions as such! Instead, arguments which seem now to be proven and well founded in the reading). Social science- and health-related theses tend to have more explicit characteristics. They usually analyse and interpret the information and data and move conclusions forward to new stages of investigation, then come to some proven conclusions and suggest further work.

▶ Models

It will certainly benefit you to look at other people's theses in similar areas, and these can probably be found in your local university library. Do not get too embroiled in the arguments. Look at them for their shape – their abstracts, and so on.

A typical plan of a thesis is frequently as follows:

- title
- abstract
- preface/acknowledgements
- introduction
- literature review
- design of study

- a theory chapter usually developing these two previous elements
- methodology and methods explored and explained
- presentation of findings and results
- discussion of results, analysis, arguments, development of ideas based on results
- summary
- conclusion/recommendations
- appendices/statistical tables and illustrations
- references
- bibliography.

Throughout the thesis there is an argument, a narrative/storyline which develops by linking your underpinning reading, themes, theories, ideas, methods, findings and arguments together. Go back and forth through the thesis as you start to write it up and edit it to ensure that this coherence develops – taking a reader clearly and logically through your work.

▶ Your plan of the thesis – what chapters and what are their main points/arguments/role?

Complete the plan chart below, planning the stages and elements of your own thesis. This will help you think through your work to come and see how ideas and arguments develop from each other, interweave, and lead to each other.

Your plan of the thesis
1
2
3
4
5
6
7
8
9

Elements of the structure of the thesis explained – and variants discussed

Title

Put your title on a separate title-page and try to keep this to one or two lines and develop a title which is clear, suggesting the questions you are posing and assertions you are making rather than just the field of study

Abstract

An abstract is usually about 500 words, and answers the questions, 'What is this thesis about? What does it argue/prove/contend?', and so on. It should use the third person and passive verbs, for example, 'it is argued that . . . in discussing . . . using . . . evidence is presented which suggests that . . .'.

Preface and acknowledgements

Introduction

This lays out the:

- background to the thesis
- other work in the area
- general ideas and developments related to the thesis

Next, it:

- moves on to lay down and explore the theoretical bases for the thesis and your work
- contextualises your arguments and findings in background, context and theory
- discusses your research questions and the hypotheses underlying the research
- sets out the main themes and suggests what your work contributes to and develops in relation to these – what your main arguments and contributions are

Usually the introduction tends to be written last – it provides a coherent introduction to themes, arguments and findings and this is difficult to do until the whole anatomy of the thesis has been actually constructed and flesh put on the bones of each chapter.

Review of the literature

Not all theses have a separate literature review chapter. If your work all develops logically and smoothly from the reading you have done, and your research and findings follow on from a coherent body of established work in the field, and established informing theories, you will probably use a literature review at this point. It will establish the theories and arguments and discuss the main debates, research and authors who contribute to the field, contextualising your own work here.

If, however, you will be moving stage by stage and at different stages need to introduce and develop theories and reading, then you might well find several chapters begin with and interleave the literature, theory and arguments. You need to decide which variation on these versions suits your own work best. Do remember that the literature review or survey is not just a collection of all you have read. You need to weave the reading and main points and arguments made into your own discussion, using it to back up or counteract some of your arguments. If you have found a few main themes developing logically and coherently through your reading, these can help form the basis of your main chapters.

Design of the study

For the social sciences, education, and related research this is as crucial as it is for scientific research. You need to explain why and how you designed your studies – mentioning the pilot stage if there is one, decisions taken about interviews, focus groups, questionnaires, samples, and so on.

If your research is more humanities- or literature-based you might well find that you have already described what your research questions are along with your main ideas and arguments. In this case there is no specific study in logical stages, each depending on the data from previous stages, as such, but instead, each chapter takes a different theme, critical approach or point of view or different author or book, and so on.

But note that it is always preferable to interweave literature, texts, authors, and so on, rather than plodding through each one individually – relate them to each other and form your own way through them in relation to your arguments and information.

Presentation of results

This can be just a clear, annotated record of what has been discovered if your area is social sciences, education, or health. You are unlikely to have this section in a literature or cultural studies thesis. In this case your 'results' or discoveries and arguments will form part of the discussions in separate chapters.

Discussion of results

For a social sciences, health or education thesis, there is often a logical place for working through different results, putting tables, statistics and bar charts either in the main text or referring to them in the appendices, and conducting a narrative which explores and brings in different results to develop arguments and present your coherent points and findings.

For a humanities or literature-based thesis and also often for one in the social sciences, health or education, there are often *several chapters* exploring different themes and issues in a linked discussion. The results as such will be your critically informed comments and arguments on the texts, images, your readings, and so on. You might find that the main themes identified in the literature review appear here as main topics in each of your chapters.

Summary

This chapter enables you to sum up your main findings and present an argued case for your original contribution, the creative element added to the field of study. In a humanities or literature-based thesis there might well be a more *organic* structure of chapters focusing on different themes, developing issues, and authors, and a summary as such is not needed.

Conclusion

All theses have a conclusion. This establishes the importance of your work, states its contribution clearly and summarises the main points you have made: where, when and how. It rounds off your arguments, even if there are still points open for further work and questioning. At this point – in theses that seek to suggest change or development, or to contribute new ideas and strategies and so cause development and change, there could well be a section for recommendations, as there is in a standard *report*. If your work does indeed seek change then it is essential that you think throughout the research *how* you are going to make constructive and realistic recommendations based on your findings.

Appendices, statistical tables and illustrations

(These might appear in the main text, where the argument using them appears.) Ensure each item is clearly labelled and referenced to where it is used in the thesis. If they are not explained in the body of the thesis, explain them fully here.

References
If you are using footnotes they usually appear at the foot of each page, and endnotes appear usually at the end of each chapter. Some writers leave all the endnotes to the end of the thesis, collected chapter by chapter at that point and integrated with the references. References can be signalled in the text by a number,[1] which leads to the endnote and reference, or by a shortened form of the actual reference.

For example, 'Estelle M. Phillips and D. S. Pugh, *How to Get a PhD: A Handbook for Students and their Supervisors* (Open University Press, second edition, 1994)' placed at the end, in the references, can be signalled in your actual text as '(Phillips and Pugh 1994)'.

Bibliography
This is usually an alphabetical list of the books and journals that you have used. Not all theses have a bibliography but it is a handy reference for any reader.

▶ Writing chapters

Each chapter is like an essay in a linked developed narrative and argument of the thesis as a whole. As such, then, you will probably begin by *planning* it using diagrams, mind-mapping, brainstorming and the development of key points followed by notes to illustrate and fill these out.

State the main argument of the chapter in an introductory paragraph or two. If you have several main arguments, suggest here how they are linked, for example:

> *In this chapter the arguments for developing regional colleges are made clearly. Regional colleges provide a valuable service for students who cannot attend the main sites of universities owing to distance or other commitments, and their usefulness should be valued politically as well as pedagogically.*

Develop notes
Under key headings for each element of the chapter, for example, 'regional colleges', show:

- their role geographically
- their role as access providers for the region

- their political role – enabling disadvantaged or distant, etc., students to gain university/college qualifications
- the franchises and mechanisms for linking regional colleges to universities, or enabling them to remain separate – the pros and cons.

Move through the argument and the narrative of your chapter, ensuring that (a) there is coherence between the different elements and examples discussed within the chapter, and (b) that each of the chapter's streams of argument are related to the thesis arguments and themes as a whole.

You will need to ensure that there are links between arguments and examples or illustrative material, theories and abstract ideas and concepts, generalised comments, and specific, worked-through examples. Do not be afraid to introduce major arguments which contradict your own – you need to argue with these in order to show you have taken other points on board and understand their relevance. Do not just include other people's work to show you have read it, but use it in a discussion/argument.

Using quotations

If you are quoting, try to break up long quotations with discussion, and do not depend for your argument on the plan and construction of the other author's work – make those elements of their arguments you use fit in with your plan of argument – use theirs as illustrations, or points to argue with or against, setting up and pulling down points, and so on. Do not just fall into re-describing and paraphrasing, make it your own and, of course, reference it fully and carefully. Disputing and arguing with authorities is all part of developing your own contributions and ideas, as is agreeing with them. Do be careful to reference fully and so avoid any accusations of plagiarism. For students from outside Britain, the USA and Australia, where English is not the first language, different conventions often operate in relation to the use of authorities. However, if this is a thesis in English for an English/US/Australian university, you will need to follow conventions of arguing with and carefully referencing any authorities, quotations, etc., you use. Check conventions with the university authorities and guidebooks for good practice in writing.

When you reach the end of each chapter, just as in the whole thesis, summarise what you have argued and 'proved', for example:

This chapter has suggested that the development of regional colleges should be supported because of the specific access provision they present. The chapter has argued for several models of linking with universities, emphasising the importance of some autonomy in this relationship. A number of examples have been considered and their position and value explored. Issues of the assessment relationships are explored in chapter 5 and issues of overseas 'regional' colleges in chapter 6.

These last points link your chapter to the rest of the thesis and show that there is a coherent argument throughout.

Language

Think of your audience's needs. Check conventions. Many university departments do not like the use of 'I' or 'we' but others recognise that the research has been carried out by you/you and others and that you wish to place your own views and arguments here, and so to signal them with the first person. Adopting distanced and stilted language can be off-putting for readers.

If you are using technical language, of whatever sort, explain acronyms on their first use and explain complex technical terms (unless they are clearly in everyday use among specialists such as yourself and the readership you expect). When in doubt, explain them on first use and if there are a great number of unusual terms, also include them in a glossary in an appendix.

Avoid 'fog' which is very (unnecessarily) dense language. This is common, especially in scientific writing, and even in the social sciences and literary criticism. Those who write theses are sometimes as guilty as anyone else in 'fogging up' their expression with too many unnecessarily long and complex words when a straightforward word would do just as well. Do not sacrifice technical terms, but do ensure that there are limited numbers of words of several syllables explaining the most straightforward elements of your argument, especially when they are all gathered in the same sentence which includes technical terms. If too many long, complex, unusually specialist words and technical terms come together the reader will experience 'fog'. They will not be able to get through the density of your prose to your argument. It is not impressive, it is confusing.

Try out early parts of early chapters on colleagues who are semi-expert in your field – if they are entirely happy, then it is probably readable prose.

Task

Expression
Look back over the research questions you have formulated and the brief outline of what you feel your thesis will be about, or at your developed proposal, especially the theoretical perspectives element.

- How clear is this?
- How logical?
- Is the language unnecessarily filled with long words in addition to technical terms?
- See if you or a colleague can summarise your arguments easily.

Try this exercise on someone else's writing.
Consider what it tells you about readable prose, which is nonetheless working at a high level and making a complex argument.

▶ Submitting the thesis – forewarning for good practice (see final chapters for further discussion)

Drafting, redrafting, changing, editing, and so on, take a long time – do allow for this. Various things can go wrong with your data collection and analysis, and even with your hypothesis and the arguments you were exploring – you will need to discuss why and how you changed your mind and some elements of your focus, and you will also need to reschedule if this happens.

Finally, however, you can proceed to submission.

To sum up, a few points to bear in mind as you are working:

- Your supervisor should have read *all* of your work before submission and can advise on layout, as well as more complex arguments, and so on.
- Ensure you have read the university guidelines about layout, typeface, presentation, binding (or not, until after the viva) and references and that your work conforms to all of these. Many theses have difficulties just because of their presentation – which is a waste if the hard work has been done and the presentation quality lets this down.

Conclusion

We have looked at:

- Planning your study
- Organising your work habits
- Stages of the thesis
- Writing chapters
- Getting ready to work towards writing up

Further reading

Phillips, E. M., & Pugh, D. S. (1994). *How to Get a PhD: A Handbook for Students and Their Supervisors*, 2nd ed. Buckingham: Open University Press.

21 Analysing Data and Thinking about Findings

> This chapter looks at:
>
> - *I wouldn't start from here . . .*
> - *Organising your data – quantitative and qualitative*
> - *Recognising how the data collected relates to the questions asked and the conceptual framework of the research*
> - *Methods of data analysis*
> - *Deducing findings from analyses*
> - *Where to end?*

There is no substitute for having a clear idea of what you are looking for (your research question(s)), and continuing to stay as close as possible to the data as it emerges raw from the participants so that you can get a 'feel' for what is emerging. Then you stand back, clarifying the areas of questions, the theories and the conceptual framework and start to put it all into some kind of order so that your data can genuinely be analysed, and findings drawn from it which relate to your original questions and conceptual framework.

In my work with colleagues on a postgraduate development programme for cohorts of PhD students, mostly from Israel, we run a session called 'What do I do with all this data? This session mimics how I and so many others felt when faced with the over-rich results of our hours of carefully planned research method application fieldwork, the collection and ultimate stockpiling of material – both quantitative (largely numbers) and qualitative (largely words) – arising from research. Of course, you would not start from here! The data that you have collected, which probably looms up in what Miles and Huberman

(1994) have described as an alpine shape, that is, in a large mountain (probably about to become an avalanche!), is a product of your research design.

Your research questions are clarified and organised by your conceptual framework, which is actioned and enabled by your research methods and your data, once collected.

But you will probably have far too much data to fully incorporate into your thesis and could ask questions of it for several years to come. At this stage, remember the initial comparison of your research to a *slice* of cake – there is a bigger cake there and other people can take slices and find out, analyse, make deductions, carry on with the work and eat them later. You need to focus on *your* slice of the cake and make sure it is neat, clear, clean, tasty and wholesome, and satisfies the needs you set about satisfying in the first place. *Don't* use everything. Do be selective and checked in your analyses.

So you need to be managed in terms of organising what data you have to date, ruthlessly selective in focusing on what is really relevant, and clearly focused on finding out what it really all 'means', that is, what the findings are and how they relate to your questions and outcomes.

One important thing to remember during your research is to ensure that you have your data analysed as far as possible when it is available – in batches. This enables you to integrate it and see whether you need to change your work direction, but it also indicates what kinds of findings are emerging. This can be a useful and comforting guide when you are faced with the avalanche.

You will probably have a great deal of raw data, but these – questionnaires, transcribed interviews, transcribed focus groups, observation, schedules completed, and so on – are not findings. Findings need to be derived from the analysis of this data, which means:

- managing the data – reduce their size and scope, find the 'slice of cake' that fits your own enquiries so you can report on this usefully
- analysing the managed data – ask them analytical questions, abstract and generalise from them, using them to back up the arguments and indications they seem to present. You need to integrate them in order to analyse them.

You may also find that much of the analysis and interpretation of your data is a repetitive and even monotonous activity because you are very carefully labelling, counting, charting data and carrying out analytical activities over and over, and are categorising and recording meticulously what you find. Remember that if you are not careful and meticulous, your findings might be questionable. If you are slipshod and your findings unreliable, there is nothing worse when giving a presentation on your findings to have a query from the audience which picks a huge hole in your analysis and the figures you have presented – just because of a few mistakes or lack of concentration at this stage.

▶ Managing data, both quantitative and qualitative

You need to code the data – preferably this should be done as they are collected. Indicate the date of the questionnaires, who completed them and the number of returns. You need to categorise your data at this stage too, for example, in relation to gender; female (1) and male (2), or origin: Malaysian (1), European (2), African (3). Ages are commonly expressed in ranges, for example, 21–30. Much of this kind of categorising should have been done on the original questionnaire, but it needs coding in now you have the data so that data matches coding.

For more open-ended questionnaires or semi-structured, open-ended interviews, you will need to read them through carefully and code them after the event, that is, code in relation to the kinds of answers, themes and issues, and categories of response (keeping a note of what the codes refer to). When you are collecting data concerning people you also need to be careful about the Data Protection Act. You are not allowed to keep the names of your respondees in close enough contact with their responses for them to be attributed, and you must find a way of coding names against numbers and numbering responses, then keeping the list relating the two in an entirely safe place. Do check with university regulations and the details of the Data Protection Act.

▶ Annotating

This is a process of managing some of your data. If you are collecting documentary evidence or taking notes from books, and so on, you will need to develop a process for keeping marginal notes, taking notes from sources (see Chapter 11) and then pulling these items of information together.

You will also find it useful to annotate thematically on the side of transcribed interviews (see below). Labelling the important themes or issues as they appear helps you to draw different responses together, and to draw together responses from the different sources, for example, documents, interviews and texts which relate to the same areas or themes of your enquiry when you write them all up.

▶ Summarising and generalising

From the whole range of your data you need to draw some relative generalisations (rather than conclusions). Ask: What kinds of responses keep recurring? What are the deviations from these? Are there themes emerging? Contradictions? Summarise and generalise, using figures and quotations to illustrate your summaries and generalisations. The use of examples is a product of selection and you need to focus on a few cases or examples which illustrate the points you are making. As a result of analysing your findings more broadly, you may find someone whose behaviour is typical, or a new person whose work and behaviour fall into a set of extremes or contrasts. Then *you* could take this person or persons as cases or samples to select and emphasise (keeping the selection of individual cases anonymous, for confidentiality). This helps to illustrate and highlight your findings, because, as with journalism, others reading your work respond well to the individual case, which represents an example of the argument.

▶ Example

Much research combines a range of methods to approach research questions, and often begins with a broad survey, perhaps by questionnaire, narrowing down to individual cases for a more in-depth enquiry. For example, in a piece of research on the learning of postgraduate students (see Chapter 8) its was discovered that there was a set of significant responses. A significant number of students tended to be taking accumulation of surface learning approaches but seeking transformational outcomes. While this was true to a small extent for most of the students surveyed, it was true for a very great extent for 6 individuals out of 50 surveyed. These 6 were then selected for further closer scrutiny in order to illustrate the problem, define it, and start to share it with the students so that they could deal with its implications in relation to their own learning. The analysis was carried out by categorising numbers of questions, in relation to certain categories of which accumulation approaches, meaningful learning approaches and transformational outcomes were the main areas focused on. Questions in these categories were then scrutinised in relation to the initial overall frequency analysis of all responses to all questions.

For a broad-brush response, categories of questions could be grouped together to indicate patterns of response – showing up those proportions and percentages of students taking accumulative approaches, meaningful approaches and transformational outcomes. However, it was important to put these three items in relation with each other. Some cross-tabulation was necessary to indicate where the students taking an accumulation approach were also stating a transformational outcome. We needed to add to these certain rigorous questions, directed to the students themselves, in discussion (in focus groups). Their responses were collected together and scrutinised. The individual students taking these 'problematic' approaches in relation to transformational outcomes could then be alerted to the potential problems arising from their approaches, and supported towards developing learning behaviours which could help *avoid* the potential problems. The potential *problem* was that if you accumulate large amounts of data as your main approach, you could find it difficult to then leap to conclusions which suggest a change, or transfiguration – the hoped for outcomes of the research aims of these students. Various strategies could help overcome the problem – different methods, links between collection and analysis, analysis in the drawing of findings, in the research design – are two very *obvious* strategies here.

Let's look at some rules for coding up your data so that you can use and interpret it. Fielding insists:

- codes must be mutually exclusive
- codes must be exhaustive
- codes must be applied consistently throughout.

And he identifies five stages in the coding process:

- developing the coding frame for both pre-coded and open questions
- creating the code book and coding instructions

- coding the questionnaires
- transferring the values to a computer
- checking and cleaning the data. (Fielding 1993: 225, 220 in Denscombe 1998: 194)

If yours is quite a small-scale study you will probably not need to go beyond the description of your statistics and the relation between a few variables. These variables might include, for example, the age of respondents and their likelihood of saying 'yes' to certain questions about what they buy in a supermarket, or, for example, the relation between the gender of respondents and their indication of how many hours they work each week. In all cases you will need to contextualise what you find. It is probably the case when looking at the latter example (gender and hours of paid work) that women respondents might seek part-time work or are only able to take part-time work because of childcare responsibilities. You would need to have some idea of this (from interviews, from sociology, background information, and so on), in order to make sense of the statistics that show women in a certain group having part-time work and men having full-time work in greater proportions.

But the data which arise from a questionnaire are much richer than such a set of questions. We could scrutinise them again and ask – is there any pattern of approach and outcome which relates to gender? Or to ethnicity? Or context? Or age? If we have asked these questions in the first place and seek the answers because they seem to be meaningful when subject to more complex statistical analyses, then diagrams can be produced which show overall norms and deviations from the norms, and patterns which indicate where individuals are very far outside the norms, when presenting your findings. If you wish to carry out such complex *statistical* analysis you will find it useful to consult such texts as Robson (1993), Blaxter, Hughes & Tight (1993) and texts more directly engaged with statistical analysis, the detail and complexity of which lie outside the range of this book.

Quantitative data analysis usually involves statistics because it uses numbers. But for those squeamish at the thought of number crunching, qualitative data analysis is not an easy option! It involves words, which are always produced in context, and then contrast affects their interpretation (even more so than questionnaires). Their interpretation is related to the intentions of the researchers as well as the relations between researcher and those interviewed/surveyed in a focus group (see Chapter 15).

▶ Qualitative data activity

Analysing qualitative data involves close and thorough reading and coding, as does quantitative data analysis. If you had a mountain of transcriptions from various interviews, one way of managing this data would be to read through most of them, referring back to the reasons behind the underpinning questions lying behind the questions you asked in the interview. Look for themes in the responses of the interviewees, and categorise the responses in relation to these themes.

You can do this logically:

- Read or look back at the underpinning questions.
- Look back at specific questions.
- Determine a range of those that relate to these questionnaires, the issues to which they relate.
- Colour-code responses, for example, blue for one of them, green for another, and so on. Try blue with two stripes and green/red, and so on, if you have lots of themes – but do not let yourself become too overwhelmed with different categories or you will find it difficult to draw any conclusions or say anything about your data.

If you can put your qualitative data through computer programmes such as Nudist or NVivo, you will find that, guided by you, these programmes can help with the thematic analysis. You need to read carefully, first to determine categories and themes, and indicate to the programme key words and phrases that appear in these themes so that it can pick them out. It will then pull these together in a continuous run of labelled paragraphs so that you can both see the amount and type of responses in the thematic area and refer back to the whole transcript because it is coded into each of the quotations.

Robson has developed useful tactics for drawing conclusions from qualitative data which I use here. You will need to count numbers and frequency of responses (for example, themes, issues); recognise and develop patterns, so that you can draw differing responses together because of their similarity and frequency; cluster them; and bring them together because of their relation to a limited number of factors. You will need to relate certain variables together to make sense of the data, and both build up networks of causal relations between items, and then, very carefully relate your findings to the theoretical frameworks from which they spring, into which they fit, and into which others can fit them. Robson suggests (1993: 401):

1 Counting and categorising data and measuring the frequency of occurrence of the categories.
2 Patterning and noting recurring patterns or themes.
3 Clustering groups of objects, persons, activities, settings, and so on, which have similar characteristics.
4 Factoring and grouping of variables into a small number of hypothetical factors.
5 Relating variables. Discovery of the type of relationship, if any, between two or more variables.
6 Building of casual networks. Development of chains or webs of linkages between variables.
7 Relating findings to general theoretical frameworks. Attempting to find general propositions that account for the particular findings in this study.

▶ Documentary analysis

This is not merely reading and taking notes but the careful identification of key issues, labels and themes. One student working on internal organisational documents within a school to chart the decision-making processes and decisions made over a four-year period carefully:

- read through every single one of the documents
- read both quantitative and qualitative analysis
- labelled up the categories of response, discussion in committee meetings, decisions, themes, rules, and those involved in the decision-making processes
- carefully analysed and labelled the themes in relation to the decisions made
- read through all of this again and came to some careful conclusions about the relationship of decisions made from committee discussion and the specific power relations of the head of the school and their close team.

Task

Documentary analysis
Find an internal document from your university, college, organisation, or local group, as appropriate.

Continued

- What would you need to know about its context?
- How could you both summarise the key points and recognise the themes and issues as they present themselves here?
- What other information would you need about timing, reason for the prediction of the document, audience, results, in order to make sense of it?
- How can it be labelled up in relation to a line of enquiry, for example, the decision-making processes or the frequency and kind of decision made regarding the use of school committees?

So what does all of this mean? Findings:

As you analyse your data and start to produce some findings that could be shared with others, you will need to think about the different parts of the findings and conclusions 'jigsaw'. As Judith Bell (1987: 128) reminds us:

> Any conclusion which can justifiably be drawn from findings should be made, If you do *not* find what your research set out to seek, you will not be able to claim it – you could not back it up with the necessary analysed data. You might well find some very interesting and relevant things you did not set out to find.

For example, in analysing the data about the learning of a cohort of PhD students, I discovered (Wisker 1999) that some students were largely motivated not by the example set by parents, friends, or by religion and a sense of civic duty (as were younger students in the first instance and social workers in the final instance), but by beliefs that learning can advance you professionally, and that learning and research can effect important social change. Perhaps these are the kinds of motivations we would expect from more mature and established students!

In a sample of social work undergraduates a surprising result was their lack of motivation in terms of duty to others. In spotting the low responses on questionnaire items related to duty, their tutor then began to focus on the issues of social duty with them in class – because one of the results of their involvement in studying learning approaches and motivation was to enable the curriculum to better suit both student and the learning outcomes of the subject area. Certainly, a lack of a motivation which involved duty was perceived as a problem (Wisker et al. 2000).

You need to consider:

1 **The significance of your findings** – in statistical terms this means the likelihood that a result could have been discovered by chance or how statistically significant it is. If it is a result that represents a genuine occurrence spotted by the research, in more general terms the term 'significance' means it has some meaning with some weight, with some importance in terms of your arguments, in terms of life.

2 **Generalisability** – one of the elements which makes a piece of research of high postgraduate level, particularly PhD research, is the generalisability of the research findings. You have discovered something interesting, but how can other people relate it to what they are finding or what they are doing? If you have carried out a very detailed study of a small-scale group (see the case-study work in Chapter 16), for example, you would need to ensure that others could see your model and findings and replicate your study or feed it into their own – build on it, develop it and generalise from it.

3 **Reliability** – reliability relates to how well you have carried out you research. It is considered reliable if another researcher carrying out the same research activities with the same kind of group would be likely to replicate your findings – although their findings need not be identical.

4 **Validity** – this is absolutely central to the whole issue of the cohesion in your work between conceptual framework methods, questions and findings. If your methods, approaches and techniques really fit with and measure the issues you have been researching then the findings are likely to be valid. If you have used inappropriate methods you are likely to find they are less valid or totally invalid. For example, if you wished to chart behaviour and change in a volatile situation, it would be very inappropriate to do so with documentary analysis of some legal documents only loosely connected to the change, and then make a huge leap from these to statements about the change. Similarly, it would be inappropriate to rely on a poorly developed questionnaire which asks single 'yes' or 'no' answers to decide complex and changing patterns of emotional response. Some of these more sensitive, human-orientated issues need capturing through a mixture of qualitative and quantitative data vehicles or through qualitative analysis, in context.

Task

Look at the jigsaw diagram of these four elements of research conclusions and findings below. Can you briefly note responses about *your* research in each of the parts of the jigsaw? How is *your* research valid, reliable, generalisable, significant? Provide a brief defence and some information. You are likely to find this very helpful in writing up, and in defending your thesis.

(Diagram – complete the jigsaw of these four elements)

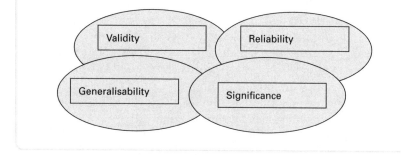

Write up your findings – indicating what your findings and evidence show and mean.

You now have an idea of how significant, generalisable and important your findings could be and need to share these with your readers and examiners. Writing up is covered in the following chapters, but it is important at this stage to consider how you are going to organise your findings and evidence in order to be able to share it in a coherent fashion, and share your enthusiasm for it too!

Task

Looking back now at what your findings have been so far, can you address these categories and see what kind of points you could make? Each category is followed by a prompt in italics.

- Link your findings together and show how they flow from the research questions. Indicate how your findings relate to the research questions – do ensure that your findings enable you to provide satisfactory answers to your questions and to engage with the questions. Indicate why some elements of the answers are satisfactory and others thwarted. *Are your findings linked to your questions? Do the findings provide satisfactory answers? If so, why, and if not, why not?*

- Ensure that your findings can be related back to your methods and your conceptual framework. *Make a brief argument about the coherence and link between your findings and the conceptual framework overall and questions of methodology/methods...*
- Explain how your findings exceed (carry on further) the research of others and can be carried on even further by others carrying out similar research activities later. *How does what you have found fit in with others' work? What else could other researchers take forward in relation to your work/areas to be developed?*
- Do not make unsubstantiated assertions and do illustrate and 'prove' all your assertions with reference to your findings. *What assertions can you make? Make a couple and indicate in note form which bits of data and findings you would use to prove them.*
- Acknowledge weaknesses in your findings and acknowledge ways in which the context, and so on, could have limited the findings in terms of reliability, scope and so on. *What are the limitations and weaknesses in your research? Why?*
- Make appropriate assertions of the importance and significance of what you have found. *Why is what you have found through your research important as a contribution to knowledge? And in furtherance of the field? And to other people?*

Answers to these questions about how your findings flow from your questions, and the *scope* of your research and its significance will all feed into (a) your claims in the *Abstract* for your thesis or dissertation and, (b) your conclusions which emphasise the significance of your work and its contribution to the field of knowledge.

Conclusion

We have looked at:

- Some essential issues and questions in analysing your quantitative and qualitative data
- How you might pull together and defend your findings
- How to justify the importance of your findings in your research

Further reading

Bell, J. (1993) *Doing your Research Project*. Buckingham: Open University Press.

Blaxter, L., Hughes, C., & Tight, M. (1993) *How to Research*. Buckingham: Open University Press.

Denscombe, M. (1998) *The Good Research Guide*. Buckingham: Open University Press.

Miles, M., & Huberman, M. (1994) *Qualitative Data Analysis*. London: Sage.

Robson, Colin (1993) *Real World Research*. Oxford: Blackwell.

Wisker, G., Tiley, J., Watkins, M., Waller, S., Maclaughlin, J., Thomas, J., & Wisker, A. (eds.) (2000) Discipline based research into student learning in English, Law, Social Work, Computer Skills for Linguists, Women's Studies, Creative Writing: how can it inform our teaching? In C. Rust (ed.), *Improving Student Learning Through the Disciplines*, pp. 377–97. Oxford: Oxford Brookes University.

22 Writing Transfer Documents and Progress Reports for EdD, MPhil and PhD Theses

This chapter looks at:

- Writing transfer documents for a move from MPhil to PhD
- Writing progress reports for EdD, MPhil and PhD
- Future developments and time scales
- The differences between EdD, MPhil and PhD

If you are undertaking an MPhil or a PhD you will probably be expected to provide a programme report on your progress, and usually you will need to write this after one year's study, if not more regularly. Students on EdD or professional, probably educational doctorates are expected to provide a series of progress reports, culminating in a long one at the point of transfer to the second stage of the EdD, the writing of the actual final thesis. MA students tend to deliver oral reports on their progress.

This chapter describes a fairly large progress report undertaking which suits MPhil transfer, universities which require large reports to confirm candidature, and the final longer report for the EdD At your own university, you might only be asked for a one-page summary, so do check on the breadth and scope of what is expected of you. EdD study is very structured and varies between universities, but the example of that of the Open University (UK) below can serve as illustration.

▶ The Open University (OU) EdD

For the Open University (UK) EdD, part A comprises an MA-level study which potentially provides the appropriate level qualification for entry to Part B, as it does for entry to many PhD studies at other universities. A research proposal forms part of this entry to Part B, as does entry to a PhD or MPhil in other universities. Part B comprises two stages: in **stage 1** the assessment is a series of shorter, then longer progress reports, four in all, the first three at 3000–4000 words, the fourth at 12000–15000 words, a draft of which forms the **stage 1** final report. In **stage 2 year one** there are three progress reports of 4000–5000 words. Two in **year two** are of the same length and the tenth progress report at the end of **stage 2** is a final dissertation, the major assessment for stage 2, at 40000–50000 words. This is comparable to the final thesis in a PhD Note, however, that this chapter can help you to determine the structure of your progress reports throughout your EdD study, while further chapters will be more suitable for the final stage year two, stage 2 dissertation for the OU EdD and any final thesis for other universities' EdD programmes.

This chapter looks at progress reports, and also looks at transfer documents. Transfer documents tend to contain the same elements as progress reports, but, for those registered on an MPhil who wish to transfer to a PhD, they crucially act as proof or documentary evidence that you have been carrying out doctoral research. The reasons for each document remain basically the same, however, to report on progress to date, noting how far you have worked towards and achieved some of the underlying aims, answered the questions, and conducted the research, and met and dealt with problems of the research you have been undertaking. In the case of an oral report or a progress/transfer document backed up by discussion with a supervisor or peer session, you will need to take full note of the feedback given to you about developing your work further. The discussions below should help you to compile your report, whatever length or format are required.

The following areas of progress reports and transfer documents are covered:

- Reasons for transfer documents
- Reasons for progress reports
- Where do they fit in the development of the higher degree thesis?

- What should be reported and explored, and what should be evidenced and planned in a transfer document or a progress report?
- Transfer document and progress report stages
- Models
- Submitting transfer documents and progress reports – the process, including referees and university research degree committees.

It is common practice in UK universities to expect:

- students registered for an **MPhil with the aim of transfer to a PhD** to complete and submit a transfer document to the research degrees committee, or equivalent, approximately one year after being registered for the research
- students registered for a **PhD** to complete and submit a progress report document to the research degrees committee, or equivalent, approximately one year after being registered for the research
- students registered for the **EdD** to complete several shorter, then longer progress reports during their three years of study, which then lead into the final dissertation.

The main aims of a transfer document or progress report are to ensure:

- that good progress has been made on the research
- that the scope and range of the research have been appropriately shaped
- that the work carried out to date is organised and has achieved some of the planned stages
- the work to date can be summed up
- that where refocusing, extending or cutting back, reshaping the topic and its objects of study, changing or developing further the necessary methods, this is recognised, understood, explained and planned for in the future work
- that the research student now focuses on the rest of their PhD research and effectively plans ahead to its completion.

The transfer document or progress report provides an excellent opportunity for taking stock of work to date and for the future. In it the researcher can sum up their work to date, put a shape to it, and indicate what plans they have for the future to complete their research and to write up their thesis.

▶ Transfer to a PhD

In the past, many university postgraduate research students have registered for an MPhil with the possibility of transfer to a PhD and have usually exercised that option, making the transfer when they had completed enough work of the right quality to argue the case for a PhD level of work. Your supervisors will advise you on your readiness for transfer. When your supervisors are convinced that you are working at PhD level, an application to transfer can be submitted to the appropriate research degrees committee. The arrangements for the transfer of a candidate's registration from Master's to Doctor will appear in the university's information on research degrees.

Let us look at the similarities between transfer documents and progress reports, both of which enable you to take stock of work so far, write it up, refocus if necessary, plan ahead, and negotiate all of this with your supervisors. The supervisors then advise you to submit your work to the research degrees committee, and gain the support and agreement that you can proceed with your research as designed and defined in your transfer document/progress report in relation to your original PhD proposal.

If you do not have to write a transfer document, you will certainly have to produce progress reports, as everyone registered for postgraduate degrees normally has to do this. Let us look first at progress reports. Below is a typical progress report outline for a PhD, and probably also for an EdD (though these are of varying lengths for EdD (see above). Note also that length requirements for all progress reports vary from university to university, so do check the details).

▶ Progress reports

With your supervisors' guidance you should produce a progress report (of 3000–6000 words) consisting of:

- a critical review of the research so far
- a statement of intended further work for the PhD programme, including details of the original contribution to knowledge. Once the progress report, *plus an ABSTRACT of not more than 500 words* are agreed by your supervisory team, you can apply to the appro-

priate research committee to transfer to the PhD by completing the appropriate form.

- The supervisory team must sign the form (giving the reasons why you are ready to transfer to the PhD). The *abstract* of the progress report must be included as part of the application.
- As before, details (name, address and telephone number) of an independent academic who is willing to complete a specialist report on the application must be provided with the application, which must be submitted *at least five weeks* before the appropriate committee meeting. The secretary of the research committee will send the external referee a copy of the application form, including the main progress report.

(adapted from Anglia Polytechnic University documentation)

Some universities provide for an alternative way of indicating the scope and success of your work to date, through submission of actual completed work and parts of the PhD (see below).

As an exception, you may submit a minimum of two completed chapters of your proposed thesis in lieu of a progress report. One chapter should deal with theoretical foundations upon which the research is based; the other may either be a chapter on either the methodology or the fieldwork.

▶ Transfer to a PhD

- Transfer to a PhD provides a vital opportunity to receive constructive feedback on the research project and the plans to progress to PhD It is the responsibility of supervisors to recommend independent referees who can provide specialist advice on the application to transfer and the viability of the proposed research.
- Your director of studies (or second supervisor) will be invited to attend the Research Degrees Committee meeting to discuss your application. A member of the committee will act as the 'designated reader' to open the discussion. All members of the committee will have received copies of the application (but not the full progress report), plus the assessor's report.
- If appropriate, the Research Degrees Committee will normally recommend approval of the transfer proposal. You will receive written notification of the outcome. In some cases, approval may be conditional on submission of additional material or, in certain

instances, the committee may decide that a revised application must be submitted in your best interests.

(adapted from Anglia Polytechnic University documentation)

▶ Transfer criteria

It is most important that you discuss with your supervisory team the criteria used in your discipline to determine whether research is of a doctoral standard. Some evidence of the following is normally required:

- originality and/or creativity
- the exercise of independent critical powers
- a significant contribution to subject knowledge in the research field
- training in research techniques and methodology.

In particular, for a transfer application to be approved, a convincing case (with evidence) must be made that you have:

- chosen an appropriate doctoral research topic of sufficient scope
- gained satisfactory knowledge of the background literature and are able to relate the project to existing scholarship and research in the field
- started to work at a PhD level, especially in terms of theoretical insights and conceptual frameworks
- planned a suitable research programme to achieve a successful doctoral conclusion.

You should also have reviewed the proposed doctoral programme in accordance with the ethical, legal and safety requirements set out by the university.

▶ How to refocus and concentrate on scoping ready for writing your transfer document or progress report

At this stage, the focus and scope of the research possibly might be cut back realistically, extended or reshaped.

An extension might include another sample, another questionnaire, the addition of a focus group, adding interviews with individuals, considering the necessity of looking further into a different but related appropriate field of study, and so on.

More probably, you will be cutting back and reshaping. This is a time to look critically at the research to see whether some of the work is possibly too ambitious or a little redundant – for example, too many questionnaires and tests planned on too many children. Often, then, at the *transfer document* or *progress report* stage the research becomes more restricted and more clearly focused and defined.

This is a key moment in the development of your own work at postgraduate level. Certainly, taking time at this point to focus on what progress has been made and the scope of the research will help you in particular, and also your supervisor, to:

- take stock
- check progress
- evaluate your work so far
- pull your work together
- see where it has been going
- see what has been achieved
- see what is still to be achieved
- see what has been successful
- see what has been unsuccessful
- see what needs to be dropped
- see what needs to be extended
- see what needs to be refocused.

Most of all, it is a way of capturing in a fully organised form what has been achieved to date and what is to be done in the future.

Transfer documents and progress reports have very much the same structure and aims. But for the transfer document, where it is used, there is a very definite sense of reapplying now for a higher level of postgraduate award, and so this is a formal resubmission moment.

▶ Transfer documents

In the case of the transfer document, this is a critical moment.

Referees are asked to comment on:

- the suitability of the candidate for transfer to a PhD
- the research progress achieved so far
- the planned work for the PhD programme
- other factors to bring to the attention of the Research Degrees Committee, including guidance for strengthening the proposal.

▶ Transfer documents and progress reports – some questions to ask yourself about achievement so far

Task

Consider:

- Looking back over the original proposal, how far have you achieved the overall aims and outcomes so far?
- What has been your research process – what have you done?
- What have you discovered so far from the literature in the subject that is feeding into the research?

Also:

- Indicate the literature themes.
- Summarise your literature review chapter, and particularly indicate how this has fed into your research planning and activities and has helped you to contextualise your results to date.
- What elements of the research activities have you carried out?
- What methods have you used?
- How appropriate and successful (or otherwise) have they been in
  - defining the field?
  - collecting the right kind of information?
- What have you found out regarding outcomes and findings so far?
- Have there been any surprises, problems or blocks to the research?
- Have you had to refocus your research, cut it back or extend it?
- What new avenues of thought and focus have you followed because of what you have found out to date?
- Why is this a PhD?
- Provide justification for the award. Look at the definitions of what constitutes an MPhil or a PhD.

Then think of the following issues and jot down a short explanation or defence in relation to each.

In particular, for a **transfer** application to be approved, a convincing case (with evidence) must be made that you have:

- chosen an appropriate doctoral research topic of sufficient scope
- gained a satisfactory knowledge of the background literature and are able to relate the project to existing scholarship and research in the field
- started to work at a PhD level, especially in terms of theoretical insights and conceptual frameworks
- planned a suitable research programme to achieve a successful doctoral conclusion
- reviewed the proposed doctoral programme in accordance with the ethical, legal and safety requirements set out by the university.

In general you need to think of the contribution your work has made to the field, and what you intend to do next. So you need to ask yourself:

- What has your postgraduate research and writing up to date to do with 'originality'?
- What progress have you made towards achieving important outcomes?
- What are the critical ideas and information with which your research is providing the field/subject areas/discipline?
- What is the important work still to be done which will make your PhD a major contribution to the field of study?
- Where do you now think the research is going?

▶ Plan – suggesting future developments and time scales

Once you have completed your progress report or transfer document, you will need to take stock of future work. For the EdD, the future work for the immediate future is the next progress report leading up to the final long report. For a PhD you will be thinking of that long final piece of work now and will need to replan and scrutinise your time scales and decide what is realistic, what new activities need planning in, and what parts of the original research plan can be carried out and when. You also need to decide what parts are unrealistic and where work has taken another direction due to interim findings, a change of sample, or other things which have affected your work since you began.

Task

Provide a detailed plan for the next year/to completion of the PhD/ EdD and discuss the stages of this plan in detail:

- what do you hope to find out about now and to continue finding out about?
- what do you intend to do?
- which methods will you use?
- indicate any need for further extended study, or curtailing of the study
- indicate the need for refocusing because of any problems and contradictions or new lines of discovery.

Task

Produce a time plan – a critical path analysis – to help you to replan realistically and indicate where your work is going to go in the next year so, to completion. Consider key dates, and key activities such as collecting data, analysing it, writing it up and giving presentations. Think also, as you replan, about what else is happening in your life, what family, friends and work demands could affect your research and so what period of time might be less useful for undisturbed work. Some things you cannot plan in – the unforeseen activities – but you can plan some spare time just in case something goes wrong. Be realistic! Look back at Chapter 8 for an example of a critical path analysis and time plan.

You will probably be expected to submit your time and progress plan along with the full transfer document or progress report, but if not, keep it as a guide for yourself.

▶ MPhil, PhD and EdD scope and differences

When considering transfer from an MPhil to a PhD it is useful to consider the differences in *scope* between the two. It is also useful to consider the differences between progress reports demanded in a PhD study and those in an EdD study:

What is the difference between an MPhil and a PhD thesis?

MPhil and PhD degrees are postgraduate awards gained by undertaking research with the submission of a thesis, normally assessed by an oral examination (viva voce). The PhD degree is the more advanced qualification than the MPhil, requiring a longer period of research and a thesis of greater length. The MPhil degree is an award of a higher degree in its own right.

Other general characteristics normally include the following:

- **MPhil degree:** candidates must submit a substantial thesis (maximum length 40000 words) which shows evidence of instruction in research methods appropriate to the field of study, as well as sound knowledge of scholarship relevant to their particular subject.
- **PhD degree**: candidates must submit a substantial thesis (the university has a maximum word length of 80000 words). It will have the different components of the MPhil, but display research work of greater scope and creativity and make an original contribution to knowledge in the field of study. Originally, the doctorate was seen as the passport into academic life as a university lecturer. While there are now wider career aspirations and other reasons for acquiring a PhD, the doctorate is still often associated with subject authority and the ability to push the frontiers onward and upwards.

(adapted from Anglia Polytechnic University documentation)

Your supervisor should discuss with you what makes a PhD Often students have supervisors (usually one, sometimes two) who are external to the university awarding the degree, and it is important therefore to make sure that your supervisor is entirely familiar with the rules and regulations of the university awarding the degree (these do vary from university to university). You may find it helpful, therefore to ask them to:

- familiarise themselves with the university's regulations on this issue – that is, what constitutes an MPhil or a PhD, the significant differences in level, and so on, between the two (as well as the regulations and codes of other universities, if they are going to be a PhD examiner)
- provide opportunities for you as an MPhil/PhD candidate to examine appropriate completed MPhil/PhD theses (some of these may be available in the library, while others, possibly those closest to your own field of study, can be borrowed on inter-library loan, having first been identified by looking at abstracts of theses)
- discuss the nature of the PhD qualification with your (and other) supervisors, especially the concept of originality, where applicable, and also issues of what constitutes a PhD in your subject area.

What is the difference between an MPhil, a PhD and an EdD?

> The **EdD** is characterised by its professional orientation, its substantial taught element, and its modular structure. The EdD is designed to meet the needs of professionals in education and related areas who are seeking to extend and deepen their knowledge and understanding of contemporary educational issues (hence the significant taught element), to develop appropriate skills in educational research and enquiry, and to carry out original research in order to contribute to professional knowledge and practice. (extract from Open University documentation)

The series of progress reports required for the Open University EdD are matched by a series of long linking essays in other universities. Most EdD studies require a long progress report to ensure a move or transfer into the final stage, where the dissertation or thesis is written. In the EdD, the shorter and longer progress reports form a large part of both the work and the words towards this final dissertation or thesis, even as a progress report would form a part of the final write-up for a PhD thesis. But note that progress report lengths differ for the EdD, and the progress report which enables a transition to the final stage of the EdD (when the final progress report or thesis is written) is likely to be much longer than any progress report required for the PhD (12 000–15 000 words for the Open University EdD progress report, enabling the student to move between stage 1 and stage 2.) For the Open University EdD the *final* 'progress report', no. 10, at the end of the final stage, stage 2 (40 000–50 000 words) is actually *equivalent* to the finished thesis for a PhD student. Do check length requirements carefully with your university, and also check the specific demands of each stage of the work, each kind of essay or progress report.

We have discussed in this chapter the kind of progress report which contains a substantial amount of information about your work to date, your progress along your intended research, as a way of noting methods and findings, and which will contribute to the final thesis by being merged in with later work. It does not describe the kind of free-standing essay common in some EdD programmes.

▶ Presentation issues to bear in mind as you carry on with your work

MPhil, EdD and PhD theses (or the final long progress report/ dissertation stage of the OU and similar EdD) must be the candidate's own work and presented in a satisfactory manner. This involves concentrating on your work throughout, and as you move towards completion, on:

- grammar
- punctuation
- spelling
- clarity of expression
- logical argument
- appropriate language.

It is also important that a thesis has a technical apparatus to support it. This refers to the shape and organisation of the thesis and involves the following:

- abstract
- preface and acknowledgements
- footnotes

- references
- appendices
- statistical tables
- diagrams
- illustrations
- bibliography.

These must be set out according to the conventions of the field of study. There are, for example, different conventions of referencing between literature theses and social science documents which provide layout and referencing guidelines for fields of study, and for that particular university. Look at past theses to see how these are organised and laid out. Check also with your supervisor.

One of the responsibilities of your supervisor is to draw these requirements to your attention and discuss how these can be met.

Particular attention must be given to the writing, editing and correction of the final draft before submission. Check issues of organisation and layout as you write up and submit to your supervisor. When you start to approach completion, check it out with a colleague as well – you could even use a professional proof-reader if that would be helpful. Most word-processing packages include good quality spell checks and even grammar, syntax and punctuation checks. Do use these but do also ensure they are correcting the right things.

Use the writing of progress reports as a way of taking stock, seeing how your research and your writing up are progressing, and ensuring that all you do still fits in with the conceptual framework of your initial proposal.

Conclusion

We have looked at:

- Taking stock
- Transfer documents
- Progress reports

23 Writing Up: Definitions and Qualities of a Good MA, MPhil, EdD and PhD Thesis

This chapter considers the features of successful research dissertations for the MA and theses for the MPhil, PhD and EdD and looks at how you can turn your work into a successful thesis of merit. It concentrates on definitions and important elements of a successful thesis and dissertation and contains advice on organisation, layout, editing and submission.

This chapter looks at:

- *The Master's dissertation and quality*
- *The EdD, Master's and doctorate levels*
- *The definitions of a good dissertation and thesis (positive features)*
- *The coherence and structure of the thesis*
- *The presentation – your reader*
- *The shape of the thesis, writing an abstract and other elements*
- *'Telling the story' – relating back to the proposal and ensuring coherence throughout*
- *Ensuring a conceptual framework underpins and runs throughout all you do*
- *Organising, explaining and rewriting*

▶ The Master's dissertation or thesis

Both taught Master's and Master's by research require a dissertation or thesis. The differences lie in the length, breadth, depth and scope of the work being constructed and presented. For a taught Master's, coursework will comprise a large and regular form of the assessment, with possibly the equivalent of one 5000-word essay/report/video and an analytical/critical write-up each semester, or each 30-credit module. Usually there is also a dissertation or thesis which can be of 30 or 60 credits in length and would normally be substantial – perhaps 20 000 words for a 60-credit dissertation and half that for a 30-credit one. Every scheme has its own rules, so you would be well advised at this stage to look back at the rules on length and layout, and the house style in terms of presentation, references, diagrams, bibliographies and appendices. Issues such as how much of your quoted material counts in the word count really matter if you are about to produce a work which may go over length. Issues about the quality of diagrams matter if you have limited access to technology and are relying on hand drawing or photocopying.

You might also need to recruit help from friends at this late stage if there is an overwhelming amount of work to be done. I hand drew dozens of graphs for a scientist friend in the late 1970s and in the early 1980s another friend typed up my bibliography from index cards on the eve of the printer shutting for Christmas, with an early January deadline. Later still, another thesis found two of us photocopying in a north London shop which hires out weird novelty costumes (the nearest photocopier), to get the work in on time. Checking the details of presentation as well as those of timing and submission can save you such awkward moments.

Quality in Master's work

The diversity of Master's programmes means that there are some difficulties in defining what a high-quality Master's award would comprise. While a more academic Master's course would demand research, creative output and independent study, a professional Master's, which sought to upgrade in a different or more practical area of the subject, would be more likely to seek a useful, practical, well-structured project or product from the Master's. One key issue is that the examiners of Master's programmes should recognise both the kind of Master's programme they are, and therefore what constitutes quality at the different ends of the continuum and all points in between.

▶ The EdD

The EdD or doctorate in education is an increasingly popular route for education practitioners to gain a doctorate and it is generally characterised by its professional orientation, its substantial taught elements and its modular structure.

To undertake the EdD, you will first have completed the Open University's taught MA in Education (or similar) which acts as **part A** of the EdD and comprises four taught modules.

Part B is the doctoral level work, and lasts for two years:

Stage One – literature reviews and progress reports (1 year, 60 points).
Stage Two – dissertation (2 years, 120 points).

The EdD is credit rated and the shape of any specific EdD on which you are studying will vary. For example, in the Open University this is 50 000 words, and it builds on a number of progress reports, each between 3000 and 15 000 words long.

Your writing of the progress reports can be guided by the comments in Chapter 22, while the final dissertation can be guided by comments on MPhil and PhD theses in this chapter.

▶ Definitions of a good dissertation or thesis

Task

Consider:

- What makes a good and successful Master's dissertation or thesis?
- What makes a good MPhil thesis?
- What makes a good PhD thesis?
- What makes a good EdD thesis?

▶ Positive features towards which you can aim and advice on how to get there

Master's or doctorate – levels

Winter (1993) bases his definitions of doctorate-level work on statements produced by staff working with a variety of students on research by thesis or taught by coursework in professional areas and in the more interdisciplinary areas. Winter's definitions of doctorate-level work builds developmentally upon Master's level work, so do look at his definitions of Master's work and then at the differences between this and doctoral-level work. This will help you make your case for the doctoral level of your own work. Critical reflectiveness is a key element in defining a Master's course outcome. Winter defines a Master's as having the following criteria:

- a balance is maintained between original and secondary material
- methodology and data analysis are clearly separated
- different investigative paradigms and their methodologies are understood
- it includes a critical self-appraisal of existing practices/beliefs
- it reaches a synthesis based on creative connections between different aspects of a problem/topic
- it is committed to/engaged with a project/discipline/body of reading ... set alongside theoretical and ethical grounding.

All of these elements of quality will also be found in an MPhil or PhD thesis, but in Winter's accumulative model, there are also some extra, deeper and more complex outcomes which help define the higher level of the work.

Task

Look through the different categories of achievement and quality necessary in a Master's or MPhil/PhD and ask yourself the questions about relevance to your own work and thesis at MPhil, EdD or PhD level.

- Does your work have these positive qualities? If so, where could you prove/show they exist?
- If not, could you write up your thesis to ensure that these qualities do exist within it?

Winter (2000: 15–19)

▶ Positive features of postgraduate work and additional elements present in a successful MPhil and PhD The same elements will be present in an EdD

Section 1: Positive features
Intellectual grasp

- grasps the scope and possibilities of the topic
- shows diligence and rigour in procedures – catholic and multifactoral approaches to problems
- shows readiness to examine apparently tangential areas for possible relevance
- grasps the wider significance of the topic – how the analysis is related to its methodological and epistemological context
- shows iterative development, allowing exploration and rejection of alternatives
- possesses an internal dialogue – plurality of approach/method, to validate the one chosen
- a broad theoretical base is treated critically
- demonstrates a coherent and explicit theoretical approach, fully thought through and critically applied – that is, noting its limitations
- gives a systematic account of the topic, including a review of all plausible possible interpretations
- demonstrates full mastery of the topic, that is, that the candidate is now an expert in the field
- indicates the future development of the work
- maintains clear and continuous links between theory, method and interpretation
- presents a reflexive, self-critical account of relationships involved in the inquiry and of the methodology
- connects theory and practice
- displays rigour.

Question
Check your thesis against these criteria and ask the general summary questions of it:

- In what way does your developing thesis show coherence, rigour and reflective self-critical elements?

- How far does it connect theory and practice?
- How far does it indicate possible future work?
- How and where does it show mastery of the subject?
- How coherent is the argument, use of information, analyses, ideas, and so on?
- How far does it incorporate awareness of alternative arguments, incorporate and deal with alternatives?

Coherence

- displays coherence of structure (for example, the conclusions follow clearly from the data)
- skilfully organises a number of different angles (required by the extended length of the work)
- is cogently organised and expressed
- possesses a definite agenda and an explicit structure
- presents a sense of the researcher's learning as a journey, as a structured, incremental progress through a process of both argument and discovery.

Question
How far does your developing thesis show explicit structure, organisation and coherence and present a sense of your learning as a journey – that is, structured and directed development?

Engagement with the literature
- displays comprehensive coverage of the field/secure command of the literature in the field
- shows breadth of contextual knowledge in the discipline
- successfully critiques established positions
- engages critically with other significant work in the field
- draws on literature with a focus different from the viewpoint pursued in the thesis
- maintains a balance between delineating an area of debate and advocating a particular approach
- includes scholarly notes, a comprehensive bibliography and accurately uses academic conventions in citations.

Question
How far does your developing thesis:

- show a comprehensive coverage of the field?
- show an ability to criticise, engage critically, debate, and advocate a scholarly approach?
- show awareness of other approaches?
- use bibliographies, citations, and so on, as appropriate?

Grasp of methodology

- the methodology is clearly established and applied
- the methodological analysis indicates the advantages *and* the disadvantages of the approach adopted
- uses several methodologies for triangulation.

Question

- Does the methodology show itself to be clearly defined and aware of alternatives?
- Is it triangulated for greater quality assurance?

Presentation

- the thesis is clear, easy to read and is presented in an appropriate style
- it contains few errors of expression
- it displays flawless literacy.

Question
How far can you say that is a well-presented thesis in terms of its articulation, literacy and expression?

Section 2: Originality and publishability
These two terms are often used as the fundamental 'criteria' for a PhD This section attempts to give more guidance on how to interpret them. An MPhil might have less emphasis on these elements.

Originality
- pushes the topic into new areas, beyond its obvious focus
- makes an original contribution to knowledge or understanding of the subject, in terms of topic area, method, experimental design, theoretical synthesis or engagement with conceptual issues

- solves some significant problem or gathers original data
- reframes issues
- is imaginative in its approach to problems
- is creative yet rigorous
- goes beyond its sources to create a new position which critiques existing theoretical positions
- uses the empirical study to enlarge the theoretical understanding of the subject
- contains innovation, speculation, imaginative reconstruction and cognitive excitement – the author has clearly wrestled with the method and tried to shape it to gain new insights
- is comprehensive in its theoretical linkages *or* makes novel connections between areas of knowledge
- opens up neglected areas or takes a new viewpoint on an old problem
- something new must have been learned and demonstrated, such that the reader is made to rethink a stance or opinion
- shows 'a spark of inspiration as well as perspiration'
- shows development towards independent research and innovation
- is innovative in content and adventurous in method, obviously at the leading edge in its particular field, with potential for yielding new knowledge
- makes a personal synthesis of an interpretative framework
- shows depth and breadth of scholarship, synthesising previous work and adding original insights/models/concepts
- argues against conventional views, presents new frameworks for interpreting the world
- applies established techniques to novel patterns, or devises new techniques which allow new questions to be addressed.

Questions

Consider all the categories above generally and ask yourself in brief to what extent:

- your thesis is creative and original?
- it provides a personal argument?
- it applies established technique to new areas and problems?
- it adds something well planned and coherent but original and creative?

Publishability

- demonstrates publishable quality or potential for publication
- publishable in a refereed journal with a good scholarly reputation
- written with an awareness of the audience for the work
- stylishly and economically written.

Questions

- How publishable is your thesis?
- Is it stylish?
- Is it directed appropriately at a chosen audience?
- Does it read fluently?

A thesis of merit will have all these aspects, or most of them, that is, publishability, coherence, sound methodology and a good grasp of the literature it engages with. It will possess originality and a sound intellectual grasp of the issues, the reading, the concepts and an original contribution to the fundamental and important arguments within the area.

▶ Writing up

The writing-up process should be started as early a possible – you can always revise, develop and change, but trying to capture several years' worth of thoughts, analysis and processes all at once is too daunting a task for many students. In the past, this has led to non-completion – you have been warned! The importance of writing up your research from the start is very important. Another reason to continue to write about what you are doing is that it keeps up the writing momentum. If you leave it all until the end the task is overwhelmingly daunting. Some people find it very difficult to commit thoughts and comments to paper because this seems like a finished statement. Think of it as a draft, think of it as working out your thoughts and experiences and research more clearly by having to articulate them through the writing – it is an aid to a final write-up. Trick yourself into writing parts you feel you can handle first, and writing what you do perhaps in the form of a journal, so that there is a lot of written work before you start to formalise it into the shape of the thesis itself. These tricks should help you to clear up your thoughts by articulating them in writing, and overcome writer's block by having some elements written up as you go along.

If you look back at your research proposal you should be able to consider how far you are filling out the contents which you outlined in your contents page at the beginning. Perhaps the thesis has changed shape to some extent, and you need to acknowledge this. Your initial research 'map' laid out questions, the conceptual framework, methods, and so on, and now as you approach writing up you will need to fill out each of these sections, and write up the analysis into findings. As you start to write up and as you go along, compile 'to do' lists reminding you of what you need to write next. Leave 'pick-up points' (Nightingale 1992, in Zuber Skerritt 1992: 115) – some memos in your writing to indicate how and where you left off and what needs to come next. These tricks all help you to structure, signpost, and maintain the flow in the sections you are writing up. See if you can visualise these as a whole when written as a coherent piece. There are several tasks involved in the writing.

▶ Coherence and the structure of the thesis

The thesis needs to be coherent overall – underpinning/driving questions need to be explicit and need to inform the exploration/investigation/examination that is the research. They need to be contextualised in terms of the field and in the theories that inform, underpin and drive the set of questions and the area of investigation. The research methodologies and methods need to flow obviously from the questions, the reading and the theories as the clearest (defined) ways of investigating and asking the questions. Then the findings need to be discussed, figures, graphs and tables should be integrated into the discussion, explored and explained, analysed and contribute to the overall argument. Finally, conclusions need to reiterate the introduction or produce the thesis in short, and round off and clarify the effects and the importance of what has been found, what it means, why it matters and what might be done with it. At this stage in the writing up the level of the research should be clear – the justification for the award emerges from the coherence of the work, the importance of the questions, and the significance of the findings as finally tied together and made explicit in the conclusion.

Structurally there needs to be a logical flow of information and argument between the different sections of chapters and between the chapters themselves, and tables, figures and graphs need to fit comfortably with the text. They should be explored and explained rather than left to stand alone or laboriously described – use them to drive the argument and illustrate the points you make.

Headings and subheadings should indicate the significance and linking of different key parts of the chapters, so that a reader can see how the headings relate to each other and follow a flow between items or sections.

Avoid 'fog', or excessive complex language, when more straight-forward and accessible language would suffice. This is *not* to deny the importance of technical terms – they do, after all, usually put an idea, concept or point in exactly the right form for the subject area. However, avoid unnecessary jargon, which is there for its own sake, and avoid unnecessarily confusing language – think of your reader!

Check on grammar and spelling using the facilities on your word processor, but do check yourself as well, because word processors make mistakes and don't understand what you are saying in context. Some amusing errors (such as 'urinal' for 'journal'!) might be less amusing in the middle of a highly intellectual discussion in your thesis. There is nothing to be gained by confusing your reader or writing in such an elevated way to impress that no one can really work out what you are saying.

▶ Use of the first person

Many readers fear writing as 'I' or 'we', and you need to check the norms and conventions of your university and your subject in your choices. But there is a great difference between using 'I' when you are just asserting an opinion and using 'I' when you are recording the research you have actually carried out. 'I interviewed three people in order to discover . . .' 'we carried out a series of surveys of . . .' are much better than, for example, 'a series of surveys were carried out to discover . . .', which sounds a little distanced from the actual experi-ence, not as active (it is in the passive form), and rather formal. It gives the impression that the words have been written by an unseen third person who observes and knows all. If you feel uneasy about writing in the first person, then remember that feminist researchers often argue that the subject (you – the self) needs to be replaced in experience, which is recorded. So the first person is a sound device for this, and certainly if you are using yourself as a case study in your own work, or researching your own creative or performative work in relation to theory, it would be absurd to hide this with a third-person record.

▶ Presentation

Ensure the pages are numbered, check the visual layout so you don't have headings appearing at the bottom of some pages, and very carefully check all your referencing, being consistent throughout. Get a trusted colleague or friend to proof the whole thing – we often do not see our own mistakes when we are too close to the writing.

▶ Thinking of your reader – the shape of the thesis

A thesis ideally represents an interaction and communication between you, your work, the field, and your reader(s). You need to explore:

Researcher/writer focus
⇓
What you set about to do
How and why you did it
What you did
What your results were
What the results mean in theory, what the results mean in practice
How other readers might link with and benefit from these results and findings
What they might want to go on and do further or with your results
⇑
Reader focus

Robert Brown (in Zuber Skerritt 1992) suggests that research students tend to write in a 'suspense' format and need to think instead of a journalist or report writer format. In the suspense format, the thesis would start with a title, abstract, introduction, literature, research, methods, results and discussion, so leaving its finding, its importance and revelations to the end.

Actually, for the benefit of the reader, a different format might be preferable. In a chapter at the outset, outline what the major arguments and findings are and why they matter, and craft and build the elements of the thesis to highlight and relate to these main points. What are the key benefits and points of each chapter? And of the thesis as a whole? Brown talks about the 'journalist's pyramid' where a good journalist knows they must capture and retain the interest of their readers, so they put the main point first, followed by the next most important point, and so on, down. The reader is captivated by the main point and moves on to see what research methods and activities helped to produce it, but when they open the chapter they need to see immediately what it is about, what its punchline is, and the explanation of the key points. Actually, good report writing does this, since it starts by explaining who asked for the report and what it solves, what kind of problem or what kind of questions are being asked, and why they matter. Methods to ask the questions and interrogate the situation follow, and the summary and conclusion indicate what has been discovered. Any recommendations follow from that.

When you have looked through your thesis and seen whether or not and where it does fulfil these expectations, you can prepare a defence of its sound elements ready for the viva. Alternatively and additionally, you can look at some of its weaknesses and work on them. Make it more coherent, with linking paragraphs, and pointing out what seems obvious to you but less so to a reader. Ensure that you have emphasised the original contribution and what and how it contributes to the concepts, arguments and knowledge of the subject area. Make a case for your thesis and its contribution to the area of knowledge, skills, and so on. If you find that there are areas of weakness such as coherence, originality or presentation quality, plan out how to tackle these now and work on the weaknesses so that you end up with a good thesis that makes an original contribution.

Shape of the thesis

You might find it useful to look back over earlier advice about the shape of a thesis and see if yours is a variation on this or if anything is missing, if it is too short, too long, and so on. Consider this and if you can, discuss it with your colleagues or a friend.

▶ Elements of the structure of the thesis explained and variants discussed

The shape applies to the MA, MPhil and PhD – only the lengths will vary, so do be sure to check these out with your university and supervisor.

Do be aware that, if you are undertaking an arts or humanities dissertation/thesis, there are differences in their overall construction and structure. Look back at Chapter 17 for a more detailed discussion of why this is the case and of the actual structure. See below for comment elements, that is, title abstract, introduction, main body of the chapters, conclusion, references, bibliography, and so on.

Title

This should appear on a separate title page. Try to keep it to one or two lines and make it clear, suggesting the questions you are posing and assertions you are making, rather than just the field of study.

Look at the example of an abstract below. Can you spot its qualities?

Abstract

This is usually about 500 words. It answers the questions, 'What is this thesis about?' 'What does it argue, prove, contend?' and so on. Use the third person and passive verbs, that is, 'It is argued that . . . in discussing . . . using . . . evidence is presented which suggests that. . . .'

At the writing-up stage, the abstract is a very important part of your work. By offering a clear, coherent summary of the aims, developments, route and findings of the thesis, the abstract gives the reader, the examiner, your supervisor and yourself a clear idea of the plans, decisions and achievements of your research.

Note how it states the aim, focus and the field of study. It establishes a clear conceptual framework. It also states briefly what the major findings and contributions have been to date.

Task

Example of an abstract:
Look this through and consider how it addresses the following areas:

- what the writer is/was aiming for
- what their research questions are/were
- how their methods and research activities flow from the questions
- how their findings follow from the research activities
- how the different parts of the dissertation/thesis represent and argue through this learning 'journey'
- making the case for discoveries and the importance of findings, major points, what could be done with the findings/how the research contributes to knowledge and in the subject field.

Abstract

Recognising and overcoming dissonance in postgraduate student research

Action research conducted with Israeli and UK postgraduate students 1997–2001 indicates that dissonance in approaches to research as learning produces potentially significant difficulties for students at different stages in their work. These difficulties emerge principally when developing a proposal, deciding on research methodologies and methods, undertaking the research, and maintaining the links between findings, analysis and conclusions, specifically those which aim to lead to transformation. This research into postgraduate learning is grounded in well-established theories of how student approaches to learning affect learning outcomes (Entwistle and Ramsden 1983, Biggs 1993). Including how students' concepts of what learning is – what are their perceptions of learning in scientific subject areas, how they go about their learning, how they know when learning has taken place, their outcomes and their motivation, affect the quality and kind of learning (Dahlgren and Marton 1978, Meyer and Shanahan, 1999). Significantly, research into postgraduate learning is a relatively new field of exploration and yields interesting information related to levels of learning and movements between these levels. Inflections on learning relate to students' origins, particularly the experiences of international students whose 'tertiary literacy' could prove an issue in articulating and engaging in debate with complex concepts at postgraduate level (Marton, Dall'alba and Beaty 1993, Todd 1997, Meyer and Kiley 1998).

Quantitative and qualitative research vehicles (Entwistle and Entwistle 1992) have been employed in an action research format. The Reflections on Learning Inventory (Meyer and Boulton Lewis 1997) enables data to be gathered relating to students' conceptions of learning, knowing the learning has occurred, learning approaches, motivation and outcomes. The Research as Learning questionnaire (Wisker 1998 – analysed using SPSS) specifically designed for this research enables information to be gathered about students' perceptions of what research is as learning and how their own research operates as learning (seeing it as creative learning, cause and effect, finding out known facts, problem solving, and so on). Focus groups and workshop activities (taped, transcribed and analysed using NVivo) engage students as aware, reflective participants concentrating on the stages of their research and learning, and links between approaches to research as learning and outcomes. Supervisory dialogues (taped, transcribed and analysed used Nvivo) indicate different kinds of supervisor interactions which do or do not enable, empower and direct students, as appropriate, to continue with their research in effective and potentially successful ways.

The action research format enables the postgraduate students to be fully involved in shaping the research, and reflecting on the implications for their own learning and research development of the research

Continued

findings. For the researcher and colleagues working with postgraduate students, it enables a direct focus on the usefulness and success of research development and support programmes, and the appropriate forms of supervisory dialogues.

Findings have indicated that student research-as-learning approaches can lead to dissonance, particularly (i) those taking accumulation approaches (acquiring numbers of facts) while seeking transformational outcomes and (ii) those who take negative and postmodern approaches (seeing *everything* as relative and relevant). These approaches are at odds with the development of a cohesive focus and coherent, managed research. Other elements of dissonance have emerged in student/supervisor interactions when dialogues occur which *disable* students from writing their work and proceeding clearly with it in different stages. They also exist between the work carried out and findings developed in the context of the overall conceptual framework of the research itself. This can emerge when clear developmental links between the conceptual framework (the questions, theoretical background, underpinning methodology, methods, findings, and so on) and the conclusions made from the research are at odds or unclear.

Both development programmes and dialogues are focused on as sources of the research and, in their developmental stages, act as part products of the research findings. The development programme and the supervisory dialogues are being developed as models which, when refined, should help students to overcome the dissonance between approaches and outcomes, and empower them to be more effective and successful in their research, as appropriate.

This thesis details action research carried out with students between 1997 and 2000, and makes a case both for the importance of action research with students to identify, investigate, and deal with dissonance in their approaches to learning and research, and to suggest possible models of developmental programmes and supervisory dialogues which assist in this supportive practice.

- Now you need to produce your own example of an abstract. Remember it must be in the third person, and should detail what was set out to be done and what was achieved, rather than suggest you are about to embark on this journey. It is the first thing a reader reads, and it suggests to them the main areas and claims of your work. It whets their appetite to read more.
- The abstract needs to be able to stand alone, as something to invite a reader into the work. It needs to make a case about the importance of the research and its findings, and how it contributes to the field of knowledge generally.

Preface and acknowledgements

Who do you want to acknowledge and to thank? Who helped you and enabled your work on the thesis and on the research?

Introduction

The introduction:

- lays out the background to the thesis
- briefly describes other work in the area
- outlines general ideas and developments related to it
- moves on to lay down and explore the theoretical bases for the thesis and your work
- contextualises your arguments and findings in background, context and theory
- discusses your research questions and the hypotheses underlying the research
- sets out the main themes and suggests what your work contributes to and develops in relation to these and what your main arguments and contributions are
- usually, the introduction tends to be written last as it provides a coherent introduction to themes, arguments and findings. This is difficult to do until the whole anatomy of the thesis has actually been constructed and flesh put on the bones of each chapter.

Review of the literature

Not all theses have a separate literature review. If your work develops logically and smoothly from the reading you have carried out, and if your research and findings follow on from a coherent body of established work in the field and have established informing theories, you will probably use a literature review at this point. It will establish the theories and arguments and discuss the main debates, research and authors who contribute to the field, contextualising your own work. The literature review is liable to take up much of your introductory chapter as you interweave background reading, theories and critical views.

If, however, you will be moving stage by stage and at different stages need to introduce and develop theories and reading, which is normal, then you might well find several chapters begin with and interweave the literature, theory and arguments. You need to decide which variation on these versions suits your work best. Remember that the literature review or survey is not just a collection of all you have read. You need to weave the reading and main points and arguments made into your own discussion, using it to back up or counteract some of your arguments. If you have found a few main themes developing logically and coherently through your reading, these can help form the basis for your main chapters.

Design of the study and methods

For social science, education and related research, this is as crucial as it is for scientific research. You need to explain why and how you designed your studies, mentioning the pilot stage if there was one, decisions taken about interviews, focus groups, questionnaires, samples, and so on (see Chapter 14).

If your research is more humanities- or literature-based you might well find that you have already described what your research questions are along with your main ideas and arguments. In this case there is no specific study in logical stages, each depending on the data from the ones which have gone before as such, but that, instead, each chapter takes a different theme, critical approach or point of view, or different author or book, and so on.

But note that it is always preferable to interweave literature, texts and authors, rather than plodding through each one individually. Relate them and form your own way through them in relation to your arguments and information.

Presentation of results

This can be a clear, annotated record of what has been discovered in the areas of social sciences, education and health. You are unlikely to have this section in a literature or cultural studies thesis. In this case your 'results' or discoveries and arguments will form part of the discussions in separate chapters.

Discussion of results

For a social science, health or education thesis there is often a logical place for working through different results, putting tables and statistics, bar charts and so on, either in the main text or referring to them in the appendices, and conducting a narrative which explores and brings in different results to develop arguments and present your coherent points and findings.

For a humanities or literature-based thesis and also often for a social sciences, health or education-based thesis, there are often *several chapters* exploring different themes and issues in a linked discussion. The results as such will be your critically informed comments and arguments on the texts, images, your readings, and so on. You might find that the main themes identified in the literature review appear here as main topics in each of your chapters.

Summary
This chapter enables you to sum up your main findings and present an argued case for them, for your original contribution, for the creative element added to the field of study, and so on. In a humanities or literature-based thesis there might well be a more *organic* structure of chapters focusing on different themes and developing issues and authors, and a summary as such is not needed. The summary could also be part of the *conclusion* chapter.

Conclusion
All theses have a conclusion. This establishes the importance of your work, states its contribution clearly and summarises the main points you have made where, when and how. It rounds off your arguments, even if there are still points open for further work and for questioning. At this point – in theses that seek to suggest change or developments, to contribute new ideas and strategies and so cause development and change – there could well be a section for recommendations, as there is in a standard report. If your work does indeed seek change then it is essential that you think throughout the research *how* you are going to make constructive and realistic recommendations based on your findings.

Appendices, statistical tables, illustrations, and so on
These might appear in the main text where the argument using them appears. They may however, all appear in the appendices. Ensure each one is clearly labelled and referenced to where it is used in the thesis. If they are not explained in the body of the thesis, explain them fully here.

References
If you are using footnotes they appear at the foot of each page, and endnotes appear usually at the end of each chapter. Some writers leave all the endnotes to the end of the thesis, collected chapter by chapter at that point and integrated with the references. References can be signalled in the text by a number[1] which leads to the endnote and reference, or by a shortened form of the actual reference. For example, 'Phillips, E. M. and Pugh, D. S. (1994), *How to Get a PhD: A Handbook*

for Students and Their Supervisors (2nd ed., Buckingham: Open University Press)' (placed at end in references) can be signalled in your actual text as '(Phillips and Pugh, 1994)'.

Bibliography

This is usually an alphabetical list of the books, journals, and so on you have used. Not all theses have a bibliography but it is a handy reference for any reader.

Ensure you have read the university guidelines about layout, typeface, presentation, binding, references, and so on, and that your work conforms to all of these. Many theses have difficulties just because of presentation, which is a waste if the hard work has been done and the presentation quality lets this down.

You will need to be able to marshal (pull together) a clear and coherent defence of your thesis, ready for the viva. We will look at preparation of the viva next.

Please note:

If you are undertaking an arts or humanities dissertation or thesis, you will find it useful to look back at Chapter 17. The shape of these works is different from those in the social sciences, although all contain a:

- title/abstract
- introduction
- chapters defining the exploration/investigation/research
- conclusion
- references/footnotes
- bibliography.

▶ Presentation – some final issues

You will need to pay particular attention to the quality of the presentation, since it would be a great pity to jeopardise your chances of attaining your PhD, MPhil, EdD or Master's because of slapdash bibliographical details, inconsistencies and poor presentation which detract from the argument, coherence and originality of the thesis itself.

The greatest presentation problem is one aligned to rigour, cohesion and originality. If you have only gathered information – rather than moving the boundaries of the study onwards and having something original to add, contextualising your work – then this will show in the thesis and its lower-level quality will be recognised. It is perfectly satisfactory to describe, relate, list and chart in some subjects at GCSE level – certainly not at PhD level – but beyond that, it is necessary to concentrate on coherence, articulation and clarity.

Task

- Review your own dissertation or thesis so far.
- How far does it conform to the desirable qualities of work at this level?
- What will you still need to do to get it to conform to them?
- Organise a 'to do' list to bring your work up to the required level, including running it past a trustworthy, critical friend for comments on the content, coherence and presentation.
- Make sure you know the dissertation or thesis really thoroughly.
- Try producing a two-page outline of it, containing the abstract and a short version of methods, context and findings. Then answer the questions: What has been discovered and developed? Why does it matter?
- This will start to make it manageable for you to prepare for the viva.

Conclusion

We have looked at:

- The shape of a Master's, MPhil, PhD or EdD thesis
- Qualities of content, presentation to consider
- What makes a good MA, MPhil and PhD in terms of shape and content
- The structure of an effective thesis

Look at Chapter 24 for how to match the developed shape of your thesis against your initial proposal, and elements of writing style.

Further reading

Marton, F., Dall'Alba, G., & Beaty, E. (1993). Conceptions of learning. *Journal of Educational Research* 19 (3): 277–300.

Meyer, J. H. F., & Kiley, M. (1998). An exploration of Indonesian postgraduate students' conceptions of learning. *Journal of Further and Higher Education* 22: 287–98.

Winter, R. (1993). *Continuity and Progression: Assessment Vocabularies for Higher Education.* Unpublished research report data. Chelmsford: Anglia Polytechnic University Faculty of Health and Social Work.

24 Preparing Your Thesis and Dissertation

> This chapter looks at:
>
> * Completing your thesis or dissertation
> * Ensuring everything springs from and fits in with the conceptual framework
> * Reviewing the proposal to define your achievements and complete the thesis or dissertation

You should have been writing up drafts of your work as you proceeded with the research so that:

* You do not have to write the whole thesis or dissertation up in a rush at the end (a very daunting task!).
* You will have worked out some of the difficulties and some of the complex thoughts and expression as you write.
* Some of your work could be shared with a supervisor and some published or delivered at conferences/to your peers at 'work-in-progress' sessions.

Think about the writing of your thesis or dissertation as 'telling the story' of your aims, questions, the context in which your work has been set, the research methods and research work carried out, and the findings resulting from your research. It also makes a point about why you carried out the research and what kind of a contribution the research makes to knowledge in the field. It is like a story following a route or plan and it shows development and achievement.

Most importantly, you need to ensure that your conceptual framework, the framework of the ideas, themes, questions and methods you have developed:

- relate closely to the main research question(s) you are asking and enable them to be asked
- are clearly underpinning, informing and 'driving through' the whole thesis so that all of it fits in with the conceptual framework, the methods act as vehicles to discover what you set out to discover, and the findings and analyses all spring logically from it.

The conceptual framework is a framework of the thesis as a whole. As you near completion of your thesis it is useful to look back at the original proposal. Of course, much of what you have completed will differ from that proposal because, in active research, our plans change, results make us change direction, and access to information and responses cause us to pursue variations on lines of thought and action. Not all of your research activities nor your findings will conform to your original plan and proposal. In fact, if you have only found what you set out to find and there have been no risks, no revelations, surprises or developments in your thought along the way, your work might well be in danger of being neither demanding nor original enough for a PhD or EdD (if that is what you are problem solving and studying for. Originality can be less of an issue with an MA and MPhil). However, your supervisor will have been advising you about originality and development, and so you should have a good sense of how well developed and original your work is before you start to write up for the final time. The important thing now, at this final stage, is to review your proposal, capture the whole process of the research and set about describing and explaining this, and then detailing, analysing and drawing conclusions from your findings.

Task

Look back at the requirements for the proposal – this will give you a sense of the actual structure of the thesis itself. Remember, you need to explore and express your plans about all these key areas. Thought-provoking comments – about how you can respond *now* to how the elements of the proposal relate to your work as you start to write up finally – appear in italics:

The proposal – revisited

In your proposal you needed to address the following areas (or similar):

- **Indicative title** – What will you call your thesis? It is better to pose questions and to make a suggestion about links in argument rather than to give a single word or area of study. *At the writing-up stage you might want to refine your title, but before you do so, check whether this is possible in your university regulations. You might have to stick with the original title.*
- **Aim and focus of the study** – This should suggest the underlying research area and your main question and sub-questions. Eventually it hopes to form the abstract of your thesis. Think about it carefully. What are you really exploring, arguing, trying to find out, hoping to find out and then suggest? What links with what in your mind? *Has your focus changed? Can you explore this as you start to write your abstract and your introduction? It might well have changed for very good reasons in relation to what you have discovered and a need for a change in direction. You will need to talk about this in the early parts of your thesis.*
- **Context for the research** – What issues, problems, history, background, others' questions and work carried out elsewhere so far in this field provide a context, an academic culture, and an ongoing set of questions, thoughts and discoveries for your own work? How is it contributing to academic work in this area? *Ask yourself now – how is it making a contribution? You will need to state this quite clearly in your abstract. The ground describing others' work and how yours will relate to it and take it on further will be laid in your literature review chapter and in your introduction (these might be one and the same). The closing parts of your thesis will make a case for your contribution to knowledge and thought in these areas. What your work does add to the field of knowledge is a key issue in deciding whether it is of Master's or of doctorate level.*
- **Theoretical perspectives and interpretations** – Where have you taken your theories from? From what kind of framework? What are the underpinning theoretical perspectives informing your ideas – for example, feminist theory or Marxist theory? *How clearly do you feel you have expressed your theoretical underpinning? How far does your work , as explored and described in the thesis, genuinely seem to be underpinned by theories and obviously flow from them? It is important to explain this in the abstract briefly, and in the introduction or theory chapter, and throughout the thesis it should be clear and logical. It is this kind of coherence that an examiner will be looking for.*
- **Research design** – How will you go about collecting information, carrying out literature searches, and so on? Provide an outline of the

Continued

different activities you will undertake at what points in your research and do a critical path analyses of this. *This will be explored in your methods chapter. You need to check that your research design underpins the whole process of the thesis and runs throughout the writing up. If you changed some of your research design as you proceeded with your work, you need to explore how and why this happened, and what it has led to.*

- **Research methodology and methods** – What is the research methodology underpinning your research? What methods or vehicles and strategies are you going to use and why? How do they link with and help inform and develop each other? *You will need to outline this briefly in the abstract and explore it in the methods chapter, if you have one. (If you are doing an arts thesis you will probably not have such a separate chapter.) As with 'research design', above, it is important to ensure that you explain why and if you have developed or changed your methods. The decisions you made to add/remove a questionnaire, add a focus group or expand into another area of work are important ones and need explaining and exploring.*

- **Ethical considerations** – Many dissertations, and theses have ethical considerations, and these will be particularly complex when you are using human subjects. Obviously if you are involved in medical research this would be so, but it is also true of protecting the identities of those who give you information from questionnaires, focus groups or interviews. You will need to take care when asking certain sorts of personal questions or using documents which refer to people alive or dead, and so on. *Your completion of an ethics statement might have to be in addition to the thesis and will also form part of your introductory discussion and inform the whole thesis. That is, the ethics need to be clearly in place and in practice in your work.*

- **Outline and plan of study** – This part of the proposal asks you to indicate what you think would be the timeline for your research activities and/or main features of each of your chapters. It would be useful to revisit this at different points in your ongoing research and consider how they are developing, if any early findings are changing these. *Look back and see whether the chapters flow from this outline plan and if not, you might well need to explore and explain why this is so, or even reorder some of them if this makes the thesis more coherent. You will probably talk about this in your abstract.*

- **Justification for level of award** – An MPhil or PhD usually involves this question. You will need to describe and discuss what you feel your research will contribute to the field of knowledge, the development of arguments and the research culture. What kinds of practices, thoughts and arguments can't move forwards? How can it make a difference? Why does it matter and why is it obviously at this level? Is it serious, broad, deep-questioning and original enough? Such comments go into the abstract, and into your conclusion. *You do not need at this stage to make a **direct claim** about the level of the award as this is assumed in your submission for an MPhil, PhD or EdD, but* *you do need to make sure that it is clear throughout your work, set out in the abstract and rounded off in the conclusion. The level of your research, its contribution to knowledge and thought in the field of study, its originality and its clear development are all important elements of your work. They need mentioning throughout the thesis and need to be very clear throughout the thesis in its organisation and logic.*

- **Primary references** – 10 or 12 of these will be included in your submission. You will need to check that you have all your references in the end of your chapters or end of your thesis.

Task

Please consider on your own, then share with a colleague or friend (if you can) your thoughts about your own work in relation to these areas of the proposal. You will find it useful to consider them for about five minutes each and then answer these questions:

Looking back at the outline (above) for the proposal, at the shape of your own proposal and at the thoughts and suggestions in italics, determine:

- How far has your work for this research achieved these aims?
- How far does its shape conform to the broad shape of the proposal?
- How far has it found out what it set out to find out or found out other things?
- How far has it taken the expected decisions in the process of the research, or has it taken different decisions?
- How far has it pursued the expected route of the research and produced the kinds of results you expected? How far has it pursued different routes of research, in practice, and produced somewhat different results? Why?
- What do you feel you have achieved with your research?
- Does your work matter and if so, how does it matter?
- What does it contribute to knowledge and thought in your field?

These are important questions.

As you start or continue to write up your thesis in its final form you will need to think not only about the process of the research itself but the shape of the thesis. Again, looking back at the shape of the proposal will help you with this since much of the outline work carried out at that stage will be similar to the shape of the completed thesis.

Conclusion

We have looked at:

- Ensuring a clear and coherent conceptual framework underpins all your dissertation or thesis as you finally write it up
- Rewriting elements of the proposal to see if they have been achieved in the final thesis or dissertation

25 Preparing for and Undertaking Your Viva

If you have been working for an MPhil, PhD or EdD, you will need to be 'vivaed' on your work. This involves answering questions on, and defending your work to examiners in an organised session based around your thesis.

It is important as you prepare for your viva that you know your thesis well and that you have had some experience in explaining, exploring and defending it.

This chapter looks at:
  Being prepared for your viva by:

  * *knowing your thesis very well in order to defend it*
  * *managing stress before and during the viva*
  * *having a brief outline of the viva*
  * *knowing what to do during the viva*
  * *knowing your abstract well*
  * *knowing your thesis (so far) very well*

Task

Think about the following questions as you prepare for your viva and fill in some of the spaces below:

* What is really important about my work? What kind of contribution does it make to knowledge in the field in which I have been working? What might others do with it?

Continued

- What are the questions underpinning the research? (try one or two *short* points)

- What is the conceptual framework of my work?

- How are questions underpinned and asked by way of the theories and literature?

- How do the methodology and methods enable me to ask and consider the questions and deal with the ideas?

- How do the findings fit in?

- What methodology have I used (interventionalist or non-interventionalist, single or multiple methods)?

- What kinds of processes and methods have I used in my work? For example:
  - interviews
  - questionnaires, document analysis – asking questions
  - observations, case studies – observing and reflecting
  - reflective journal
  - experimentation, pre- and post-test, establish a test, models – experimenting.

- What kinds of problems have I had in my research? What kinds of drawbacks, changes and new questions? How did I deal with and overcome any problems?

- What have been the major findings from my research so far? Try to establish a few *short* points.

Now move on to speculate a little. You will need to know *who* your examiners are in order to answer these questions:

- What might my examiners be interested in/want to ask about?

- What are their specialist areas?

- What is really typical in my field?

- Is there anything contentious in my work?

▶ Being prepared

You need to prepare to explain the conceptual framework and how it underpins and drives everything in the research. Generally, describe the main issues and answer questions about interesting or strange problems. Describe the importance of your findings, why the research matters and what it contributes to knowledge and understanding in the subject.

Have some very brief notes handy for when you go into the viva (use the sheet of questions you have just completed). Be sure you know where some of your answers could be found in the thesis.

(a)   make reference points in your notes/answers and
(b)   place post-its in the thesis where you think you could be asked questions, or where you want to make specific points.

▶ Stress management

A viva is a potentially stressful experience. Think about ways of managing your stress so that you can perform well in the actual viva. Persuade a friend to undertake a mock viva with you so you can practice your defence and learn to manage any stress. It is possible that your university offers training in preparation for the viva. If so, do take advantage of this. Although it is *not* an interview, it has similar stresses and being prepared will help you deal with these.

- Make sure you are not stressed. Let your stress drive you, rather than overwhelm you.
- Control your breathing consciously – breathe deeply and slowly.
- Practise relaxation.
- Concentrate on repeating and rehearsing your main points, so that you are engaged and coherent.
- Make sure you are well rested and have ingested food and drink appropriately.
- Don't wear clothes that are awkward or too tight. You need to be alert but also relaxed.
- Remember that you would not have got this far if your work was not passable and interesting.
- Relax before you go into the viva. Get some fresh air and sit quietly and reflectively.

- Take with you a copy of your thesis, with annotations (for example, on post-its – but not too many – stuck in the thesis) and a summary sheet of your main points, and so on.
- Make sure you really know your own work – its conceptual framework, how each part fits together and what you have achieved.

▶ The viva voce – a brief outline

Present:	• Two external examiners (or one internal and two externals) • Possibly chaired by a university research degrees committee member or similar • The candidate (and translator) • Supervisors – at the discretion of the candidate. Supervisors may not speak
Duration:	Unspecified – 30–90 minutes or more
Room:	A comfortable and informal setting (tea, coffee and water should be available)
Atmosphere:	Friendly, collegial and non-inquisitorial
Purpose:	• To examine the academic content and scholastic level of the thesis • To provide candidates with the opportunity to defend their thesis • To explore and explain the design, methodology and outcomes of the research • To discuss the research from the perspective of 'experts in the area' • To provide evidence to help the external examiners arrive at a judgement about the defence of the thesis • To enable the external examiners to make a recommendation to the university about the thesis.

(Adapted from a handout by Dr Vernon Trafford, Anglia Polytechnic University, 1999.)

Useful tips during the viva
You might find these ideas and tips useful.

- Sit down and place the thesis at hand, but don't open it.
- Thank the examiners for the opportunity to talk with them about your work.
- Answer questions clearly and concisely.
- Use the arguments, ideas and examples from your thesis in answering the questions.
- Back up your cohesive and coherent piece of research by making it clear how the conceptual framework links questions, themes, methodology, methods, fieldwork, findings and conclusions.
- Be able to refer to key texts you have used and agree or disagree with.
- Use eye contact.
- Do not fumble through your thesis – use book markers to allow you easy access to pages you feel might be useful (but not all of the pages. Mark key chapters, problem points and any original points you would like to discuss).
- If the examiners do not seem to mention what you think are key issues, new findings or important contributions, mention them and ask what they think about these issues. Engage them in conversation.
- If they point out problems, think on the spot and let them know if you do not know/agree/disagree/or indicate that these issues led to further work beyond the scope of this thesis.
- Don't try to answer questions that you don't understand. Ask them to clarify them.
- Don't introduce new information and new ideas that are not in the thesis (this could lead to suggestions that you go off and do more work now) but do recognise (and say) that other people might be interested in pursuing these ideas and areas, or that you might do so at postdoctoral level.
- Make sure you relate to and answer the questions of each examiner.
- Thank the examiners at the end of the session.
- It is rather like a job interview – but you are not in competition with other people. It is all about your work.
- If everyone relaxes and talks as intellectual equals about your work, you will probably have very little else to do to it.
- Good luck!

Remember – many candidates have to make revisions (some large, some small), so don't be dismayed if you are asked to revise. You will need to clarify the work required, schedule it in and get on with it.

Conclusion

In this chapter we have looked at:

- Preparing for the viva – knowing your thesis and the viva process
- How to do well in your viva
- Managing revisions

26 Presentations, Conferences and Publishing

> This chapter looks at:
>
> * Work-in-progress seminars
> * Presentations – with colleagues
> * Presentations – at conferences
> * Seeking publication

An important part of your work as a research student is sharing and presenting your work in progress with others. Research is a contribution to knowledge and to ideas in the subject(s), and as a researcher you are part of a larger research community which shares its ideas and moves forward through that sharing. Additionally, sharing your work with others helps you to clarify, control and evaluate it. It also enables you to seek analytical responses from others and this can help you develop in your work. You might well be worried that such sharing can show up the faults in your work, and you could also be rather apprehensive about the public appraisal presentation seems to offer. But a well-planned presentation of work in progress can provide immensely useful feedback to help you in your research work. Attending the presentations of others can enable you to stand back from your own work, advise them on points in theirs, and reflect on the ways which you can develop your own, illuminated by strategies others have adopted. Sharing your work in a research community is not about giving it away but about supportive, analytical critique for constructive purposes. If you decide to become involved in work-in-progress seminars, it is important to ensure that a structured, constructive response is part of the ground rules.

Give (1) work-in-progress presentations and (2) conference presentations at various points during your research, as it is useful to share your work with your peers and probably also your supervisor. It is also important to share your work with the wider academic community, once you feel you have a contribution which they will find useful (do not be too modest, and do not wait too long to do this). There are both informal and formal opportunities to present these as there are a number of differences in terms of formality, length and activity involved. Let us explore these in the first instance:

1 **Work-in-progress presentations** – these are essentially a matter of you sharing the work you have carried out to date, the ways you have approached it and why, and what you have discovered. The presentations provide an opportunity to ask questions and to seek support from your peers on some of the developments, issues, points and problems you might have come across. Certain information is possible and some interaction would be a good idea.

2 **Conference presentations** – these take several forms. You might be giving a whole paper or running a seminar that consists of a formal paper, followed by questions and prompts for a reaction – rather more like presenting to your peers. You might also be running an interactive workshop session in which, after you have introduced some of your work, you can involve participants in active questioning, trying out activities, engaging with and reflecting on some of your ideas or findings.

The idea behind a poster presentation is to produce a visually striking and appropriate summary of the main issues, questions and findings of a piece of research or other development. The content is often rather like an abstract with summarised findings. Your role at a conference is to present your point to whoever is interested in hearing about your work and discussing it with them so you need to put up your poster, stand by it, and talk about it to whoever shows interest.

Whatever the type of format or context of your presentation, you need to:

- define the area of your research that you wish to share and explore
- clarify the questions which this addresses
- contextualise this piece of research in relation to questions for your research so far
- clarify the research strategies and methods you are using

- define and clarify the investigations, questions and findings to date
- organise your information and arguments into the format of a presentation
- invite appropriate others/join in a series of seminars and offer your presentation
- plan to deliver your work several weeks or months ahead so that you have plenty of time to prepare the whole presentation
- decide who else needs to be involved to help you with OHTs (overhead transparencies) and handouts.

In the more conventional presentations you should find the following presentation tips helpful.

Task

Decide on an element or part of your research that could form a short presentation. Look below at the planning, preparation and presentation stages and consider what you would need to think of and produce to present your work.

▶ Consider the four Ps

- plan
- prepare
- practise
- present.

Plan

Decide when and where you want to present, and to whom. Find out all you can about your audience and their interests and needs. In the case of a research community, find out who else works in your area. Who else is using similar research methods? Who might be interested in your research? Who might be only marginally interested and who might know much more than you do? Who will need introducing to basic concepts before the full presentation?

Decide on the plan and aim of your presentation. (a) To introduce others to your work, select a part of your work and explore it as an example. (b) To enable you to explore the full shape of your research to date. Be precise.

- Commit yourself to a title and a date for your presentation. Select an area that will be of interest to yourself and to others.
- Select a coherent part of your work.
- Decide what kinds of questions you hope can be approached in the work.
- Decide what kinds of questions about your work in progress can be answered or agreed with by your audience.
- Select a manageable part of your research work to date.
- Decide on the main point of your presentation or argument.
- Carry out a critical path analysis, assessing what work you need to carry out and when, in order to produce a good quality presentation of part of your work to date.

Prepare

Gather together all the information you need. Carry out the appropriate research to help you answer your questions and fill in facts and information. Ask questions, investigate on the Internet, carry out any research needed, and consult your notes and drafts of papers to date. Carry out any necessary extra reading, but do not become so embroiled in extensive new work that you lose sight of the subject of the paper to be presented.

There are many shapes to a presentation, as is suggested in the many different purposes suggested above. There are also many different ways to organise yourself for this presentation. The two main ways are:

1. to collect and produce an outline and headings, then fill them in with information
2. to produce a full paper, with headings, and so on, then to extract these.

Either way, you need a more or less full (but not necessarily finished) text with some elegant phrasing and a shorter way of presenting it, so that you can talk to it. Remember that a written text is not in presentation format. Spoken language is much simpler than written language and you can ensure the more complex parts of your talk/'presentation' are delivered through handouts, and so on, rather than word for word in the talk itself. Audiences find it difficult to follow the complexity of written prose when it is read out rapidly in a presentation.

Audience
Thinking about your audience is not just a matter of working out who could be there and what their interest might be. It also involves producing spoken English at the level at which people can hear and understand your main points, if necessary providing written handouts as backups.

- Organise your points under headings, starting with an introduction and selecting main points.
- Decide how to structure your presentation: what will come first, what follows, where to place OHTs, charts and handouts, where to show slides, video clips or music, and whether to use a visualiser to show a model.
- Organise the charts, slides, video clips, handouts and OHTs as necessary and write up the presentation.
- You would be well advised to organise your arguments and ideas under headings in the main text and then to separate them from the main text, perhaps on index cards or in bold, and to collate your points separately on OHTs.

OHTs are very useful for highlighting main points but they need to be carefully produced, as do handouts.

Handouts
We all use handouts if we teach, and also when we give presentations, but why and to what ends? What types are there?

- lecture/presentation outlines
- full lecture/presentation note handouts
- background information
- examples, samples, cases, extracts and images
- gapped handouts for completion of notes and answers to questions considered in the course of the presentation
- interactive handouts which ask audiences to complete a task

Some dos and don'ts in putting handouts together
Do ensure handouts are:

- legible in terms of copying, layout and clarity of images and words
- laid out in the most appropriate format and shape to make movement around and use of them straightforward and appropriate to the format of the class
- logical layout, for example, first things first, then what follows, then summaries and further work.

Don't produce handouts that are:

- ugly or badly designed
- cluttered and confusing
- irrelevant to the task, content and context
- illegible – retype and re-copy.

Task

- Choose any element of your research so far or a favourite topic not connected to your research.
- Decide on a specific context for presenting your work.
- Consider the reason for the handout, for example, information and so on (see above).
- For how long would you like this handout to be used – in interaction, as a record forever, or just to provide shape to a talk for now?
- Do you want to use colour, images and interaction?
- What kind of layout, shape, amount and kind of content would best suit your audience in terms of the context and your own presentational strategies?

Design a one-page handout which would be suitable for these design needs in this context. In a rough plan, indicate layout, shapes and content. Then define and evaluate why it is useful and appropriate and what, if any, were the difficulties and questions raised while designing and producing it.

In your design and layout decide:

- Who is this handout for?
- When is it for?
- What are the learning outcomes it serves?

Are the content and the shape intended:

- to inform?
- to illustrate?
- to prompt thought?

- to prompt individual or group interaction?
- to aid a record/act as the full record or prompt some further record?
- to encourage further study?
- for another purpose?

Do you want to use:

- colour?
- images?
- bullets?
- large fonts?
- spaces to complete interactions?
- desktop publishing formats?

Designing and using OHTs

For a 20-minute talk you need to have no more than four or five OHTs, otherwise all anyone will do is read them. If you want to show charts, statistics, and so on, these can be produced separately or on handouts for people to look at later. One thing to remember is that audiences learn and respond immediately through what they hear and see, and later use the material in their own work if it has been delivered in a transportable fashion with paper and handouts. They do not want to be copying down complex figures and notes, so keep this to a bare minimum. This is why photocopies of your OHTs are useful, to enable them to follow the flow of the points you are making when they review the session later, as well as while they are listening and jotting down the odd key point.

The rules for designing and using OHTs are very similar to those of handouts. It is important that they should serve the learning outcomes, be pitched at the right level for the audience, be clear, legible, visible, and well laid-out, uncluttered and totally appropriate.

OHTs can be used to:

- provide an overall shape to a talk or session
- indicate main points and key moments to summarise and move on
- give instructions and the essential information
- suggest reading and suggest interactions and activities
- trace development and movement, for example, through overlays.

How to use them
- Do ensure that the projector is clean, clear and focused. Ensure that there is a spare bulb in case the bulb blows.

- Never project an OHT onto a white board as this reflects, and also can intermingle with your previous writing on the board! Project it onto a screen.
- Ensure that the distance between the OHT and the screen is suitable to make the words readable and clear at the back – adjust the clarity of the OHT when you move it, and avoid 'keystoning' – a shape that disfigures the wording and is caused by a flat rather than a slightly angled screen.
- Indicate on the OHT using a pen or pointer, and avoid looking at the screen or blocking the screen while doing so. If you are happy using pointers on the screen, e.g. the magic eye of a laser pointer, then do use one but try not to move it around confusingly. Normally you would not be pointing at the screen but facing the audience and pointing at the OHP.
- Keep a paper copy of your transparencies to read from so that you are not turning round to squint at the screen.
- The ideal font size is 24 point – no smaller, and preferably a font which shows up well, such as Times or New York, with gaps between words, well laid-out. If using bold throughout helps, use it.

Using PowerPoint

The ability and opportunity to use PowerPoint is increasing today. PowerPoint can be used to construct whole layouts of OHTs for sessions. It will help you to order these and run off a shrunken version of the OHTs so that they can sit alongside your notes.

PowerPoint can also be used in conjunction with a laptop to deliver a lecture onto a screen, making notes on the screen and interacting with the presentation.

It can enable you to update your notes and OHTs and to add comments from the session onto the originals as you proceed.

Drawbacks

- It is rather static and pre-prepared. You need to proceed at the pace of your individual OHTs, which can be too slow.
- The tendency to make a separate headline for each transparency means it can take an age to get on to anything complex.
- Running a PowerPoint presentation from an OHP in the dark can reduce concentration.

Your script

Organisation
Write out your opening paragraph clearly, with well-chosen words, and memorise it. This will enable you to feel comfortable, to maintain eye contact with your audience without depending on notes, and to get into your stride. You would be well advised to write out a closing paragraph to which you can jump when your time is up, in the event this might happen before you have completed all you have to say. A neat closing paragraph summing up your main points can enable you to round off the presentation and leave a lasting and positive effect in the minds of the audience.

Practise

It is important to practise the presentation – not to memorise it and practise too much so you will feel artificial, but enough to ensure that it is not too long and that the points flow logically and clearly.

If there is enough time for you to use the OHTs and slides, and so on, you might prepare to identify in your master text (the bit with all the headings on) exactly where you might show a slide. Annotating your master script as if it were a production copy of a drama is a good idea – for example:

'OHT 2 here'
'now refer to handout 3'

and so on. When you are in full flow you might forget key elements, so the wise thing to do is make notes while the timing doesn't matter. Then, when the timing is crucial, you can jog your mind with such notes and so stick to the coherent organisation you have planned.

You need to assure yourself that if all the technical equipment fails you, you still have the handouts and your script, with bold headings, in colour or underlined, or on card index files. You can talk to this.

As you practise, consider all the elements of the actual presentation.

Presentation

- Just prior to the presentation, you need to check the room, the projector, other audio-visual aids, the quality of your handouts and to ensure your notes and OHTs are in order.
- Make sure you know where to stand in relation to any audio-visual aids so that you are not blocking them, do not get yourself hemmed

in behind too much machinery and too many bits of furniture, and give yourself the kind of space you feel you will need. If this is not possible (that is, you are in a group of four, each of whom will speak, and you will have to negotiate getting around each other to the OHP), talk to yourself about the negotiations so that none of it upsets you when it is your turn to speak. Plan what you will do to overcome any physical difficulties this might throw in your way.

In the presentation you will need to ensure that you:

- Engage the attention of the audience. Introduce yourself and your topic, thank them for being there and explain what you hope to achieve in your short presentation.
- Ensure they have sufficient copies of any handouts. Check with them that they can see the OHT and hear you at the back (if it is a big auditorium, this is essential).
- Try not to gabble your information too quickly or speak so slowly that little is said.
- Place your notes in a position so that you can see them – preferably not on a lectern, as this seems to cut you off from an audience. However, a lectern does ensure that your notes stay at eye level so that you can see them and maintain eye contact with the audience, so even if you walk around a lectern it is a good place to put your notes.
- Ensure your OHTs, and so on, are in the right order and are accessible to the place where you will show them when the time comes.
- Speak very clearly and write or spell, or have handouts for difficult words, terms and names.
- Emphasise the main points by repetition and by indicating them on the OHT with a pencil, pointer or your finger.
- Do not face the OHP screen or any other screen but stand slightly behind the projector.
- Try not to block it. Indicate which part of the OHT you are talking to. Some people learn to reveal parts of an OHT one by one, but this can irritate some other people. However, if you put up a very cluttered slide, the audience might spend the whole of the time trying to decipher and copy it down. So do keep the OHT slides very clear and simple.
- Try not to just read the text out although, if you mention it very briefly, then it does actually give you the kind of visual structure on which you can depend.

- Ensure that you keep eye contact with the audience. This means not fixing your gaze on one single person, however positive their responses might be, and ensuring that you at least give the impression that your can see all around the audience and are engaging their attention.
- Avoid appearing like a nodding dog, or a spectator watching a game of tennis, looking from side to side, making eye contact. Avoid unnecessary personal habits such as jangling keys and change in your pockets (men), adjusting necklaces and dropping beads (women), pacing back and forth, swaying from side to side, marching, tapping or mangling paper clips and Blu-Tac which happen to be lying around.
- Avoid irritating speech habits such as saying 'in a manner of speaking' or making 'um' every other word. Audiences tend to concentrate on the mannerisms rather than the content if there is an excess of mannerism over content. These mannerisms are often just personal traits. So you do not want to be superhuman or faceless – an automaton – but ask yourself if they are excessive and if they might be distracting your audience, rather than helping to emphasise what you are saying. If this is so, try and keep a voice in your head that warns you off them and tells you to concentrate on eye contact, pace, tone of voice and presenting your arguments clearly.

Time yourself and try to ensure that you do not run beyond your allotted time, especially if there is someone speaking after you. Ensure that you finish with an organised conclusion so that you feel you have rounded off your points. It's possible, even if you have prepared and practised, that the timing of the presentation will be different, especially if anyone asks questions.

After the presentation, you can invite questions and be prepared to answer them. Quite often a rather stiff presentation becomes much more lively at this point, when you are asked about your findings and some special issues and engage directly with the audience. This can be an interesting moment of engaging with the audience. Think about how to deal with difficult questions, however.

▶ Dealing with difficult questions

There are several sorts of difficult questions and difficult questioners, so do be prepared.

1 The difficult questioners who are merely here to ask you to explain what you have said or a part of it. It is a matter of being well rehearsed and familiar with your work. This is not the real difficulty. The really difficult questions are from people who want to take issue with your points or with your statistics, and you need to think how to deal with these often mischievous interruptions.

2 If someone asks a question part of the way through, and this is not the conventional response in these circumstances, ask them to wait until the end or you will lose your flow – unless it is a simple question that is easily answered. Consider not only the questioner but the other listeners who want to hear you develop your thesis and to back it up.

3 If questioned about your statistics, which you cannot actually explain there and then, or if the questioner raises a substantive issue that isn't covered in your research (it can happen!), you would be well advised to thank them for this and to suggest that you discuss it later. Otherwise, it will hold up the presentation. This prevents them from taking over. You will need to use your initiative to spot whether you feel this is the case, but there are people out there who are good at asking awkward questions – do not be put off by them! Say you have noted their interest and will tackle it later.

Be prepared to give or send members of the audience your whole paper after the presentation. Make sure they have your full referencing details so they can cite you should they use your work in their own.

▶ Publications

- Why publish?
- Where to publish?
- What to publish?

Getting your work published while you are working on a thesis is desirable and probably a necessity, but it needs carefully managing and steering. It is a necessary part of research as it enables you to contribute to the research culture in which your work is placed, as well as getting your name known in the field among other specialists.

You will need to start thinking about publishing articles from your thesis as you write it. There is a safeguard here to be careful of, and that is that only a proportion of your work submitted for the thesis can actually be published (or it is considered already published work rather than a thesis). Also, beware that you might be sacrificing the coherence of your thesis to a desire to get in print. You need both thesis and publications. Producing publishable articles and conference publications while also writing your thesis will require very careful time planning and a certain ruthlessness. Once you have finished your work, submitted it and passed, then you may publish as much of it as you can.

▶ Getting published

Task

If you have already published, identify:

- What were the stages of getting published?
- What were the problems and pitfalls?
- What are the tips and guidelines?
- What one specific piece of advice would you give a colleague seeking to be published?

Stages of getting published

Some practical guidelines, tips and examples of good practice developed and shared:

- Be clear about the area(s) in which you wish to write.
- Your favourite subject might not be topical and interesting to others.
- Can you give a favourite subject a topical spin?
- Can you find something else that is topical and interesting, or of major importance, on which you are working?

Your PhD or Master's thesis or your lecture won't be published as it stands!

Find at least one suitable outlet or forum. Read carefully through any work published here already and identify:

- what sort of area of work they usually publish
- any special treatment and angle likely, any particular flavour or preferred kind of writing
- the tone
- the audience
- complexity and specialist elements
- length, presentation, layout, footnotes, endnotes, referencing, and so on.

Approach these outlets/forums with a suggestion.

- Identify who to contact – specialist areas and specialist responsibilities.
- Some publishers like a personal approach first to discuss areas of interest.
- Some like recommendations from someone they know.
- Some accept papers/books out of the blue (but this is pretty rare).

Draft a proposal and include specimen material or the draft paper/a chapter and send it to the commissioning editor/relevant person.

Eventually you will possibly want to publish your work as a book. One main tip is that very few (if any) dissertations or theses go straight into print. They all need reshaping for a different audience:

Draft outline/frequently expected elements of a book proposal

Proposal/outline
An introductory piece outlining the main area of argument and interest in the book. Make this accessible in style but containing the main arguments and main conceptual points you wish the book to put across.

Rationale and audience (can be separate)
Explain why this is:

- topical and interesting. What kinds of readers it might expect (be as full as possible and relevant)?
- worth doing right now. What will it contribute to the field of knowledge and ideas?

Market

Carry out market research
What other books, articles, conferences and so on are there on this? Identify, list and evaluate them and detail why your work is different, how it adds to theirs and how it improves on it.

Draft chapters and contents
Include a draft contents page, outlining the major chapters in your book.

Give information on topics and the arguments they develop, some of the work they will refer to (a short paragraph for each).

Include a draft chapter. This can be the introduction, but more usually it would be a chapter from the rest of the book.

What happens next?
Absolutely nothing:

Chase it up.

If it all comes back months later, turned down flat, with a shallow excuse (irritating you):

- Contact them to thank them and ask for ways in which it might be better directed at their market. Then redo it.
- Or dump it.
- Or find another outlet and start to gear it all up again towards this outlet. Look back through the stages and see if you can spot where it went wrong.

Where could it have gone wrong?

- The editor you sent it to was too busy skiing!/moving/working on another topic.
- The commissioning editor is conservative/radical/it is not their field.
- They have someone else working in this field already and have invested in this/they are more important than you/they have a track record.
- You didn't make it clear how topical and appropriately written your book was going to be.
- It needs a sponsor.
- It was a bad idea anyway.
- It was not well worked-out in the proposal.

If they like it and they want you to write more about it so they can judge it better:

- Weigh up the investment. Carry out the writing unless you don't want to go any further (intuition and long conversations help here).
- Send them the next version with a letter.
- Usual wait time, and so on.
- Follow up with a call.
- Follow up again.

If it is accepted

- Be very clear about the terms and conditions of any contract.
- Who owns the copyright?
- Is there an advance?
- How do you get royalties? Will you have to pay the advance back out of your own pocket if the book is pulped within six weeks?
- Are there any overseas rights and what is your cut of these?
- Do they intend to go into paperback too?
- What is their practice with regard to publicity, marketing and distribution?
- How many free copies will you get?
- Can you complete an author's form to detail who should be referees? Who would like to hear about it?
- Is there advance publicity and if so, can you get hold of it?

Writing your book

- Time your planning and critical path analysis so that you can work out how long each phase might take.
- Carry out research and start to draft in parts.
- Contact anyone whose information is needed in advance. Leave plenty of time for gathering information that is crucial but time-consuming to gather.
- Do you know the field very well? Or will you benefit from a literature search?
- Do you need any new skills or de-rusting?
- Whether you work directly on a PC or if it needs typing up will affect timing.

- Leave plenty of time for graphs, statistics and so on to be drawn up appropriately.
- Draft and redraft.
- Test it out on a friend and colleague for sense and interest.
- Test it against your market – colleagues and students for accessibility and interest.
- Ensure the references are all in the same format and the layout is the same.
- Edit, edit and edit.
- Ensure it looks really well presented.
- Photocopy it twice. Send two copies of the manuscript to the editor and keep one for yourself. Do you need to send a disk too?

Writing for a journal or other outlet

- The main advice is to select your outlet, your journal, and find out about the tone, audience, find a sponsor who will write a letter. Read the journal to gauge the kind of pitch, the kind of essays it usually publishes.
- See if they are interested in the idea of the essay first and send an A4 outline to them, with a copy of other work you have done, if relevant and well presented.
- Some never get back to you – chase these.
- Others send out to the referees even for the proposal/for the essay.
- When comments return, decide how to deal with them. Most will need to be taken on board, but sometimes intuition will tell you that this is a hint that they don't want it.
- In this case, find another outlet and possibly rewrite for it.
- Or/and when you do get the paper accepted, ensure you know all about their guidelines for layout, length, timing and so on.
- Write it.
- Check it.
- Edit it.
- Test it.
- Send off two copies. (Do they need a disk?)
- They will probably contact you with other minor changes and some proofing questions. You will probably be asked to sign a contract. Check if you will receive payment, offerings or a copy of the journal.

Task

Please identify the kind of help and ideas that have emerged from reading through these materials.

- Which elements of your work could you usefully develop now to publication?
- What would you need to do to your current work in order to carry out the writing?
- Where might you send it? Why?

Conclusion

We have looked at:

- Organising your work for presentation at conferences and work-in-progress seminars
- Organising your work for publication in books and journals

27 Life after the Research

Depending on where you are in your research project, you will probably want to or *not* want to consider what happens when you finish. Indeed, 'is there life after the research?' is not such an ironic question. A research project that lasts the best part of a year (MA) to up to eight years (PhD – but preferably three years) quite simply takes over your life, or part of it. Once you have been successful in your submission and assessment and in your viva, and if necessary, resubmitted or revised, you will probably feel all or some of the following:

- elated! This is *the* major achievement
- ready to rejoin the human race – the family and your friends
- ready to do all those things you have been putting off
- bereaved.

You live with your research and your thesis for a long time, like a recalcitrant pet animal. For some people it is actually impossible to stop, give it up, hand it over, bring it to a close. There *was* no life after research for the nineteenth-century British novelist George Eliot's Casaubon in *Middlemarch*. He could not imagine completion and he never completed. But you have finished and the world awaits you.

If you are looking ahead to this chapter at the *beginning* of your research career, you will see that the planning and time-management issues stressed throughout should include some planning of work and ongoing activities which take you beyond the research. Research-based degrees are, after all, *not* an end in themselves. They are qualifications that recognise achievement but also confer a kind of licence to practice. They are a training ground for, and an indication of, the future likelihood of further research. So do think about staging your withdrawal, celebration and future development based on your research degree.

First of all, celebrate! Then, take a holiday or at least an intellectual break, or you will become stale. Friends and family, expecting your return to normality, will have calculated tasks both physical and emotional for you to be engaged in, and/or you will find they are piling up for you by your own planning. Obviously they include things like painting the kitchen or cooking regular meals again. But they also should include developing elements of the research, following up avenues, picking bits out – and publishing, giving conference papers and seminars, and putting in for research method posts and research funding. You might find you need quite a long break before you get on with this last area of work but you might also find that, unless you *do* throw yourself into some projects (*after* a break), you will feel rather bereaved. After my own PhD, I did the following within 18 months – moved house, moved to a new job, started an advanced diploma, and had a first baby. Not everyone needs to be quite so obsessive, of course. For me, publication approached gradually and not all of the thesis ever saw the light of day in publication, though its ideas have fed into much of what I do daily, and into my teaching. So, in terms of the work/research areas involved, do consider:

- selecting elements of the thesis or dissertation to develop and rewrite for publication
- selecting elements of the thesis for conference presentation

(do these two quickly)

- update your CV and gradually look for openings/seize immediate openings for job improvement (if that is your aim).

If none of these necessarily appear immediately:

- update your CV
- appear at conferences.

Then when you are ready – but do not wait too long, even research into ancient history becomes superseded by newer research into ancient history – seek research funding, and with or without it, carry on.

Task

Draw up a brief plan of *ten* things you intend to do upon completion of the research. Make some of these just for your own benefit, some for friends and or family, some work-related and research-related. Do ensure some are easily managed, and others less easily obtained.

Once you have drawn up the list, consider what you can do to work towards them.

Life after research list

Things to do – goals	What to do to achieve this
1.	
2.	
3.	
4.	
5.	
6.	
7.	
8.	
9.	
10.	

Conclusion

We have looked at:

- Life after your research
- Celebrations
- Further work

Bibliography

Alavi, C. (ed.) (1995). *Problem Based Learning in a Health Sciences Curriculum.* London: Routledge.

Anderson, G., Boud, D., & Sampson, J. (eds) (1996). *Learning Contracts: A Practical Guide.* London: Kogan Page.

Andresen, L. W. (1997). *Highways to Postgraduate Supervision.* Sydney: University of Western Sydney.

Bales, R. F. (1950). *Interaction Process Analysis: A Method for the Study of Small Groups.* Cambridge, MA: Addison-Wesley.

Bell, J. (1993). *Doing your Research Project.* Buckingham: Open University Press.

Biggs, J. B. (1978). Individual and group differences in study processes and the quality of learning outcomes. *British Journal of Educational Psychology* 48: 266–79.

Biggs, J. B. (1999). *Teaching for Quality Learning at University: What the Student Does.* Buckingham: Open University Press.

Biggs, J. B., & Rihn, B. A. (1984). The effects of intervation on deep and surface approaches to learning. In J. R. Kirby (ed.), *Cognitive Strategies and Educational Performance*, pp. 279–93. London: Academic Press.

Blaxter, L., Hughes, C., & Tight, M. (1993). *How to Research.* Buckingham: Open University Press.

Brookfield, S. (ed.) (1986). *Self-Directed Learning: From Theory to Practice (New Directions for Continuing Education 25).* San Francisco: Jossey-Bass.

Brookfield, S. D. (1986). *Understanding and Facilitating Adult Learning: Comprehensive Analysis of Principles and Effective Practices.* Milton Keynes: Open University Press.

Carr, W., & Kemmis, S. (1986). *Becoming Critical: Education, Knowledge and Action Research.* London: Falmer.

Cooper, H. M. (1985). *The Integrative Research Review: A Systematic Approach.* London: Sage.

Cooperrider, D. L., & Srivastra, S. (1987). Appreciative Inquiry into Organizational Life. In W. A. Pasmore & R. W. Woodman (eds), *Research into Organizational Change and Development*, vol. 1. Greenwich, CT: JAI.

Cottrell, S. (1999). *The Study Skills Handbook.* Basingstoke: Macmillan Press – now Palgrave.

Delamont, S., Atkinson, P., & Parry, O. (1997). *Supervising the PhD A Guide to Success*. Buckingham: Open University Press.

Denscombe, M. (1998). *The Good Research Guide*. Buckingham: Open University Press.

Denzin, N. K., & Lincoln, Y. S. (1998). *The Landscape of Qualitative Research, Theories and Issues*. Thousand Oaks, CA: Sage.

Dewey, J. (1963). *Experience and Education*. New York: Collier.

Dunleaky, P. (1986). *Studying for a Degree*. Basingstoke: Macmillan Press – now Palgrave.

Eliot, G. (1965). *Middlemarch*. (1871). London: Penguin.

Entwistle, N. J., & Ramsden, P. (1983). *Understanding Student Learning*. London: Croom Helm.

Evans, L. (1998). *Teaching and Learning in Higher Education*. London: Cassell.

Evans, P., & Varma, V. P. (1990). *Special Education*. London: Falmer.

Fisher, J. (1996). *Starting from the Child: Teaching and Learning from 4 to 8*. Buckingham: Open University Press.

Fisher, S. (1994). *Stress in Academic Life*. Buckingham: Open University Press.

Flanders, N. A. (1970). *Analysing Teacher Behaviors*. Reading, MA: Addison-Wesley.

Gibbs, G. (1981). *Teaching Students to Learn*. Buckingham: Open University Press.

Glaser, B., & Strauss, A. (1967). *The Discovery of Grounded Theory*. Chicago: Aldine.

Gordon, William J. J. (1961). *Synectics: The Development of Creative Capacity*. New York: Harper.

Graves, N., & Varma, V. (eds) (1997). *Working for a Doctorate: A Guide for the Humanities and Social Sciences*. London: Routledge.

Hodge, B. (1995). Monstrous knowledge: doing PhDs in the new humanities. *Australian Universities' Review* 38 (2): 35–9.

Holland, J. (1991). *Learning Legal Rules: A Student's Guide to Legal Method and Reasoning*. London: Blackstone Press.

Holland, J., & Ramazanoglu, C. (1994). Coming to conclusions: power and interpretation in researching young women's sexuality. In M. Maynard & J. Purvis (eds), *Researching Women's Lives from a Feminist Perspective*, pp. 125–48. London: Taylor and Francis.

Hollway, W., & Jefferson, T. (2000). *Doing Qualitative Research Differently, Free Association Narrative and the Interview Method*. London: Sage.

Honey, P., & Mumford, A. (1986). *Using your Manual of Learning Styles*. Peter Honey Publications.

Kolb, D. A. (1984). *Experiential Learning: Experience as the Source of Learning and Development*. Englewood Cliffs, NJ: Prentice-Hall.

Lacey, C. (1976). Problems of sociological fieldwork: a review of the methodology of 'Hightown Grammar'. In Shipman, M. (ed.), *The Organisation and Impact of Social Research*. London: Routledge & Kegan Paul.

Lee, R. (1995). *Dangerous Fieldwork*. Thousand Oaks, CA: Sage.

Mailer, N. (2000). *Why are we in Vietnam?* USA: Picador.

Marton, F., Dall'Alba, G., & Beaty, E. (1993). Conceptions of learning. *Journal of Educational Research* 19 (3): 277–300.

Marton, F., Hounsell, D., Entwhistle, N., & Mckeachie, W. (eds) (1984). *The Experience of Learning*. Edinburgh: Scottish Academic Press.

Marton, F., & Säljö, R. (1976). On qualitative differences in learning. I – Outcome and process. *British Journal of Educational Psychology* 46: 4–11.

Melamed, L. (1987). The role of play in adult learning. In D. Boud & V. Griffin (eds), *Appreciating Adults Learning: From the Learner's Perspective*. London: Kogan Page.

Meyer, J. H. F., & Boulton-Lewis, G. M. (1997). Reflections on Learning Inventory.

Meyer, J. H. F., & Kiley, M. (1998). An exploration of Indonesian postgraduate students' conceptions of learning. *Journal of Further and Higher Education* 22: 287–98.

Mezirow, J. (1985). A critical theory of self-directed learning. In S. Brookfield (ed.), *Self-Directed Learning: From Theory to Practice* (*New Directions for Continuing Education* 25). San Francisco: Jossey-Bass.

Mezirow, J. (1990). *Fostering Critical Reflection on Adulthood: A Guide to Transformative and Emancipatory Learning*. San Francisco: Jossey-Bass.

Miles, M., & Huberman, M. (1994). *Qualitative Data Analysis*. London: Sage.

Moses, I. (1989). *Supervising Postgraduates*. Sydney: HERDSA.

Orna, E., & Stevens, G. (1995). *Managing Information for Research*. Buckingham: Open University Press.

Over, R. (1982). Does research productivity decline with age? *Higher Education* 11: 511–20.

Phillips, E. M., & Pugh, D. S. (1994). *How to Get a PhD: A Handbook for Students and Their Supervisors*. 2nd ed., Buckingham: Open University Press.

Prosser, M., & Trigwell, K. (eds) (1999). *Understanding Learning and Teaching: The Experience in Higher Education*. Buckingham: Open University Press.

Ramsden, P. (1979). Student learning and the perception of the academic environment. *Higher Education* 8: 411–28.

Ramsden, P. (1992). *Learning to Teach in Higher Education*. London: Routledge.

Rendel, M. (1986). How Many Women Academics 1912–1977? In R. Deem (ed.), *Schooling for Women's Work*. London: Routledge.

Robson, C. (1993). *Real World Research*. Oxford: Blackwell.

Rogers, J. (1989). *Adults Learning*. Buckingham: Open University Press.

Rossi, C. (1995). *Problem Based Learning in a Health Sciences Curriculum*. London: Routledge.

Säljö, R. (1997). *Learning and Discourse: A Sociocultural Perspective*. Leicester: British Psychological Society.

Schmeck, R. R. (1988). *Learning Strategies and Learning Styles*. New York: Plenum Press.

Schön, D. (1983). *The Reflective Practitioner*. San Francisco: Jossey-Bass.

Strauss, A. (1987). *Qualitative Analysis for Social Scientists*. Cambridge: Cambridge University Press.

Strauss, A., & Corbin, J. (1990). *Basics of Qualitative Research: Grounded Theory Procedures and Techniques*. London: Sage.

Svensson, L. (1977). On qualitative differences in learning. III – Study skills and learning. *British Journal of Educational Psychology* 47: 233–43.

Svensson, L. G. (1987). *Higher Education and the State in Swedish History*. Stockholm: Almqvist & Wiksell.

Swinnerton-Dyer, H. P. F. (1982). *Report of the Working Party on Postgraduate Education*. London: HMSO.

Tenopir, C., & Lundeen, G. (1988). *Managing Your Information*. New York: Neal Schuman.

Thomas, P. R., & Bain J. D. (1982). Consistency in learning strategies. *Higher Education* 11 249–59.

Tight, M. (1983). *Education for Adults Volume 2: Opportunities for Adult Education*. London: Routledge.

Watkins, B. (1981). *Drama and Education*. London: Batsford.

Winter, J. (1995). *Skills for Graduates in the 21st Century*. London: Association of Graduate Recruiters.

Winter, R. (1989). *Learning from Experience: Principles and Practice in Action Research*. London: Falmer.

Winter, R. (1993). *Continuity and Progression: Assessment Vocabularies for Higher Education*. Unpublished research report data. Chelmsford: Anglia Polytechnic University Faculty of Health and Social Work.

Winter, R. (2000). Assessment vocabularies for higher education: practice-based PhDs. *Journal of Further and Higher Education* 1.

Winter, R., & Guise, S. (1995). *The Ford ASSET Project: the report of a two year collaborative project to introduce work based learning within an honours degree level award in engineering undertaken jointly by Ford Motor Company Ltd & Anglia Polytechnic University*. Chelmsford: Anglia Polytechnic University.

Wirter, R., & Sabiechowska, P. (1999). *Professional Experience and the Investigative Imagination*. London: Routledge.

Wisker, G. (1999). Learning conceptions and strategies of postgraduate students (Israeli PhD students) and some steps towards encouraging and enabling their learning. Paper presented to the 2nd Postgraduate Experience Conference: Developing Research.

Wisker, G. (2000). *Good Practice Working with International Students.* SEDA Occasional Paper 110. Birmingham: SEDA.

Wisker, G., & Sutcliffe, N. (eds) (1999). *Good Practice in Postgraduate Supervision.* SEDA Occasional Paper 106. Birmingham: SEDA.

Wisker, G., Tiley, J., Watkins, M., Waller, S., Maclaughlin, J., Thomas, J., & Wisker, A. (eds) (2000). Discipline based research into student learning in English, Law Social Work, Computer skills for linguists, Women's Studies, Creative Writing: how can it inform our teaching? In C. Rust (ed.), *Improving Student Learning Through the Disciplines*, pp. 377–97. Oxford: Oxford Brookes University.

Zuber Skerritt, O. (1992). *Action Research in Higher Education.* London: Kogan Page.

Index